Spitfire Mark V in Action

Spitfire Mark V
in Action

RAF Operations in Northern Europe

Peter Caygill

9901174118/ 940·544
CIRC 2

Airlife
England

First published in the UK in 2001
by Airlife Publishing Ltd

British Library Cataloguing-in-Publication Data
A catalogue record for this book
is available from the British Library

ISBN 1 84037 248 6

Typeset by Phoenix Typesetting, Ilkley, West Yorkshire
Printed in England by MPG Books Ltd, Bodmin, Cornwall.

Airlife Publishing Ltd

101 Longden Road, Shrewsbury, SY3 9EB England.
E-mail: airlife@airlifebooks.com
Website: www.airlifebooks.com

ACKNOWLEDGEMENTS

Without the enthusiastic support received from many former Spitfire pilots this book would not have been written, and I would like to take this opportunity of thanking them for sharing their memories with me. I am deeply indebted to the following:

64 Squadron	Ted Andrews, Tony Cooper
92 Squadron	Neville Duke, Walter Johnston
118 Squadron	Johnny Freeborn, 'Paddy' Harbison, Stan Jones, Sid Watson, the late 'Bertie' Wootten
234 Squadron	Roy Fairweather, Dave Ferguson, Dave Glaser, Charlie Potter, George Sparrow, Ray Stebbings
350 Squadron	Robert Laumans
403 Squadron	George Aitken, Don Campbell, Eric Crist, Norris Hunt, Charles Magwood, Jack Parr, Roy Wozniak
416 Squadron	Doug Booth, Doug Love, Al McFadden, Dan Noonan, Art Sager
611 Squadron	Ian Walker

In particular I would like to thank Walter Johnston for recording his wartime memories, Ray Stebbings for supplying material on 234 Squadron and Patricia Kingaby for allowing me to quote from her father's unpublished autobiography.

I would also like to thank Tony Cooper and Philip Jarrett for providing photographs from their excellent collections, the staff at the Public Record Office and all the many individuals who have helped me along the way.

PREFACE

Generally regarded as one of the all-time classic fighter aircraft, virtually every superlative in the dictionary has been used to describe the Supermarine Spitfire at one time or another, and for many it continues to be a source of fascination sixty-five years after its first flight. In the past few years I have been privileged to meet and interview many Spitfire pilots who have described their feelings for this particular machine. On numerous occasions the word 'love' has been used to describe affection for the Spitfire, its looks and handling qualities producing emotions that belie its role as a weapon of war. It seems almost inconceivable that anything derogatory could be said of the Spitfire, yet the Mark V has attracted its fair share of vilification.

Its story is inextricably linked to the Focke-Wulf Fw 190 which entered *Luftwaffe* service in the late summer of 1941 and caused Fighter Command such a profound shock. Following an extremely difficult period in which combat losses were worryingly high, the Spitfire V received a lifeline courtesy of Rolls-Royce which allowed it to compete on more or less equal terms, although restricted to operations at low to medium levels.

Built in greater numbers than any other Spitfire variant, the Mark V served in all theatres of war and was instrumental in winning the battle to save the island of Malta, a feat that has been well documented. In northern Europe its history is less well known, especially in the mid- to late-war period. Although it was progressively replaced by the Mark IX from June 1942, there were still ten front-line squadrons flying Spitfire Vs at the time of D-Day, a full two years later. Despite its age and predictions of impending obsolescence, it was to continue in the firing line until the end of the European war.

As an operational history, this book tells the aircraft's story from the viewpoint of various squadrons and wings throughout 10, 11 and 12 Groups. Choice of individual unit is purely arbitrary, but it is hoped that there is sufficient variety to cover most of the operational flying that it undertook. Many of the actions that are described are based on pilots' combat reports which, together with intelligence reports and first-hand accounts, provide a detailed account of some of the more notable air battles that took place over northern France, Holland and Belgium. The final chapter charts the operational histories of preserved Spitfire Vs that fought in the skies over northern Europe, aircraft that are a permanent reminder of the gallantry and sacrifice of the pilots who took it to war.

CONTENTS

CHAPTER 1	Improving the Breed	1
CHAPTER 2	Into Service	7
CHAPTER 3	Biggin Hill Wing, August–December 1941	30
CHAPTER 4	Ibsley Wing, January–June 1942	51
CHAPTER 5	Channel Dash, February 1942	71
CHAPTER 6	Focke-Wulf Summer	88
CHAPTER 7	The Dieppe Raid	108
CHAPTER 8	A Present from the Enemy	119
CHAPTER 9	Coltishall Wing, January–June 1943	129
CHAPTER 10	Coltishall/Digby Wings, July–December 1943	145
CHAPTER 11	Perranporth Wing, September 1943–January 1944	172
CHAPTER 12	The Deanland Wing	185
CHAPTER 13	The Dragon Strikes Back	206
CHAPTER 14	Final Operations	221
CHAPTER 15	Spitfire V Survivors	228
APPENDIX A	Details of Selected Operations	237
APPENDIX B	Operations Logs of Spitfire V Survivors	241
APPENDIX C	Spitfire V Squadrons in Fighter Command – January 1942	253
APPENDIX D	Spitfire V Squadrons in Fighter Command – June 1943	255
APPENDIX E	Spitfire V Squadrons in ADGB – June 1944	257
Index		258

ONE

IMPROVING THE BREED

Forecasting future events is a difficult enough exercise at the best of times, but attempting to second-guess what an enemy will do next in time of war can be particularly onerous. New threats emerge which demand an immediate response and long-term plans can quickly become worthless. When one considers the evolution of the Supermarine Spitfire, had everything gone the way the Air Staff thought it would, the Mark V would not have been produced, and this book would not have been written. In the event, the Spitfire V was to be produced in greater numbers than any other mark and was to serve the RAF with distinction throughout the whole of World War Two.

Unlike the Hawker Hurricane, its partner in the Battle of Britain, the Spitfire had the potential to accept considerable development which would ultimately see it fly with engines of twice the power of the original Rolls-Royce Merlin, and with armament of four times the fire power of the eight 0.303in machine-guns of the Spitfire I.

The first attempt to increase the performance of the basic Spitfire design resulted in the Mark III, which flew for the first time on 16 March 1940. It was powered by a two-speed supercharged Merlin XX of 1,390hp, the use of which required strengthening of the forward fuselage and engine mountings. Other modifications included a general beefing up of the undercarriage legs, which were also angled forward by a further two inches in an attempt to avoid the Spitfire's tendency to nose-over in soft-field conditions. The tailwheel was also made retractable. In addition, there was considerable attention to detail: small flaps attached to the mainwheel fairings covered the portion of the tyre that had previously remained exposed when retracted, and there was a much neater windscreen design with the 'bulletproof' glazing mounted internally rather than externally. Wingspan was also reduced to 30ft 6in (and wing area to 220sq.ft), the overall effect being to increase the aircraft's rate of roll.

Almost from the word go, however, the Spitfire III was in trouble. Development difficulties with the Merlin XX led to delays, and the decision was then taken to award priority of engine supply to the Hurricane II, which would have quickly become obsolescent without it. Supermarine themselves underestimated the amount of time it would take to organise deliveries of the re-engineered fighter, but the main danger to the Mark III came from the *Luftwaffe*.

By the end of October 1940 the Battle of Britain had been won and German plans for invasion had been postponed. Despite this, their bombers continued to operate widely over Britain in the hours of darkness, and incursions over mainland Britain during the day were principally by bomb-carrying Messerschmitt 109s and 110s. Towards the end of 1940 the Me 109F was introduced into service in small numbers and its appearance in the skies over south-east England made it clear that it could fly and fight at higher altitudes than its predecessor, the *Emil*. Reconnaissance sorties were also being carried out by twin-engined Junkers Ju 86Ps, which were capable of flying at heights of up to 40,000ft. This greatly worried the Air Ministry and the conclusion was drawn that if the *Luftwaffe* were to re-launch their offensive in 1941, the resultant air battles would most likely be fought at much greater heights.

The matter came to a head early in the year when it became clear that the Spitfire III could not be produced in anything like the numbers the RAF required. The main production difficulty with the Merlin XX concerned its low-altitude blower, but ironically the RAF's operational requirement was now heavily weighted towards performance at higher altitudes. In parallel with the Merlin XX, Rolls-Royce had been developing a similar version which featured a single blower of 10.25in diameter. Known as the Merlin 45, it gave a power output of 1,440hp and promised to make the Spitfire much more effective at greater heights. As it could also be easily adapted to the Mark I/II airframe with the minimum amount of modification, the Spitfire III was effectively killed off, and on 6 March 1941 Air Chief Marshal Sir Charles Portal gave the go-ahead for the Mark V to be put into quantity production.

This is not quite the end of the story as the Air Ministry still regarded the Spitfire V as 'a temporary expedient', a short-term solution to the immediate problem of high-altitude attack. With the prospect of having to fight at heights approaching the stratosphere, it should have been supplanted by the Mark VI, which featured a pressure cabin employing a Marshall blower. Although the pressure differential of 2lb/sq.in was modest by modern standards, it meant that, at a height of 37,000ft, the pressure experienced by the pilot was equivalent to that at 28,000ft. Extended low-drag wingtips increased wingspan to 40ft 2in (and wing area to 248½sq. ft) and power came from a Rolls-Royce Merlin 47. As if to underline the fact that nothing is certain in time of war, the threat posed by high-flying bombers failed to materialise and production of the Spitfire VI would cease in October 1942 after only 100 aircraft had been delivered. All of this left the Spitfire V as the RAF's premier day fighter, a position it would hold until the arrival of the Spitfire IX, which began to enter squadron service in June 1942.

Visually there was little to distinguish the new Spitfire from earlier versions. Apart from a slightly altered nose profile, the only other identifying feature was a larger oil cooler under the port wing which was of circular instead of semi-circular section. The main improvement lay with the Merlin 45, which featured revisions to the supercharger impeller and diffuser, improving its efficiency by the order of 10%. The air intake ducting was also completely revised so that pressure losses were minimised, the overall effect being to raise take-off boost to +12lb/sq. in, with maximum combat boost increased to +16lb/sq. in, limited to a maximum of five minutes. The engine's full-throttle altitude was 19,000ft, an improvement of 3,000ft over the Merlin III of the Spitfire I.

Initially two versions of the Mark V were produced, the Va with eight 0.303in Browning machine-guns, and the Vb with two 20mm Hispano cannon and four Brownings. These were followed by the Vc, which possessed a strengthened wing employing much of the development work that had gone into the Mark III. Known as the Type 'C' or 'universal' wing, it could accommodate either of the armament options of the earlier versions, or four 20mm Hispano cannons.

During the Battle of Britain it had become clear that the days of rifle-calibre machine-guns as the sole armament in fighter aircraft were numbered. By early 1941 most combat aircraft were fitted with armour plating, which afforded protection for the crew compartment and other vital areas, and fuel tanks were of the self-sealing type. Unless attacks were pressed home to close range, the machine-gun did not possess the necessary weight of fire to bring down an enemy aircraft with any degree of certainty. As a result only 100 Spitfire Vas were produced out of the 6,479 Mark Vs that were eventually made, all of the rest being cannon-armed Vbs and Vcs.

Although there was general agreement that the 20mm Hispano cannon was a much more effective weapon than the 0.303in Browning, its detractors pointed to its abysmal reliability rate. Armament in the Spitfire was mounted well out in the wing to avoid firing through the propeller arc, and as cannon stoppages invariably occurred on one side or the other, recoil from the working gun would slew the aircraft, thus making aiming impossible. Indeed, the first squadron to take the cannon-equipped Spitfire Ib into action (19 Squadron in August 1940) did so for only a few days and quickly demanded that their old aircraft be returned!

Problems with the Hispano cannon stemmed mainly from the fact that it had been designed specifically for mounting between the cylinder banks of Hispano Suiza's 'V' type in-line engines and not for the considerably less rigid structure that made up a Spitfire wing. As the early weapons were fed by a sixty-round magazine, the gun had to be laid on its side so that the bulge in the wing to accommodate the magazine was not too large. With such an installation the gun often jammed when the empty cartridge case failed to eject properly. By the time the Spitfire V began to enter squadron service the change-over was being made to a belt-feed mechanism which proved to be much more reliable, although correct maintenance was critical and armourers needed to be careful that the ammunition belt was correctly aligned. Until the idiosyncrasies of the set-up were better known, many pilots' combat reports would continue to complain of a malfunction of their primary armament.

The Spitfire had been designed primarily as a short-range bomber-destroyer and little thought had been given to its having to engage fighters of similar performance. The RAF's regimented 'Fighter Attacks' had been formulated before the war for use against unescorted bomber formations, and many older-generation RAF officers refused to believe that the new high-performance monoplane fighters were capable of First World War style dogfighting. When it became clear that this sort of air fighting was still very much possible, Spitfire pilots began to report a number of worrying deficiencies in their aircraft.

Early aircraft were fitted with fabric-covered ailerons which tended to 'balloon' in high-speed dives over 400mph, with the result that stick forces became unacceptably high. As the Messerschmitt Me 109E/F was inferior to the Spitfire in the turn, *Luftwaffe* pilots usually flew at high speed and disengaged by diving to lower levels. If this manoeuvre was followed by a Spitfire, its unfortunate pilot soon found that he was unable to turn sufficiently in the dive to be able to bring his guns to bear. Lateral control would eventually be improved by the fitting of metal ailerons, but many months would go by before this modification became standard, and the first Spitfire Vs to enter service only received them retrospectively when sufficient sets had been produced.

Another major disadvantage of the Spitfire V concerned its Rolls-Royce Merlin engine. The Merlin was fitted with a normal SU carburettor which ceased to function in any flight conditions involving negative-G, unlike the Daimler-Benz DB601, as fitted to the Me 109, which featured fuel injection and continued to operate normally in such conditions. When attacked from behind, 109 pilots usually pushed straight into a dive, a manoeuvre that a Spitfire could not perform without the engine cutting out. The only effective response was to perform a half-roll and then pull through, so that positive-G was maintained throughout. By this time, however, a skilfully flown 109 was usually well out of firing range. This situation would remain unchanged until well into 1942 when late-production Spitfire Vs came into service powered by the Merlin 50 engine, which featured a revised carburettor with a metal diaphragm fitted into the float chamber. This simple device prevented fuel starvation and proved to be remarkably effective in combat.

Although the Spitfire was to be developed considerably in terms of power and armament, a basic lack of range was to remain its greatest shortcoming. Internal fuel capacity was a meagre eighty-five gallons, perfectly adequate for fighting defensively over home territory, but insufficient for the offensive work it was later asked to do. Spitfire pilots had quickly to learn the techniques for correct fuel management to achieve endurance, or risk a soaking in the Channel on the way back from France.

Extending the Spitfire's range had been considered as early as 1939 when trials took place with a fixed thirty-gallon overload tank under the port wing. These were eventually fitted to a number of Spitfire IIs in early 1941 and saw service with 66, 118, 152 and 234 Squadrons. The asymmetric positioning of the fuel tank caused adverse handling characteristics which led to the modified Spitfires being thoroughly disliked by those unlucky enough to have to fly them. Sergeant Walter 'Johnnie' Johnston, who would later fly Spitfire Vs with 92 and 234 Squadrons, began his first tour with 152 Squadron at Warmwell before moving to Portreath. Here he flew the LR version of the Mark II which had sufficient range to escort Hampden bombers on daylight raids against the *Scharnhorst* and *Gneisenau*, in Brest harbour.

> When we got the awful long-range Spitfires we all had very narrow escapes. Taking off was full right rudder and stick almost hard over in the same direction. This was due to the extra weight on the port wing only. Flying circuits and bumps to get the feel was dicey as it meant take-offs and landings with a full wing tank. There was no such thing as a typical curving Spitfire approach to keep the ground in sight – not with about 250–300 lb on the inner wing. So we trundled in as if the runway was that of a carrier. Some of us did forget and had hair-raising things happen. We lost two pilots who just undercooked the turn and slipped in.

When overload fuel tanks reappeared for use on the Spitfire V and subsequent marks, they were of a much neater streamlined shape and were mounted under the centre section between the undercarriage legs, thereby doing away with any undesirable handling problems.

Unlike the fixed installation on the long-range Spitfire IIs, they were designed to be jettisoned before entering combat.

All of this, of course, was still many months away when in early February 1941 92 Squadron, Fighter Command's top-scoring unit, prepared to introduce the Spitfire V to the battle for air supremacy high in the skies over France.

Two

INTO SERVICE

S hortly before the introduction of the Spitfire V into squadron
service, there were a number of important personnel changes at
the highest level within Fighter Command which saw the replacement of the two main architects of victory in the Battle of Britain. Air
Chief Marshal Hugh Dowding was replaced as AOC-in-C by Air Chief
Marshal William Sholto Douglas, and the commander of No.11 Group,
Air Vice-Marshal Keith Park, was succeeded by Air Vice-Marshal
Trafford Leigh-Mallory. Although the events of the summer of 1940 are
generally regarded as being the most glorious in the RAF's long and
distinguished history, the contentious issue of tactics has tended to cloud
the manner of victory and remains controversial to this day. Park's use
of small, flexible units contrasted sharply with Leigh-Mallory's 'Big
Wing' theories, but it was to be the latter's ideas that would prevail, albeit
used offensively rather than defensively.

With Sholto Douglas and Leigh-Mallory now in charge, Fighter
Command's posture changed to one of increased aggression, a policy
which grew in intensity throughout the first half of 1941 with improving
weather. In many ways the RAF were carrying on the tradition set by the
Royal Flying Corps, who had carried out offensive operations against
their German opponents during the First World War.

The first forays into occupied Europe were by fighters operating in
pairs on the so-called 'Rhubarb' sorties, looking for targets of opportunity
and taking advantage of cloud cover to evade defending fighters. By
spring, Spitfires were soon flying in wing-strength over France in an
attempt to draw the rival Me 109s into a battle of attrition which, it was
hoped, would prove once and for all the merits of having large numbers
of fighters concentrated in a single action. Any hope of producing large,
decisive air battles over France quickly evaporated, however, as it soon
became apparent that the Germans were uninterested in countering pure
fighter sweeps, often preferring to stay on the ground or keep a watching
brief from a distance.

This lack of reaction led to the development of 'Circus' operations, of which a small number of bombers (usually Blenheims, but occasionally Stirlings) formed the nucleus. Although the destructive capability of these aircraft was small, their presence increased the likelihood of drawing the 109s into combat, which remained the primary intention. Even so, the hoped-for dogfights often failed to materialise and the fighting that did occur usually took the form of brief skirmishes when sections became detached and inadvertently placed themselves in a disadvantageous position.

The first Circus operation took place on 10 January 1941 when six Blenheims of 114 Squadron, escorted by nine fighter squadrons (three Hurricane and six Spitfire), attacked an ammunition dump situated in the Forêt de Guines. Having made rendezvous with the close-escort Hurricanes of 56 Squadron just after midday, the Blenheims set course for Calais at 12,000ft with the Spitfires of the Hornchurch Wing stepped up from 13–15,000ft as top cover (the Hurricanes of 242 and 249 Squadrons having already gone ahead to provide forward cover). The raid was completed successfully, withdrawal being made via Cap Gris Nez where the three Spitfire squadrons of the Biggin Hill Wing (66, 74 and 92) met up with the bombers to protect them on their way home. Although a fair amount of heavy flak had been experienced, the only fighter engagements were those of 242 and 249 Squadrons who shot down two Me 109s for the loss of one of their number. From such small beginnings, Circuses would evolve into huge, integrated affairs employing up to 300 fighter aircraft in varying escort roles. As activity on such a scale demanded good weather conditions, 11 Group's squadrons would have to make do with more modest operations until the summer.

The story of the Spitfire V's actions over northern France in 1941 could be told by highlighting any one of Fighter Command's stations in the south-east, but one base was to be at the forefront of the air battles more than any other – Biggin Hill. Perhaps the most famous RAF fighter station of them all, Biggin was situated on a plateau on the North Downs to the south of Bromley, and had first been developed by the Royal Flying Corps in 1917 for wireless telegraphy experiments. Its proximity to London meant it played a strategic role in the defence of the capital, and its capacity to take considerable punishment during the Battle of Britain and keep going had been an inspiration to all.

Still bearing the scars of battle, it now housed two Spitfire squadrons including No.92, whose aircraft proudly carried the title 'East India Squadron' following the donation of funds for the war effort. It could boast more 'aces' than any other unit, the exploits of Brian Kingcome, Tony Bartley, Don Kingaby and 'Tich' Havercroft, to name but a few,

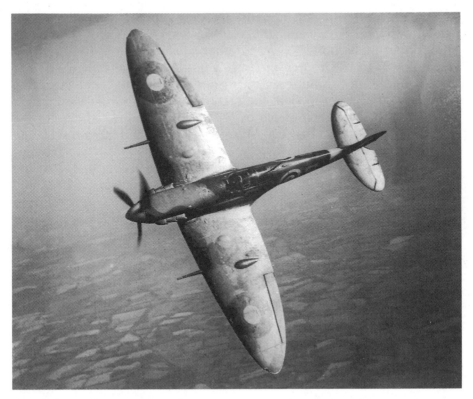

R6923 QJ-S of 92 Squadron (*IWM*)

having been widely reported in the popular press. Its Commanding Officer was twenty-seven-year-old Squadron Leader Jamie Rankin, who had recently arrived from 64 Squadron. Although relatively in-experienced, he would rapidly forge a reputation to equal any, and before the year was out would be awarded a DFC and Bar.

No.92 Squadron was chosen to introduce the Spitfire V into RAF service, but as no new-build Mark Vs were yet available they had to make do with 'interim' machines which were, in fact, their old aircraft re-engined with the Merlin 45. From the end of February, the squadron's Spitfire Ibs were sent in small batches to Rolls-Royce at Hucknall for conversion work, with the result that the unit flew a mix of Ibs and Vbs until early April. First impressions of the new variant were good, especially its improved rate of climb, and the fact that its increased per-formance was maintained to much greater heights.

No.92 Squadron was partnered at Biggin Hill by 609 (West Riding) Squadron who had moved in from Warmwell on 24 February to replace

66 Squadron, inheriting their Spitfire IIs in the process. Led by Squadron Leader Michael Robinson DFC, 609 had seen many of their most experienced pilots posted away to other squadrons and, having spent seven months in 10 Group, were largely untried. They would soon have ample opportunity to improve their combat efficiency, and come the summer would begin to rival the record of their distinguished neighbours. The wing was completed by 74 'Tiger' Squadron which, for the time being at least, was based at Manston. Both 74 and 609 would begin to fly the Spitfire V in late May.

In the meantime the East India Squadron was seeing just what the Spitfire V could do, but the trials were not without mishap. On 19 March eleven aircraft, led by Squadron Leader Rankin in X4257, took off from Biggin Hill to patrol Hastings at 36,000ft. Once at altitude Rankin soon found that he was unable to control his engine speed due to a malfunctioning of the constant speed unit (CSU), a device intended to regulate rpm automatically by altering the angle of attack of the propeller blades. He then lost consciousness due to oxygen starvation and only came to again in a dive at 12,000ft. Normally limited to a maximum of 3,000rpm, his engine had over-revved to 3,800rpm and he was forced to carry out a crash-landing near Maidstone. Two other Spitfire pilots suffered similar problems, Sergeant Jerrold Le Cheminant in R6897 and Sergeant de Montbron, who crash-landed R6776 near Chatham.

Failures had already occurred during trials carried out at the Aeroplane and Armament Experimental Establishment (A&AEE) at Boscombe Down where operations in extremely cold air at high altitude had led to oil in the de Havilland CSU freezing. Examination of 92 Squadron's Spitfires shortly after their premature return to earth revealed ice accretion on the spinner and propeller boss, which pointed to the same problem. Modifications to solve the defect would obviously take some time to complete, so until then pilots were requested to work their throttles more than normal when flying at altitude so that the CSU was given plenty of exercise to keep it free. In addition, heavier flyweights were installed and a number of Spitfires had their de Havilland propellers replaced by Rotol units.

With the acceptance that fighter operations over France were to be carried out in wing strength it was clear that each wing would need an experienced leader, one who possessed a high degree of tactical awareness and was capable of 'flying' thirty-six aircraft so that the formation maintained its integrity during manoeuvring. The new post was officially termed 'Wing Commander Flying', although incumbents were more often referred to as Wing Leaders. The first two appointments were

Douglas Bader, who took over at Tangmere, and Sailor Malan, who was elevated from his position as CO of 74 Squadron to fly at the head of the Biggin Hill Wing.

Malan had joined the RAF in early 1936 from his native South Africa and had been flying with the Tigers since December the same year. His reading of the tactical situation as it evolved during large-scale operations over France proved to be of the highest order, and much of the success achieved by the Biggin Hill squadrons can be attributed to his expert leadership. Malan was also an excellent shot, and come the summer he would claim twelve enemy aircraft destroyed, with two others shared (all Me 109E/Fs), making him one of the top-scoring Spitfire V pilots of the war.

By the end of March the final batches of 92 Squadron's Spitfire Ibs were being flown to Hucknall to be up-graded to Mark V standard, and on the 30th Flying Officer 'Tommy' Lund, Pilot Officer Geoff Wellum and Sergeant Ream delivered R7161, R6908 and R6770. These were followed on 7 April by R7195 and R6923 flown by Squadron Leader Rankin and Flight Lieutenant Wright, the two pilots returning the same day in R6908 and R6770.

Bad weather during much of March and early April had resulted in 92

R7161 first flew on 6 March 1941 and carried the presentation title *Mombasa*. (*Author's collection*)

Squadron flying a preponderance of defensive patrols, a situation that was finally broken on 11 April when reports were received just before midday that a German seaplane was under tow back to the French coast. Four Spitfires were scrambled, led by Squadron Leader Rankin in R6882, and located their target just before it was able to reach the safety of Boulogne harbour. The seaplane, a Heinkel He 59 used for Air Sea Rescue duties along the Channel, was quickly sunk, damage also being inflicted on its tow ship. A sharp exchange then took place with a number of Me 109s of III/JG51, during which Sergeant Gaskell was shot down and killed in X4062.

Recently returned from Hucknall, R7161 saw a hectic couple of days towards the end of April commencing on the 24th when it was flown by Squadron Leader Rankin on a patrol along the south coast from Dover to Dungeness. Partnered by Pilot Officer Brunier, he shot down an Me 109 in flames, its pilot (*Feldwebel* Gunther Struck of 2/JG52) baling out to become a prisoner. Two days later R7161 was flown by Pilot Officer Ronnie Fokes on an offensive patrol over the French coast during which he shot down the Me109F of *Unteroffizier* Werner Zimmer of 4/JG53.

With the coming of better weather, the so-called 'Fighter Nights' were reinstated, whereby day fighters flew night patrols at set heights in an attempt to intercept raids by the *Luftwaffe*'s medium bombers. Britain's night defences were still woefully inadequate, and even with perfect conditions, successful interceptions by Spitfires at night were usually only achieved by a large slice of luck. Night duties were carried out in turn, and at 2000 hrs on 8 May, 92 Squadron flew over to West Malling to await the arrival of any nocturnal visitors. With German forces preparing for the invasion of Russia, however, night raids were becoming much more sporadic and the night passed without incident.

As was usual after night operations, the squadron arrived back at Biggin before breakfast the following morning and was then released until the evening, when a patrol was carried out from Dungeness to Ashford at 30,000ft. After an hour in the air, six Me 109s were seen manoeuvring above Red section, four of which dived to attack, with the other two maintaining their height to act as cover. Squadron Leader Rankin turned the section to meet the attack but his No.2, Sergeant Hugh Bowen-Morris, stalled out and was immediately pounced on by one of the 109s. His evasive action very nearly took him into the path of the German fighter, which then continued its dive towards France. Bowen-Morris followed it down and fired several short bursts with cannon which produced twin streams of glycol, and it was last seen at around 3,000ft diving vertically towards the sea.

Yellow section also had their problems when their 'weaver' lost consciousness due to oxygen starvation and had to be replaced by Flying Officer T.S. 'Wimpy' Wade in R7219. Shortly after taking up position, Wade spotted a single 109 climbing up to attack him from below and proceeded to carry out a series of violent turns, having warned the section of the potential threat. During his manoeuvres his windscreen iced up completely leaving him little choice but to dive to lower levels. The pilot of the 109 attempted to follow but he too was in trouble, and soon after his aircraft's control surfaces broke up, forcing him to take to his parachute. During the brief exchange Wade's Spitfire had been hit in the starboard ammunition drum, and shell splinters had also damaged the glycol pipelines.

No.92 Squadron's exclusive use of the Spitfire V did not last long as 74 Squadron received the first of its new aircraft on 16 May. No.74 had been part of the Biggin Hill Wing since October 1940 and was commanded by Squadron Leader John Mungo Park DFC who had taken over from Sailor Malan on his elevation to Wing Leader. After operating from Manston for a couple of months, they were now based at Gravesend, a small grass airfield that had been the start and finish point for Alex Henshaw's epic return flight to the Cape in 1939. With the outbreak of war it had been requisitioned by the Air Ministry for military use and became a satellite station of Biggin Hill. Although it had minimal facilities, officer pilots could at least relax in the opulent surroundings of Cobham Hall, a stately mansion dating back to Tudor times, complete with its own landscaped gardens. NCO pilots were not quite so fortunate, having to sleep in a small bungalow about a mile away, their mess being squeezed into a semi-detached house on the airfield boundary.

Even by mid-May weather conditions were still preventing Fighter Command from launching its long-awaited offensive against *Luftwaffe* units based in the Pas de Calais, and apart from a few sporadic Circus operations, much of its flying had been of a defensive nature. This allowed high-flying Me 109Fs to take the initiative on occasion, a typical example being 16 May, when several small formations tested the effectiveness of British defences along the south coast.

No.92 Squadron flew two patrols in the Dungeness–Dover area commencing at 1145 hrs, and was engaged on both. During the first, Sergeant Don Kingaby DFM (R6882 – Black 1) damaged an Me 109 but then had to break off combat due to the attentions of two more. The second patrol, flown shortly afterwards, produced a number of encounters and once again Kingaby was in the thick of the action. Seeing a 109 diving towards France, he set off after it at full throttle and eventually caught it up, having attained an estimated 470mph during the chase. Renowned as one of the squadron's best marksman, his fire caused severe damage to the 109's starboard wing and very soon it crumpled up and broke off. The attack took place at 7,000ft about five miles off Calais. On his way home Kingaby saw another 109 going down vertically trailing thick black smoke having been engaged by other members of the squadron.

Throughout the first half of 1941 much intelligence information had been gathered, from Ultra and other sources, which pointed to a massive German military build-up in the east that would ultimately lead to the invasion of Russia. The offensive was launched on 22 June under the code name Barbarossa and took the Russians completely by surprise, despite the fact that every piece of evidence concerning the German preparations had been passed on by British Intelligence. There was little that could be done to provide assistance for the Russians; Bomber Command's night raids were still largely ineffectual and Fighter Command's efforts were limited to the fringes of occupied Europe. Even so, Circus operations were carried out with much increased intensity from mid-June onwards in an effort to tie down as many *Luftwaffe* fighter units as possible.

A period of hot, sunny weather which lasted, with only occasional breaks, until the end of July, allowed the squadrons of the Biggin Hill Wing to operate one or more offensive missions over France on most days. During this period they were credited with having shot down more enemy aircraft than any other wing in 11 Group, their first major success occurring in the afternoon of 16 June when they operated on a fighter sweep along the French coast from Le Touquet to Boulogne. Although 92 Squadron claimed two destroyed with two probables, on this occasion it was to be out-scored by its rivals from Gravesend.

Having made rendezvous over Biggin Hill at 1550 hrs at 7,000ft, the wing climbed overland and set course for France via Beachy Head with 74 Squadron now at 25,000ft. Just after crossing the French coast north of Le Touquet, four Me 109Fs were seen turning in behind 92 Squadron and 74 dived to attack. As they did so approximately sixteen more 109s came in from their port side and a general dogfight ensued. Squadron Leader Mungo Park engaged one Me 109 to devastating effect, his cannon shells ripping off its entire tail assembly. Almost immediately he came under attack himself and received a number of hits on his aircraft's fuselage, and a cannon shell in the engine. He climbed as best he could but when crossing the coast on his way out he was attacked again, this time by five 109Fs which had apparently been guided to him by red-coloured flak bursts.

Ironically, his crippled machine gave him an advantage at first as the leader of the 109s completely misjudged his attack and overshot. Taking full advantage, Mungo Park fired the remainder of his ammunition into the Messerschmitt which burst into flames and fell away. By now his engine was sounding extremely rough but he managed to maintain speed in a dive and evaded the attentions of the other 109s by performing aileron turns and firing occasional bursts at them with his machine-guns. Fortunately the 109s turned for home in mid-Channel, but at 6,000ft, when still two miles off Folkestone, his engine seized completely, leaving him insufficient height to make Hawkinge and forcing him to crash-land in a field nearby.

Back over France, the rest of the squadron were heavily engaged and during a hectic dogfight Pilot Officer W.J. Sandman (Red 2) fired a short burst at a 109 achieving strikes along the length of its fuselage. Glycol immediately poured from the machine and as he passed over it Sandman was convinced that his fire had disabled its pilot. Sergeant Yorke got behind another 109 which was turning to attack a Spitfire and delivered a two-second burst which hit the engine. With its propeller blades wind-milling, the machine turned over on its side and went into a steep dive, eventually disappearing into the haze below.

By now the action was a general free-for-all and Sergeant Stewart dived on three 109s which were following a solitary Spitfire 500ft below. Two of the enemy aircraft saw him coming and turned to meet his attack but after a brief turning fight he succeeded in getting onto the tail of one of them and fired a four-second burst from close range. Pieces fell off the 109 and there was an explosion near the cockpit. It then rolled over and fell into a spin, emitting dense clouds of black smoke. Stewart attempted to follow but was unable to close sufficiently to open fire. Although it was not seen to crash, Stewart's combat film was impressive enough for him to be awarded with its destruction.

All in all it had been a very successful day for the Biggin Hill Wing, with five Me 109s claimed destroyed and another four probables. Apart from Squadron Leader Mungo Park's crash-landing, the only other misfortune befell Flight Lieutenant Brian Kingcome of 92 Squadron, whose aircraft was badly shot up over France. Both Spitfires suffered Cat. Ac damage but returned to the fray after repair.

In researching Royal Air Force history, one of the aviation historian's primary sources of material are the Squadron Operations Record Books (ORB), which were kept on RAF Forms 540 and 541. He is, however, very much at the mercy of the compiler and some considered their duties to have been carried out satisfactorily having included the barest minimum of information. At the other end of the scale are the writings of Frank Ziegler, 609 Squadron's Intelligence Officer, whose work shows a conscientiousness and an eye for detail equalled by few others. The entry for the squadron's operations on 22 June is a good example of his diligence:

Today was notable for Germany's invasion of Russia, for the shooting down of four 109s by 609 Squadron, and for the successful rescue of P/O De Spirlet from the drink. 12 Blenheims were raiding Hazebrouck yards (Circus 18) with Biggin acting as forward and withdrawal Wing. 609 were flying in three independent sections at 20/25,000ft inland from Dunkirk when Blue Leader (F/L Bisdee) saw about nine Me 109Fs flying down the coast from the Dunkirk direction. He gave the tally ho and attacked one pair which turned to port and left the pair in front unguarded. Closing to point blank range behind one of them (which took no evasive action) he fired with m.g. continuously. Its engine caught fire and pieces of red hot metal flew off. It turned on its back and went straight down.

Blue 2 (Sgt Rigler) brought the second down from similar range (no evasive action again) then found himself alone at 8,000ft. 7 109Es were above and 2 peeled off and came dead astern of him. By throttling back and turning, he caused the leader to overshoot and firing at it, saw a flash and the e/a disintegrate. Meanwhile he himself was hit in the wing by fire from another e/a and during his evasive action he was at one time inverted with a cut engine and head pressed against the perspex. 'Rigler, if you ever get out of this, you need never fly again' he said to himself. Calling out 'Blue 2 down below in trouble', he had the impression of the a/c diving and one of his attackers going down in flames. Losing height to gain the cover of the haze of the sea, he found yet another 109 (E) flying in front at 800ft. An unseen burst of m.g. only was enough to send it down to crash near the sands east of Dunkirk. Owing to the behaviour of his engine and high temperature, he thought his glycol tanks had been hit and got ready to bale out. It wasn't necessary however and he landed at Manston.

P/O Offenberg (Red 2) again went looking for trouble on his own and eventually found himself in the interesting position of firing at an Me 109E low over the sand dunes, wiping a frozen windscreen, avoiding tracer from Gravelines and watching an Me 109F that was 'floundering around' a bit further inland – practically all at the same time. He damaged the 109E so successfully that glycol covered his own windscreen and then had to avoid the attention of the 109F.

Yellow section was jumped on crossing the coast and Yellow 3 (P/O De Spirlet) was shot down, bullets also hitting P/O Ortmans who thought the e/a was his colleague. After gliding a short distance,

P/O De Spirlet baled out with some difficulty from 800–1,000ft and began inflating his Mae West on the way down. He reached the water, got into his dinghy and fell out twice, once trying to pull in the drogue, once standing up to wave. 2 Spitfires of another squadron had been circling him and afterwards a Lysander appeared and dropped a smoke bomb. 2 rescue boats then appeared, one from the English, the other from the French coast and he feared a battle. One however turned out to be Naval, the other RAF – after an argument as to who should pick him up, the RAF boat won. After 35 minutes in the water, he was grieved to find that the crew had finished all of their rum at a party the night before. After this he spent a week or two in Ramsgate Hospital having got a splinter in his leg.

Although the 20mm Hispano cannon had been in use for nearly a year, its reliability was still extremely poor, a situation that was not helped by unsatisfactory standards of workmanship exhibited by some sub-contractors who manufactured the weapon. The Hispano was not liked by certain pilots within Fighter Command, notably Wing Commander Douglas Bader, whose personal mount was W3185, a Mark Va with eight 0.303in Browning guns. Pilot Officer Neville Duke of 92 Squadron, who after the war became Chief Test Pilot at Hawker Aircraft Ltd, recalls some of the difficulties:

We did have quite a problem with stoppages on the cannon Spits. What happened was that sometimes only one cannon would fire, resulting in a strong yaw which obviously threw your aim off. You then either tried to offset your aim in anticipation, or fired .303s only. Only once did I have both cannons fail to fire – March 1943 with 92 Squadron – however the .303s achieved their object!

One problem with the drum-fed cannon was the limited amount of ammunition available (60 rounds) and this ran out before the 0.303s which had 350 rounds per gun (but a much higher rate of fire). The later belt-fed cannon was better with 120 rounds per gun. Even with 120 rounds we only had about twelve seconds of fire compared with about seventeen seconds with the 0.303s. Short squirts were the order of the day with the drum ammunition in 1941.

Sergeant 'Johnnie' Johnston, also of 92 Squadron, recalls another problem:

With the Hispano it was not unknown for the extractor to fail and leave an empty case in the chamber. The HE shells we used were pre-set of course and if a new round was then fed into the chamber

17

you had a situation where the shell could explode in your wing. Not long after I arrived at 92, I was flying behind Tich Havercroft when this happened to him and the panel came whizzing past over my head. The Hispano was not very reliable and I cannot remember ever emptying both drums, there was always a stoppage. It was nice to have them when they worked, they did make a big hole, but the Germans made big holes in us as well!

After a modest beginning in January, Circus operations had grown considerably in scale and complexity. The core of the force, often referred to as the 'beehive', took the form of three or four squadrons acting as close escort (each stepped up at 1,000ft intervals) with three more squadrons of the escort cover wing, at similar increments in height, providing immediate protection to the close escorts and the bombers. Higher still, and stepped up into sun, were the three squadrons which comprised the top cover wing. In addition to the fighters that were tied to the bombers, further wings flew as Target Support and took independent routing to clear the bombers' track to the objective. These were given a completely free role to take on enemy formations that were likely to be climbing to get above the incoming bombers. Finally, one or more wings would act as withdrawal cover to meet the force on its way home and deal with any enemy fighters that were still in the vicinity. They were also able to provide relief for the other escorts who were likely to be low on fuel, especially if they had been engaged over France.

Up to now most operations had seen fairly shallow penetrations into occupied Europe but from June raids were carried out on targets deeper into France. The implications of this new policy for the escort fighters are discussed in the following extract which comes from *Greyhound in the Slips*, the unpublished autobiography of Flight Sergeant (later Wing Commander) Don Kingaby DFM of 92 Squadron.

Most of our operations over France up to this time had been confined to sweeps around the coastal areas and very rarely did we go more than a few miles into Hunland. On 23 June we were called into the dispersal hut for briefing – Sailor Malan popped his head into the hut long enough to say 'Target is Bethune, look it up on the map'. We looked – we looked and we looked. We were expecting a target about ten miles inside the coast and it was some time before anyone believed that that was it – fifty miles in! We had no long-range tanks then, and thirty miles in meant a darn good fight and a landing at a forward base to refuel on the way home. What would it be like taking twelve bombers in fifty miles?

Sgt Hugh Bowen-Morris who was shot down in R6761 on 23 June 1941. (*via Johnston*)

We were briefed for close escort and within an hour we were on our way. For the first time I saw not only the English coast disappear, but also the French coast fade from sight in the haze as we penetrated further into enemy territory. The Huns didn't catch up with our game until we nearly reached the target and then we had a real good scrap getting home. It was in this scrap that I lost the first of my Sergeant pals (Sergeant Hugh Bowen-Morris – R6761). He saw a 109 on the tail of a Spitfire and went down to get it. The Spitfire got away O.K. but 'Bowie' was left with five other 109s to deal with. After a stout fight he was badly wounded and was shot down. It was a tough break to buy it after helping an unknown comrade out of trouble. The show concluded successfully on the whole – all the bombers were brought back and the day's score showed ten to one against the Huns, of which 92 bagged five. [Bowen-Morris lost an arm in the encounter and was eventually made a PoW.]

19

Kingaby's reference to an extremely favourable scoreline is typical of contemporary accounts, but in fact the RAF were not shooting down anywhere near the numbers they were claiming. This does not reflect badly on the pilots involved, their reports were honest reflections on what they thought they had seen. Instead, it highlights the way the mind can be deceived in the heat of battle, when events happen with frightening rapidity. In a swirling dogfight it was possible for several pilots to fire at a single opponent, quite independently, and make multiple claims for the same aircraft. Contact with the enemy was often fleeting, but if an aircraft was seen on fire or a parachute appeared near where a combat had taken place, it was easy to assume that this was your 'kill', although in reality it may well have belonged to someone else. As the air war was now being fought over northern France and the Channel, there was no physical evidence to back up claims, although some idea of the true picture was obtained from Ultra intelligence, which gave reasonably accurate figures via *Luftwaffe* requests for replacement aircraft. To maintain pilots' morale, this information was not passed down and remained at the highest level within Fighter Command.

On the last day in June the Biggin Hill Wing provided target support to eighteen Blenheims from 18 and 139 Squadrons which raided a power station near Lens. The 609 Squadron ORB describes the action:

> Many small formations of Me 109, mostly Es, menaced them from the target area onwards without seriously attacking and whenever they did, our aircraft used their superior manoeuvrability to assume an attacking position themselves. S/L Robinson, after chasing two down to 5,000ft over Merville aerodrome, got behind five that were stalking Blue section and damaged one before they made off. It was probably the same lot with which Sgt Hughes-Rees became involved and one of which he managed to shoot down from below during a vertical climb.
>
> Over the Forêt de Nieppe the squadron was following the W/C down to investigate when Yellow section saw 4 Me 109E on their port quarter. Yellow section pulled up and each selected a victim. Yellow 2 (P/O Ortmans) attacked his with quarter, astern and finally deflection attacks as it climbed and dived and skidded till, at last, it disintegrated. F/L Richey got astern of his and despite its evasive action caused it to go down in a spiral, covered with oil and flaming from its engine.
>
> Meanwhile F/L Richey joined some other Spits at 16,000ft and saw 6 Me 109E coming down behind. After an ineffectual engagement with one, he found himself alone again and dived for a patch

of cloud at 800ft near the Forêt de Clairmarais. At ground level he saw 2 Me 109Es diving onto his tail with a third opening fire from his starboard quarter. A violent climbing turn and side-loop brought him on the latter's tail and after two longish bursts the e/a dived at full speed from 1,000ft. After eluding the other two, also accurate light flak from St Omer, F/L Richey flew home, at times below tree top level, taking a look at France.

Although intangible, one of the major assets of a fighter squadron in wartime is the collective combat experience of its members. During the Battle of Britain, many untried units suffered heavy losses almost immediately, so that they had to be pulled away from the action once again to re-form. At the opposite end of the scale, other squadrons saw action over a long period of time, but gradually operational efficiency would be reduced as pilots began to suffer the effects of combat fatigue, a condition that was very difficult to assess. As a small fighting unit, a squadron is particularly susceptible to heavy losses and its morale is likely to suffer severely, especially if squadron or flight commanders are among those lost.

Having been in 11 Group since October 1940, 74 Squadron had as much combat experience within its ranks as any, but, whether out of tiredness or just plain bad luck, three pilots failed to return from an evening sweep near St Omer on 27 June. Most significantly 74's CO, Squadron Leader Mungo Park, was shot down and killed when flying X4668. Mungo Park's death was a severe setback to the squadron as he had been with them since September 1939 and had been the popular choice to take over command following Sailor Malan's departure. The other pilots shot down were Sergeant C.G. Hilken (W3252) and New Zealander Pilot Officer W.J. Sandman (W3210), both of whom became PoWs.

For the Tigers the situation soon went from bad to worse as seven more pilots were lost in early July, commencing on the 2nd when Pilot Officer S.Z. Krol (W3263) and Sergeant G.T. Evans (W3259) were shot down during an afternoon sweep. Both pilots survived, but Krol was later murdered by the Gestapo as a result of his involvement in the 'Great Escape' from *Stalag Luft III* in March 1944. On 3 July Sergeant Cochrane (W3232) went missing over France and the following day Sergeant W.G. Henderson (W3258) was shot down and killed on a sweep near St Omer. The final reversal occurred on the 6th during Circus 35 when Pilot Officer W.M. Skinner DFM (W3208), Sergeant L.R. Carter (W3176) and Sergeant W.G. Lockhart (W3317) were all shot down, only Skinner surviving. No squadron could continue as an effective fighting force having sustained such heavy losses, and on 8 July 74 was replaced by 72 Squadron, which flew into Gravesend from Acklington in Northumberland.

72 Squadron were no strangers to the area as Biggin Hill had been their base during the climax of the Battle of Britain in September 1940. Since then they had been involved mainly on shipping protection duties along the north-east coast and were commanded by Squadron Leader Desmond Sheen DFC, who, apart from a brief spell as a photo-reconnaissance pilot in early 1940, had been with them since June 1937.

With the Biggin Hill Wing now comprising 72, 92 and 609 Squadrons, the pressure was maintained for the rest of the month, as Don Kingaby wrote in his autobiography:

> When I returned from leave I settled down to the most intensive period of ops I have ever done apart from the Normandy show. In just under three weeks I took part in twenty-three shows over France, doing three a day whenever the weather was fine enough. On my second day back I had one of the luckiest shots at a Hun I have ever had. We were just crossing the French coast on the way home when two aircraft dived down in front of my section. I thought for a moment they were Hurricanes and let them go, then I realised they were 109s and that they formed part of the Huns' old decoy trick.
>
> I looked above me and sure enough there was a small bunch of 109s with another two diving down in front of me to try it again. I knew that if I dived down after them the rest would come tearing down onto my tail, but I decided to take a chance this time and took a quick squirt at the first one. I broke away and climbed immediately to throw the 109's pals off the scent without looking to see what had happened to him. I hadn't expected to hit him as it had been such a hurried shot and I was amazed when my No.2 called up on the R/T to say that I had got two of them. Apparently I hit the first one and the second collided with him. I looked down and there were two parachutes, and then two great splashes in the water far below as the remains of their machines hit the drink. When I returned to base and checked up on my ammunition I found that I had only given a three-second burst of cannon and machine-gun to get two Huns!

During early July 1941 four-engined Stirling heavy bombers were used on a number of Circuses. Don Kingaby recalls his experiences on two such operations, the second of which took place on 8 July:

It was in July that we escorted four-engined bombers over France for the first time, the first effort was with three Stirlings which we took to Lille to bomb the steel works. Although the Hun had by this time opened his attack on Russia, there were still enough enemy fighters left in northern France to warrant an escort of twenty-six squadrons to take those three Stirlings in on what was later to prove only a shallow penetration into enemy territory. We were very impressed by the load that the Stirlings dropped and the effect it had on the target below, for they carried three times as much H.E. as the twelve Blenheims to which we were accustomed. We had no action on this particular show as we were close escort and all the other squadrons around prevented the Huns from getting anywhere near the bombers. The next show I did with the Stirlings however provided plenty of excitement.

We took off at first light to take three Stirlings in to Lens. When we arrived over the French coast the sun was still just above the horizon on our port bow. I realised that when we had reached the target and turned for home we would be in a very sticky position as the 109s would be able to come in straight and level behind us and we would not be able to see them on account of the sun. We crossed the French coast and had got about ten miles in when a 109 came in at me out of the sun and almost head-on. I only saw him at the last moment and didn't have time to fire at him. He flashed past me and fired off a verey cartridge. From that time on until we crossed out again all hell seemed to let loose. The 109s poured in from all directions and we were so busy dealing with them that it just wasn't possible to see what happened to anything we fired at. Then the Hun flak joined in with great gusto and winged one of the Stirlings. A thin stream of smoke began to pour from his outboard port engine, but he carried on and at last we reached the target which was obliterated in clouds of smoke and dust.

The bombers turned for home and then we had the sun right up our tails. Things got even hotter than before as the 109s steamed in out of the sun whilst we were blinded. The Stirling that had been hit by flak before had received another nasty knock from flak over the target and a fire now began in the outboard engine. Gradually the fire spread along the wing towards the cockpit and then she keeled over like a stricken ship and went plunging to her doom. Only three of the crew baled out and, flaming like a torch, she screamed down and plunged into the middle of a factory in a small town about ten miles from the target. We forced on and eventually reached the coast without further loss. I had fired all my ammunition

92 Squadron pilots pose for the camera, S/L Jamie Rankin at centre. (*Author's collection*)

but couldn't even claim a damaged because I had been too busy to see what happened when I fired.

After crossing the coast the attacks faded out and I throttled back to conserve my petrol which was getting pretty low. I landed at a forward airfield to refuel and just after two more Spitties taxied in. The show that morning had been laid on at very short notice and no-one had had time to eat anything – a very bad thing to fly on an empty stomach. I wasn't feeling too good myself, but when the occupants of the other two Spitfires got out of their cockpits I couldn't restrain a grin. They were as green as the sea they had just flown over and both hurriedly disappeared from sight behind the nearest building!

On 9 July the Biggin Hill Wing flew a diversionary sweep in connection with Circus 41, a raid by three Stirlings on Mazingarbe. Three red bursts of flak from the coastal battery at Ambleteuse announced the wing's entry into France and soon after several gaggles of 109s were seen below. No.609 Squadron flying at 30,000ft had a bird's-eye view of 92 Squadron diving to attack but did not see any action themselves until they were on their way back when Me 109Fs were spotted patrolling two small vessels off Le Touquet. Flight Lieutenant John Bisdee and Pilot Officer

'Pyker' Offenberg went after them and Bisdee had no difficulty in latching onto one of the 109s, his fire causing it to enter an inverted dive from which it did not recover. No.92 Squadron in the meantime were much busier and claimed five Me 109s, one each to Squadron Leader Rankin, Flying Officer Geoff Wellum and Pilot Officer Philip Archer, and two to Sergeant Adolf Pietrasiak.

A former member of the Polish Air Force's 122 Eskadra, Pietrasiak had joined 92 Squadron on 4 June having also flown Curtiss H-75As with the French Air Force. Although he was destined to be with 92 for only a few weeks, he formed a brief but formidable partnership with Jamie Rankin, with whom he often flew as wingman. Don Kingaby recalled that he had the tenacity of a limpet, and usually answered to the nickname of 'Meaty Pete', an epithet that had come about following stories of his escape from occupied territory during which he claimed to have knifed over fifty German soldiers!

No.72 Squadron's first operation in 11 Group took place on 10 July and should have consisted of a wing sweep in connection with Circus 42, an attack by three Stirlings on the chemical works at Choques. Not long after take-off, however, the controller vectored them onto an incoming 'raid', which turned out to be friendly aircraft returning from France. Rather than abort the mission, the squadron continued over the Channel but were unable to find the rest of the wing due to haze. Having flown a rough semi-circle over occupied France, they withdrew, minus three of their number who had been picked off by marauding Me 109s. Indeed, the Messerschmitts had delivered their thrusts with such precision that one of their pilots was not aware that the squadron had even been attacked. All three of the pilots shot down were killed: Flying Officer J.M. Godlewski (W3411), Sergeant A.J. Casey (P8600) and Sergeant C.L. Harrison (P8604).

No.92 Squadron also had their problems. Jamie Rankin's R/T packed up shortly after take-off, the ensuing confusion prompting several aircraft to follow him back to Hawkinge, and Sergeant C.G. Waldern failed to return in somewhat mysterious circumstances. His disappearance prompted an ASR operation which included Don Kingaby:

> I was sure that he had been with us when we crossed out from the French coast between Calais and Dunkirk so I went off with David Lloyd to escort an air-sea rescue Lysander on a search. We patrolled low down on the water, flying at slow speed and with our hoods open, straining our eyes for signs of a dinghy against the scintillating reflections thrown up from the sea by the sun. After two hours we sighted him, lolling in his rubber dinghy, and drew the Lysander's

attention to him. The Lissie dropped him additional rations and first aid equipment then rumbled off to guide a rescue launch to the spot while we returned to Manston for fuel. Waldern was back with us the next day none the worse for his ducking. He had apparently broken away from the squadron to attack a 109 on his own and had been bounced and shot down himself instead. Ten days later the same thing happened, but this time we heard no more of him. [Waldern was shot down and killed on 19 July in W3326.]

On 11 July, following a visit to Biggin by the New Zealand Prime Minister, Mr P. Frazer, the wing took off after lunch for an operation that would have Frank Ziegler working well into the night to compile a typically comprehensive report:

Circus 44 ensued in the afternoon . . . a special feature was the electrical machinations of an IFF Blenheim to deceive the enemy prior to the entry of the bombers and connected with a diversionary sweep in which Biggin took part. 609 in the lead at 27,000ft crossed the coast 7 miles east of Dunkirk and, turning towards Cassel, sighted 30–40 Me 109F climbing up through cumulus cloud, perhaps in answer to the Blenheim's ethereal vibrations. Convinced that their plan was to gain height and catch our formation from up-sun as it exited via Gravelines, S/L Robinson turned the Wing right and flew parallel with the coast about 15 miles inland, gradually converging on the enemy with a height advantage of 1,000ft.

E/a were in three squadrons line astern. The first was allowed to go unmolested then Yellow section (led by F/L Richey) attacked the second squadron and Red section (S/L Robinson) the last. The C.O. shot one down from dead astern and the pilot baled out. He followed another in a steep dive from 27,000ft to 10,000ft firing with m.g. all the way. Just as he was despairing running out of ammunition, his No.2 (the Station Commander, G/C Barwell) who had stuck with him all the way, leapt into the breach and firing cannon and m.g. turned the 109 into a ball of fire, this pilot also appearing to bale out. Previous to this the G/C, without losing contact with S/L Robinson, had fired at what must have been the third of the same formation of three and caused it to emit black smoke. Red 3 (P/O Seghers) had followed another e/a which broke to the right and dived on a Spitfire. P/O Seghers attacked and the e/a rolled on its back, smoking. He was surprised to see a parachute open.

Meanwhile Yellow section had been doing some fine team work, leader using R/T to give orders and warnings with such good effect that the section stuck together during three consecutive engage-

Sgt David Lloyd of 92 Squadron. (*via Johnston*)

ments. During the first, F/L Richey used all his cannon shells at close range on an e/a which went down pouring black smoke after making an attempt to climb, and is claimed as probably destroyed. The section then dived on another e/a only to find these were already being pursued by other Spitfires (probably Blue section). They therefore broke off this attack and using the speed of their dive, climbed up to 4 other 109s. Leaving the nearer pair to his section, F/L Richey attacked and damaged both the others with frontal and rear quarter attacks respectively. During these and other attacks Yellow 2 (Sgt Boyd) destroyed one and damaged another e/a (shattering the top of the cockpit and killing the pilot of the first). Yellow 3 (P/O Du Monceau) probably destroyed another which turned on its back and fell sideways out of control. Yellow 4 (Sgt Bramble) damaged another. During the whole engagement there was only one pilot of 609 Squadron who did not fire his guns. It was a proper bounce!

When the wing landed back at Biggin details emerged of an incident which showed outstanding bravery on the part of one of 92 Squadron's pilots and a selfless devotion to duty. While over France, Sergeant David

Lloyd (Blue 3) found that his R/T was malfunctioning and was given permission by his leader to return to base, together with his wingman Pilot Officer J. Dougall (W3183). As they crossed out over the coast Dougall became aware of three 109s closing in from behind, but, because of his leader's radio problem, was unable to warn him. Despite coming under attack himself he flew on and gradually overtook Lloyd, waggling his wings to attract his attention. By this time Dougall's Spitfire was going down on fire, but he had achieved his objective and Lloyd was able to fight his way back to make a safe landing. As Dougall had not been seen to bale out it was assumed that he had been killed, but news eventually arrived that he was a prisoner, albeit badly wounded. Indeed, his injuries were so severe that he was repatriated two years later, at which time he received the DFC.

Having been blessed with hot, sunny conditions since the escalation of operations in mid-June, occasional bad weather made life more difficult during the next few days and again it was to be 72 Squadron who suffered most severely with the loss of three more pilots. Sergeant W. Lamberton (R7219) was shot down to become a PoW during Circus 48 on the 14th, and three days later Pilot Officer L.B. Fordham (P8544) baled out into the sea having been hit by flak. He was eventually located by the air-sea rescue services, but was found to have drowned. On the 19th Sergeant R.F. Lewis (W3181) failed to return from a Circus operation, and New Zealander Sergeant G.F. Breckon was lucky to survive when he crash-landed on Ramsgate beach in the middle of a minefield.

A general improvement in the weather led to the RAF operating over a wide front on 23–24 July with attacks by heavy bombers against the *Scharnhorst* and *Gneisenau* at La Pallice and Brest, together with diversionary attacks by 2 Group Blenheims on Cherbourg, while in the east, two Circuses were flown on each day. The first attack (Circus 59) was against a target in the Forêt d'Eperlecques, with the oil refinery at Mazingarbe being raided in the evening. During the second operation, Sergeant Sika opened 72 Squadron's account when he shot down an Me 109 north of Boulogne, but the hazy conditions encountered made life difficult for both sides.

On 24 July two sweeps were flown by the Biggin Hill Wing in quick succession, operations that were timed to coincide with bomber attacks on the French ports in the west. The first sweep produced little reaction, but a number of encounters took place during the second which saw Sergeant 'Johnnie' Johnston of 92 Squadron claim two Me 109s as probables. On the debit side Sergeant S.H. Vinter, also of 92 Squadron, was shot down and killed in W3381, and Sergeant Breckon's luck finally deserted him when he was shot down and taken prisoner.

Sgt Walter 'Johnnie' Johnston of 92 Squadron with W3314 QJ-H. (*Johnston*)

Towards the end of July the met situation deteriorated once again, allowing some respite as Circus operations had to be temporarily postponed. Pilots kept their hand in with a few Rhubarb sorties, but these were largely ineffectual and little was achieved. The poor weather proved beneficial in one respect, as it allowed two of the wing's squadrons to move home with relative ease, 72 Squadron taking up residence at Biggin Hill on the 26th, with 609 Squadron moving in the opposite direction to Gravesend.

Shortly after 609's move to Gravesend a number of personnel changes took place within the Biggin Hill Wing that were prompted by the departure of Sailor Malan at the end of his tour. Squadron Leader Michael Robinson, who had led 609 with distinction since October 1940, was promoted to Wing Commander to take over from Malan, his position with the 'West Riding' Squadron being taken by Squadron Leader George 'Sheep' Gilroy, who had been awarded the DFC during service with 603 (City of Edinburgh) Squadron. The appointment of Robinson as Wing Leader would only be temporary, however, as he was also due for a rest from operations, and within four weeks he too would be replaced.

THREE

BIGGIN HILL WING, AUGUST–DECEMBER 1941

With the wing's re-organisation still only partially complete, offensive operations began once again on 7 August with two Circus operations to the aerodrome at St Omer/Longuenesse and Lille power station, although cloud build-up caused the second objective to be abandoned in favour of invasion barges at Gravelines. It was near the alternative target that Squadron Leader Rankin shot down an Me 109, his eighth 'kill' since joining 92 Squadron in February (not including shared victories).

Two days later, 92 Squadron had more success during a wing fighter sweep near Boulogne which further underlined their position as 11 Group's top-scoring unit. Having crossed into France at 25,000ft with 72 and 609 Squadrons stepped up above and behind, a number of Me 109s were seen below which tempted Blue section to launch an attack. The German fighters, however, were acting as bait, and as soon as the Spitfires dived, they were themselves attacked by more 109s which had been waiting up-sun for the opportunity to pounce. Don Kingaby (W3320 – Blue 3) was forced to break sharply and consequently lost contact with the rest of the section. He then came under attack from a group of four Me 109s, but managed to lose them by selecting maximum boost and climbing into the glare of the sun. With the tactical situation in his favour once more, he turned to deliver his own attack, but the 109s saw him coming and dived away for the safety of a layer of cloud at around 10,000ft. Kingaby followed them down but was not able to get within firing range before they disappeared from view.

Although alone, Kingaby was quite prepared to go on the lookout for enemy aircraft and positioned his Spitfire just below the cloud layer to protect himself from being attacked from above. He soon spotted two Me 109Fs climbing out of Le Touquet and proceeded to stalk them, waiting for the ideal moment to attack. Selecting the left-hand 109, he fired a two-second burst with cannon and machine-guns which caused it to 'wobble' violently before it turned over and dived vertically, pouring glycol and black smoke.

Kingaby immediately climbed up to the cloud base again, thereby restoring his height advantage over the pilot of the other 109, who was seen to be going round in a steep turn, apparently looking for his partner's assailant. When he launched his attack, rather than dive away out of trouble, the German pilot tried to out-turn the Spitfire, his only realistic chance of success being to make his opponent overshoot. However, by closing his throttle and skidding violently, Kingaby was able to reduce his speed sufficiently to tuck in behind. At a range of less than 100 yards, his fire struck the 109 on its wing and centre-section, causing it to roll over lazily and dive into the ground about five miles south of Le Touquet. Having used up all of his 20mm ammunition, Kingaby sought the sanctuary of the cloud once more and returned to Biggin, where he landed at 1850 hrs, having been airborne for one hour and thirty minutes.

While Kingaby was fighting his lone battles, Red section were continually engaged for a hectic ten-minute period during which three 109s were damaged, two by Jamie Rankin (Red 1) and one by his No.2 Sergeant Stan Harrison. Sergeant Le Cheminant (W3375 – Red 4) dived after a 109 and then found himself completely alone at 13,000ft over Boulogne. His isolation was to be short-lived as he soon spotted four 109s in his mirror and was forced to haul his aircraft around in a steep turn to the right. His turn took him directly into the path of one of the 109s which had broken away from the other three and was showing practically all of its belly. A short burst of cannon and machine-gun fire caused catastrophic failure of the aircraft's fuselage and it broke in two aft of the cockpit and fell away to crash in the middle of Boulogne.

In the meantime, further formations of Me 109s had joined the battle higher up, prompting Rankin to order a general withdrawal. As Rankin dived for home an Me 109F followed him down, opening fire 1,000ft above the sea and forcing him to break hard right. Unfortunately for the German, he was carrying too much speed and overshot, which gave Rankin the opportunity to reverse his turn and fire a burst at minimum deflection. Although he missed completely, his fire prompted the pilot of the 109 to enter a steep turn to the right during which his aircraft suffered a high-speed stall and crashed into the sea.

Other members of the squadron had an eventful time as they tried to get home, and Pilot Officer Neville Duke found himself outnumbered 2:1 at 2,000ft over Boulogne. As he was engrossed in a turning competition with a 109, tracer shells passed close by his canopy and another 109 slipped by on his right-hand side. The range between the two aircraft increased rapidly but Duke was able to fire a long burst with some

Pas de Calais

deflection which struck the 109 and caused it to roll onto its back and enter a slow spin. It was last seen as it entered cloud at around 800ft. Shortly afterwards he was jumped by two more 109s which chased him in and out of cloud to within two or three miles of Dover.

Throughout the rest of the month two, and sometimes three, operations were flown each day, weather conditions permitting, a punishing schedule that took its toll on both man and machine. Don Kingaby's logbook gives an indication of the level of activity. For the period 14–19 August he carried out eight offensive sweeps over France, two on the 14th, three on the 16th, with a further three on the 19th. Total flying time for these operations amounted to eleven hours and five minutes, the longest trip being one hour and forty minutes for a sweep from Dunkirk to Calais on the 16th, the shortest at 1 hour exactly, during the escort of Blenheims attacking E-boats in Boulogne harbour on the 14th.

Of two escort operations flown by the Biggin Hill Wing on the 18th, the first produced little of note, except for a mysterious Spitfire which joined the wing on the way back, one that still wore the old green/brown camouflage (Biggin's aircraft having been repainted in a green/grey scheme the day before). In contrast, the second operation of the day provoked a determined response and provided successes for Pilot Officer Vicki Ortmans and Pilot Officer 'Duke' Du Monceau, both of 609 Squadron.

It is interesting to note that, in the first of these operations, a new tactical formation was tried with each section in line abreast. Since engagements with the *Luftwaffe* had become commonplace more than a year before, the question of fighter tactics had been debated endlessly, but there was still considerable disagreement among Wing Leaders as to the most effective formation. As leader of the Biggin Hill Wing, Sailor Malan had favoured the use of three sections of four, each in line astern, which effectively formed two pairs, Nos. 1 and 3 being the leaders, with Nos. 2 and 4 their respective wingmen. One of the formation's main attributes was that it was relatively easy to fly – pilots had little difficulty in maintaining their position – but its biggest drawback was its lack of cross-cover. As a result, all aircraft had to fly a weaving course to clear the area behind them and invariably the effect became more pronounced towards the tail end of the formation. Consequently, the No.4 found himself manoeuvring the most and having to use higher throttle settings, and more fuel, to stay in touch. Although Malan had become Wing Leader on 10 March, it took some weeks for his ideas to be implemented. Neville Duke recalls that the old vic of three, with or without 'weavers', was still being flown as late as mid-May.

In contrast, the Tangmere Wing had gone over to using a formation similar to that flown by the *Luftwaffe* with four aircraft in virtual line abreast. This system provided excellent cross-cover and avoided the wasting of precious fuel, although there were still problems with the direction and timing of the break when the unit came under attack.

As already mentioned, the Biggin Hill Wing dabbled with the 'finger four' formation themselves and flew other systems on a trial basis, not all of which were successful, as Neville Duke recollects:

> I remember some experiments with different ideas and recall very well a complete shambles when Malan tried to lead the wing on a training flight with a formation called (for some unknown reason) 'American pairs'. This consisted of sections of two aircraft scattered all over the sky. It seemed a good idea at the time and gave good area cover with a lot of freedom of action, but was quite uncontrollable as a wing.

Despite everything, the basic line astern formation was to be retained for the rest of the year; indeed, 92 Squadron were still using these tactics when Duke met up with them again in North Africa in late-1942!

On 19 August Circus 81, otherwise known as 'Operation Leg', took place which included the dropping of an artificial leg for Wing Commander Douglas Bader who had been shot down and taken prisoner ten days before. Although this particular operation had a distinctly humanitarian element to it, the outcome turned out to be less than charitable for Vicki Ortmans of 609 Squadron whose Spitfire (W3241) was attacked by two Me 109s and set on fire near Dunkirk. He was forced to bale out in mid-Channel, his position being fixed by several Spitfires which orbited overhead until a rescue launch arrived to pick him up.

Sergeant 'Johnnie' Johnston also had an eventful day, together with his Flight Commander, Flight Lieutenant R.M. 'Dickie' Milne:

> Milne, who was to take over after Jamie got the wing, was an ex-Battle of Britain pilot but he was new to the squadron and on this day he told me he would slip in behind me after take-off to get the hang of tactics on sweeps. We were flying withdrawal cover southeast of Dunkirk when, out of the blue, he called up '109 below' and peeled off. We went down from 15,000ft to about 200ft chasing this blasted 109 but we didn't realise at the time where we were heading. All I knew was that there was an awful lot of flak coming up at us. He was on my right and we were really at nought feet when a hedge in front of us suddenly exploded. There were two multiple barrel cannons firing at us and I remember seeing a tracer round bounce off Dickie's wing and then come straight over me. We then

Sgt 'Johnnie' Johnston of 92 Squadron. (*Johnston*)

found where we were heading – straight for Calais-Marck aero-drome where we really got hammered with flak.

The two eventually landed at Manston to refuel, where Johnston counted a total of thirty-six bullet holes in the tailplane of his Spitfire.

Not long after, on 27 August, an incident occurred which, sadly, was to be repeated on many other occasions during the high summer of 1941. 'Johnnie' Johnston again:

I had been promised a forty-eight-hour pass from noon on the 27th to get home to Newcastle as the following day was my 21st birthday. The sergeant pilots of 92 used to sleep off camp for safety reasons and, as the lightest sleeper, I had the phone by my bed. I was not amused on the morning of the 27th to get a call from the CO giving me a list of pilots required for an early show which included me! I was on the wagon going up to the 'drome at around 0400 hrs for briefing for a 0530 hrs take-off.

Over France there were a hell of a lot of 109s around and Sergeant Roff (W3319 QJ-X) got hit. Now I had been hit somewhere in the tail but I knew that it wasn't too serious. Sometimes when you were hit, depending on the angle it went in, it would go round and round and rattled like a nail in a tin can, but Roff was in a much worse state than me. His prop had stopped, so I thought I would try to escort him back and got him to about twelve miles off Dunkirk. I flew alongside him once we had got offshore, but I could tell from the way he was sitting that he had been wounded. He looked up at me and turned his thumb down so there was no doubt that he was in a bad way.

His aircraft was in a gradual dive and I tried to signal to him to jump out while he had the height. I got in really close so that he couldn't misunderstand what my actions were meaning. He nodded his head very, very slowly and just as I was easing away he jettisoned his hood so I knew that he was going to come out. By the time he jumped for it he was fairly low, the 'chute opened OK but he was in the water pretty well at once. He actually released himself from his parachute just before he hit the water.

By now I was extremely short on petrol and as I was going round him he put his hand up but I couldn't understand what he was getting at. His 'chute had blown away by this time and then I realised that his dinghy was still attached to it. I tried to get mine off but it was almost impossible, so I climbed up and contacted Biggin control for another Mayday. I then went down and waved at him. He was still alive but that was it, there wasn't anything else I could do for him. I found out afterwards that he hadn't been picked up.

No.72 Squadron also took part in this operation and lost two aircraft, that flown by Flying Officer H. Skalski, who was taken prisoner after baling out over France, and Sergeant Rutherford (P8609), who parachuted into the Channel three miles off Ramsgate. Unlike Roff, he was quickly located by a rescue launch and brought safely ashore.

Since their arrival in 11 Group, 72 had not seen as much success as their counterparts but began to make amends on 29 August during Circus 88, an early-morning raid on the marshalling yards at Hazebrouck. The French coast was crossed at 24,000ft but, as was usually the case, the 109s were higher still and many condensation trails could be seen up-sun. Several enemy formations were reported and one began to assume a position that posed a distinct threat. Squadron Leader Des Sheen decided to take the initiative and entice the 109s to attack, an invitation that was quickly accepted. Very soon a large-scale action was being fought.

As more and more 109s joined the battle, the situation became desperate and the squadron's Spitfires had to fight their way out as best they could. Squadron Leader Sheen fired at the last in a *Schwarm* of Me 109Es that passed through his sights producing a spume of glycol as it fell away. He then dived for home, and apart from a brief exchange with two more 109Es near Dunkirk, his only concern came from heavy and accurate flak as he crossed out over the coast.

Pilot Officer E.P.W. Bocock was attacked from his starboard rear by three Me 109Fs but found that he was easily able to out-turn them. Although completely outnumbered, targets were at least easy to come by and he fired at two 109s which passed in front of him at about 100 yards' range. He succeeded in hitting both, bits flying off the wings and nose cowling of the first, with white smoke pouring from the engine of the second. This aircraft then fell into a spin that gradually became flatter as it went down. Bocock tried to follow, but was forced to break when attacked by yet more 109s. Pilot Officer W.J. Rosser shot down a 109 in flames ten miles south of Mardyck, and Flying Officer K. Kosinsky claimed another after chasing it down to 4,000ft and leaving it diving vertically, enveloped in thick black smoke. Having successfully evaded the attentions of a group of six more, he then fired at a single 109 which shuddered for a few seconds under the impact of his shells and fell into cloud near the coast. No.72 Squadron's excellent performance had to be set against the loss of Sergeant P.T. Grisdale (P8713) who was shot down by *Oberleutnant* Seegatz of 4/JG26.

For the first two weeks in September poor weather with mist and fog prevented any large-scale operations from being carried out, and it was not until the 17th that Circus operations could be resumed. It was during this period that 92 Squadron's Jamie Rankin took over as Wing Leader, his command passing in turn to 'Dickie' Milne. 'Johnnie' Johnston compares Rankin with one of his predecessors:

> When Jamie took over as Wing Leader things did change a little bit. Malan was a very hard taskmaster. He expected that everybody who he picked to put into a job could do it, and if they couldn't, he got rid. He was an excellent tactician, but he was ruthless and had a bit of a reputation for losing his No.2s. Quite often he would take evasive action without any warning and the No.2 was left high and dry, miles behind, which was why some of us used to find ourselves stuck on our own at times.
>
> Jamie was different. He had been a good CO, but he freely admitted that he was learning, the same as everybody else, because 92 was his first operational trip after a time as an instructor [Rankin

had in fact spent a short time as a supernumerary with 64 Squadron in early 1941]. As far as gunnery was concerned he was damn good, but the thing that impressed me the most was his flying which was absolutely immaculate. If you were supposed to be going into a turn of 110 degrees, you did 110, not 105 or 115, but 110 exactly, so personally, I found life easier with him as Wing Leader.

Shortly after the resumption of Circus operations over France, reports began to come in of a new German fighter powered by a radial engine that had been seen flying with the familiar Me 109Fs. At first it was thought that the sightings were former French Air Force Curtiss Hawk 75As pressed into service by the Germans, but the aircraft's speed quickly put paid to this unlikely theory. This was, of course, the Focke-Wulf Fw 190A, unofficially named *Wurger* or Butcher Bird, an aircraft that was destined to be one of the classic fighter designs of all time and one that was to have a profound effect on the development of the Spitfire V.

The history of the Fw 190 can be traced back to the autumn of 1937 when Focke-Wulf *Flugzeugbau* received an order from the *Reichluft-ministerium* for a new aircraft that was to push the boundaries of piston-engined fighter technology close to the ultimate. The design team, headed by Dipl Ing Kurt Tank, produced initial proposals based on the liquid-cooled Daimler-Benz DB601 and the BMW 139 air-cooled radial. Unusually for the time, the latter was given preference, despite contemporary thinking that radials were not best suited for fighter designs due to their comparatively large frontal area and high drag when compared with inline 'V' type engines. The first prototype was ready for flight testing a mere ten months after work commenced on the project, the resultant design being small and lightweight, with considerable ingenuity having been employed to reduce profile drag.

By mid-1939 early examples of the Fw 190 had already achieved 370mph but more performance would soon be available thanks to the new BMW 801 air-cooled radial. Although the new engine weighed more than the BMW 139, it was more powerful and offered much more in the way of development potential. By the spring of 1941 the first production batch of 100 Fw 190A-1s had all been delivered and top speed had now been increased to 389mph. The initial A-1 variant possessed only four MG17 machine-guns, but this inadequate armament was remedied in the A-2 where the two MG17s mounted in the wing roots were replaced by 20mm MG FF cannons. After testing at Rechlin, the first Fw 190A-2s were delivered to JG26 at Le Bourget in the summer of 1941, and by late September they were ready to take on the Spitfire V head-to-head.

Circus 103B on 27 September provided one of the first opportunities

Some of 92 Squadron's Spitfires in formation near Biggin Hill. (*Author's collection*)

for Biggin Hill's pilots to have a close look at the new German fighter; 609 Squadron's ORB describes the action:

> Fair weather heralds another bout of action and the Wing takes off as high cover wing to 12 Blenheims bound for Mazingarbe, W/C Rankin leading with 609. Crossing the coast at Mardyck at 27,000ft it became immediately apparent that Jerry is going to resist. An enormous gaggle of 109s is seen passing some 5,000ft below. The Wing dives and 609 becomes split up into sections and individuals – Sgt van Schaick is attacked 4 times. F/O Dieu becomes involved in a turning competition with a 109 until the latter makes the mistake of turning in the opposite direction thus presenting F/O Dieu with a nice beam shot (m.g. only) at 40 yds. E/a dives vertically streaming white, then black smoke.
>
> F/O V. Ortmans follows W/C Rankin to the target area and on the way back informs him of 2 109s about to attack, but the latter does not hear clearly and F/O Ortmans is engaged alone, his aircraft being hit in the fuselage. Two other Spits relieve him but by the time he leaves the French coast at Le Touquet he has only 7 gallons of petrol. Informing Controller, he bales out having reached a point

5 miles off Dover by gliding and within 15 minutes is picked up by a fishing boat, whence he is transferred to the same rescue boat which rescued him a few weeks ago.

Meanwhile Yellow section, led by S/L Gilroy, has also been engaged and has followed the beehive to the target. Off Le Touquet it becomes engaged again with 2 Fw 190s, and off Dungeness meets 2 109Es. As for Blue section, F/L Offenberg, after damaging a 109, blacks out and afterwards joins up again with Blue 2 (P/O Du Monceau). Approaching the coast they are attacked by two more 109s and 5 miles off the coast P/O Du Monceau succeeds in bringing one plunging down towards the sea.

No.92 Squadron were also engaged, and 'Dickie' Milne, their new CO, opened his account with his new unit claiming a 109 probably destroyed with another damaged. 'Johnnie' Johnston flew on this operation and explains one of the factors taken into consideration during planning:

It should be appreciated that the sun played a great part in deciding which way we went in and came out. We did not like the sun behind us when coming out for home and this decided whether the job was am or pm, if we had a choice! I had a good pair of eyes in those days and I was often put in as Red 4 with instructions to report at once if suspicious, and then it was me who would call the break. I was sitting there, minding my own business, when I saw a gaggle of black dots dropping on us from out of the sun.

We broke into the 109s to starboard and climbing, and at the top we turned port. I was lagging a bit. A very prettily marked 109 came across my front from starboard and fastened onto Beakey (P/O P.H. Beake). I hauled round, pulled through the 109 and fired a burst. It took off his rudder and a few more pieces, finally showing strikes aft of the cockpit, and then I realised I'd done this without a gunsight, I had forgotten to switch it on! We re-formed into a squadron and when nearly out we were caught again by the 109s who had also re-grouped. I claimed another probable.

No.72 Squadron claimed an Me 109 destroyed through Sergeant Falkiner, with Flight Lieutenant Hall gaining a probable, but two of their pilots were shot down and killed, Sergeant A.F. Binns (AB843) and Sergeant J.G. Merrett (P8560).

Sixty years on it is difficult to appreciate the stresses and strains, both physical and mental, that were imposed on pilots, day after day. Once engaged, to stand any chance of survival, a pilot would be forced to fly his aircraft to the very edge of its performance envelope, a situation that could lead to him being physically drained within a matter of minutes. Neville Duke remembers some of the problems:

> Despite a lot of adrenalin flowing, there was considerable physical effort involved in handling the controls during constant high-G manoeuvres while, at the same time, straining to hold off black-out. Pre-engagement, there had to be constant scanning to the rear which was pretty wearing on the neck. Chafing was relieved by wearing a parachute silk scarf. Of course it was very cold at altitude, with no heating in the Spitfire. Numb hands were a particular problem, in spite of wearing silk inner gloves and outer gauntlets. Fur-lined flying boots were the norm. Misting or icing up was also a major difficulty. Ice occurred mainly on the inside of the front bulletproof screen (I carried a rag soaked in glycol for this purpose), outside ice could be cleared by de-ice glycol spray.

'Johnnie' Johnston recalls:

> In a steep turn you were pulling an awful lot of G but you became adept at seeing a little bit of grey come across your eyes and you knew that you were about on the verge of blacking out. Then you either kept it where it was, or eased off a little bit. You could hear all right, but you just couldn't see properly. I think everyone blacked out a number of times; hauling it around you actually went before the aircraft shuddered, but with experience you were able to keep it just on the verge.
>
> We used to get up to 25/26,000ft quite regularly, but 30,000ft and above was really stretching it. On those occasions it was bitterly cold. We used to wear straightforward uniform and we all had our big white sweaters and seaboot stockings. Our wives, sweethearts or mothers used to knit big thick tubes that you could pull up so that they came from the top of your stockings up to your thighs, but it was still mighty cold.
>
> On one trip we were up high and all of us were really hanging on our props. I was flying No.3 behind Jamie Rankin and we were at the point where, if we had tried to fire our cannon, we would have stalled. Then I looked to starboard and, completely unannounced, a 109 came up alongside. He was slightly above and he knew damned fine that he was as safe as houses. He looked over and gave me a wave and then pulled up and climbed merrily away, and I thought 'My God, what would I give for that.'
>
> Our canopies used to ice up on the inside, even a turn would

change the pressure inside the cockpit, and when that happened a thin film of ice could come over your windscreen. You had to loosen your straps, lean forward and try to scratch the ice off, but it didn't really disappear until you got lower down.

Flight at high altitude demanded peak fitness, but the pressure of constant operations often resulted in pilots continuing to fly when they would have been better off staying on the ground; indeed, Neville Duke had already landed himself in hospital following a dogfight with two Me 109s. During a steep dive he felt excruciating pain in his ears and suddenly became aware that he could no longer hear the noise of the engine. When he was examined by the squadron MO it was discovered that the changes in pressure experienced during his rapid descent had cracked both ear drums. Wherever possible pilots did not fly when suffering from colds but on this occasion Duke had only been aware of having a slightly sore throat prior to the sortie. His hearing gradually came back over the next three weeks, but this was by no means an isolated incident. In comparison to the tiredness which was the inevitable result of a high cockpit workload, mental strain which gradually built up over a period of time was much more insidious, and ultimately, much more dangerous.

On occasion, pilots even had to put up with hazards during off-duty hours as 'Johnnie' Johnston recalls:

> The boffins were always trying to improve things and one time they produced something to fireproof our equipment. They arrived at Biggin to give a demo and petrol was spattered over an unwilling volunteer who stood there complete with helmet, gloves, boots and wearing a flying suit. The 'blue touch paper' was ignited and suddenly we had Guy Fawkes. Our boffins had fireproofed everything except the sheepskin showing at the top of the boots which blew up nicely! The fire was swiftly put out, but we never heard of the scheme after that.

On 2 October the Biggin Hill Wing took off at 1200 hrs to carry out a diversionary sweep routing Berck sur Mer–Abbeville–Le Treport in connection with Circus 104. Weather conditions were perfect with unlimited visibility, and as the wing proceeded north-east towards Abbeville a number of enemy aircraft could be seen manoeuvring high above. Of the three squadrons involved, 72 and 609 were at full strength, but 92 Squadron, who were flying at the lowest level, had only been able to put up a total of eight aircraft.

While over France, 92's Blue section lost position with the rest of the

F/Sgt Don Kingaby DFM in the cockpit of W3320 *The Darlington Spitfire*. (*via Franks*)

wing and were considerably lower than they should have been. This was enough to prompt an attack, and within a matter of seconds Section Leader Flight Lieutenant J.W. 'Tommy' Lund (W3459), Sergeant K.G. Port (W3762) and Sergeant N.H. Edge (W3137) had been shot down. None survived. Pilot Officer Tony Bruce, the remaining member of the quartet, was injured when a cannon shell exploded on top of the armour plating behind his head, sending fine metal splinters up into his neck and scalp. Despite this he was able to shake off his attacker and made it back across the Channel to crash-land near Ashford. Several pilots from 609 later reported that a 92 Squadron Spitfire had been seen trailing glycol prior to the attack which might account for Blue section becoming detached from the rest of the squadron. (Although some accounts have stated that 92 Squadron's aircraft were shot down by Fw 190s, it seems more likely that they fell to Me 109Fs of JG2. As yet, the only Fw 190s in service were with II/JG26, whose pilots did not put in any claims on this day).

The situation became even worse for 92 Squadron the following day when they flew as part of the escort cover wing to an attack by six Blenheims of 88 Squadron on Ostend docks (Circus 105). Again under strength, Yellow section was badly bounced by elements of I/JG26 and Sergeant G.E.F. Woods-Scawen (AB779) and Sergeant H. Cox (W3710) were shot down and killed. The successful German pilots were *Gruppenkommandeur Hauptmann* Johannes Seifert and *Leutnant* Schauder of the 3rd *Staffel.* Despite being heavily outnumbered there were no further losses, the only success of the day being that achieved by Don Kingaby (W3320) who destroyed an Me 109F low over the Channel, despite the fact that he had lost the use of his reflector gunsight due to an electrical problem.

Having been in the front line for over a year it was clear that 92 Squadron were due for a break from operations, and shortly after it was announced that they would be pulled back to Digby in 12 Group to be replaced by the Canadians of 401 Squadron. A week before the move took place, 'Dickie' Milne was able to exact retribution for the losses the squadron had sustained in recent weeks, although his success was achieved thanks to a large slice of good fortune.

Circus 108B was an attack by eighteen Blenheims of 114 and 139 Squadrons on the chemical works at Mazingarbe in the early afternoon of 13 October. The Biggin Hill squadrons formed the escort cover wing but, on crossing into France, Milne's oxygen system started to leak and it soon became clear that he would be unable to remain at altitude for much longer. Handing over the squadron to Flight Lieutenant Richardson, his 'A' Flight Commander, he dropped down to join up with a squadron lower down in the beehive, but soon had to descend even further.

As he did so a single Me 109 attacked, forcing him to turn completely around in defence, but the pilot of the German aircraft was not prepared to mix it and quickly dived away at full throttle. When Milne searched the skies around him he found that he was completely alone and the seriousness of his situation was immediately apparent. By now he was down to 9,000ft and setting course for the coast; he flew a zigzag course to clear his tail. It was not long before he saw two Me 109Es well above and behind, but fortunately he was in their blind spot and the two passed overhead, oblivious to the tempting target below. As they flew on, he got into position behind the No.2 and opened fire, black smoke and flames pouring from the stricken aircraft which rolled over and went down. Milne was also able to put in an attack on the leading 109, hitting its radiator, but it quickly dived away before he could inflict further damage. As he watched it descend he saw the first aircraft explode as it hit the ground.

Just before he was about to cross the coast on his way home, he became aware of two more 109s in his mirror and just had enough time to skid wildly to the left and slam his throttle shut before they were able to deliver their attack. The pilots of the German aircraft were not prepared for such sudden evasive action and both overshot, the No.2 turning slightly to the right as he did so. Milne swung in behind the leader and opened fire at 70 yards, his shells hitting it all the way up the fuselage which trailed puffs of grey smoke. The 109 broke to the right, but this took it directly into the path of the other Messerschmitt and the two collided, debris being flung over a wide area. The two 109s fell together, but only one parachute emerged from the shattered remains. Milne did not hang around to see the outcome and dived away to cross the Channel at wave-top height, re-arming and re-fuelling at Manston.

Throughout the rest of October 1941 the new Focke-Wulf Fw 190 was seen on many occasions and never failed to impress. On the 21st of the month 72 Squadron carried out an offensive sweep which was to provide withdrawal support to other squadrons returning from St Omer via Hardelot. The Squadron ORB records their reactions:

> Flight Lieutenant Campbell (W3511) was attacked by four aircraft all with radial engines and square tipped wings similar to 109Bs which out-climbed him very easily when he turned towards them. Several other pilots reported the amazing speed and climb of the radial-engined aircraft – no doubt Fw 190s.

Although the Fw 190s' arrival came as a considerable shock to Fighter Command, there should have been an aircraft available to deal with it. The Hawker Typhoon had been designed as the next-generation fighter-interceptor for the RAF and with a top speed of just over 400mph, much was expected of it. It entered service on 11 September 1941 with 56 Squadron at Duxford but its complex 24-cylinder Napier Sabre engine proved to be chronically unreliable. Even by the end of 1942 its time between overhaul was still only twenty-five hours – most of the early units did not get that far. If that were not enough, there were also problems with the seepage of carbon monoxide fumes into the cockpit and occasional structural failures of the rear fuselage, but of fundamental importance was the fact that its performance and manoeuvrability above 20,000ft were clearly inferior to the new Focke-Wulf. The Typhoon would eventually be developed into a superb ground attack aircraft, but for the time being it was something of a liability.

This left the Spitfire to carry on as the RAF's premier day fighter, but developed versions would not be available for many months. Although the two-speed, two-stage supercharged Rolls-Royce Merlin 61 had been successfully tested in a Spitfire III in September 1941, Spitfire IXs powered by this engine would not enter squadron service until June the following year. The larger-capacity Rolls-Royce Griffon engine, first flown in a Spitfire IV in late November 1941, would take even longer, and it was not to be cleared for operational use until February 1943 when 41 Squadron introduced the Spitfire XII. Even so, the early Griffon engines featured a single-stage supercharger and altitude performance proved to be disappointing, a situation that was not to be remedied until the arrival of the Griffon 61 in the Spitfire XIV a year later.

It was clear that in the short term there was little that could be done to combat the threat posed by the Fw 190, and in the meantime Spitfire V squadrons would have to carry on as best they could. Circus operations were gradually wound down throughout October, the last raid being carried out on 8th November. The approach of winter weather was not the only factor, however, as the whole policy of flying elaborate offensive operations over France had been called into question due to mounting losses.

During the year some of Fighter Command's most experienced pilots had been lost, including Wing Commanders Joe Kayll, Douglas Bader and Norman Ryder (Wing Leaders at Hornchurch, Tangmere and Kenley respectively) who had all been shot down and taken prisoner. In addition, Wing Commander John Gillan had been killed when leading the North Weald Wing, and a number of Squadron Commanders had also been lost. As the *Luftwaffe* had already discovered, to operate over enemy-held territory against well-equipped and battle-hardened adversaries was a daunting task. It had also become clear that the RAF's desire to dominate the opposing fighter force would be made even more difficult due to the evident superiority of the Fw 190 over the Spitfire V. For the moment, though, technical difficulties and demands from the Russian front would mean that the new fighter would not be in service in appreciable numbers in the west until the spring of 1942.

Despite this, 11 Group's losses continued to mount, and on 27 October it was Biggin Hill's turn to experience heavy casualties. Having arrived full of confidence just over a week before, 401 Squadron suffered severely at the hands of I and III/JG26 as the wing struggled to retain its cohesion during a sweep over Gravelines. Flying Officer C.A.B. Wallace (AB991), and Pilot Officer J.A. Small (AB983) were shot down and killed, while Pilot Officer C.W. Floody (W3964) and Sergeant B.G. Hodgkinson (W3955) were also brought down, surviving to become PoWs. Sergeant G.B. Whitney's Spitfire (W3452) was badly shot up but, through excellent flying, he managed to coax it back over the Channel before baling out successfully. Sergeant S.L. Thompson was not so fortunate: his parachute failed to open and his body was found near his aircraft (W3601), which crashed near Deal.

401 Squadron were relatively inexperienced, having spent much of the last six months at Digby, and had only recently converted to Spitfires from Hurricane IIbs. By chance they had come up against the cream of *Luftwaffe* fighter pilots in northern France; Sergeant Hodgkinson had become the ninety-third victim of *Oberstleutnant* Adolf Galland, *Kommodore* of JG26, and one of the other claimants was *Hauptmann* Josef 'Pips' Priller, whose score at the time stood at fifty-six. To complete a disastrous day, Pilot Officer Falkiner of 72 Squadron was shot down and killed in W3704.

No.609 Squadron could easily have suffered similar losses, as their ORB recounts:

> It is thought that a sweep by the Biggin Wing from Nieuport to Gravelines will encounter the usual lack of opposition and be good practice for 401 Squadron. It turns out far otherwise. S/L Gilroy is leading the Wing and as it is orbiting behind Gravelines to allow stragglers to catch up, he reports up to 50 e/a building up behind them. Though 401 bears the brunt of the attack, 609's Red section does well to get back intact, two of them being hit, Sgt Galloway (Canadian) by a cannon shell which puts his compressor out of action. Half-rolling he sees a 109 and 2 Fw 190s and gets on the tail of one of the latter only to find his guns will not work. He eludes them and lands at Manston without brakes or flaps. P/O Smith also suffers a damaged compressor and his guns don't work either.
>
> S/L Gilroy is engaged by 3 109s in mid Channel, comes down to sea level and up again in a series of head-on attacks. The remaining member of Red section, Lt Choron, sees 2 Fw 190s proceeding towards Manston at 5,000ft. He dives on one and after his attack it drops a wheel and dives to 2,000ft at which point Choron's attention is directed to 4 more 190s, one of which is firing at him, with m.g. only apparently. He causes this one to overshoot and firing at it from the quarter, produces a stream of white smoke. The others are not shaken off until 5 miles off Manston after an engagement lasting 10 minutes and Choron lands at Southend. The only other 609 pilot to fire is F/L Offenberg at 2 109s which come down on Blue section.
>
> Needless to say a post-mortem conference on the above is deemed highly necessary. Before it can be convened 609 are ordered off to protect two rescue boats searching the Channel for missing pilots. This proves to be almost as exciting an affair as the other and Intelligence has its worst day for months as battles

accumulate. Group agitates for reports and these become hours overdue. It might, in fact, easily have been the end of 609 (West Riding) Squadron, ops plotting no less than 3 lots of 15+, 2 of 12+, a 9+ and a 3+ with 609 and W/C Rankin as the only defence. S/L Gilroy's appeal for help going apparently unheeded until too late. Effective assistance is, however, given by the W/C who appoints himself 'high cover' to 609 and chases 15 109s back to France single handed, probably destroying one. He then draws off 5 Fw 190s and chases them back as well.

Meanwhile 609, down below near Dover, have been attacked by another lot of 15 109s. S/L Gilroy manages to get within range of the last pair and fires at both, one being seen to turn on its back and go vertically down. The effect of all this is to bring the rest of the enemy formation round into sun to attack and an exciting time is had by all till the enemy eventually decide to go home.

With reduced daylight hours, activity gradually eased off throughout November, and on the 18th 609 Squadron flew one last operation from Biggin Hill when they joined 401 Squadron in providing cover to eight Hurricanes attacking a distillery at Hesdin. In keeping with their exemplary record, they signed off with a victory when Pilot Officer Denis Barnham shot down one of three Fw 190s with whom he had a desperate struggle at zero feet all the way from Cap Gris Nez to Dover. Shortly afterwards 609 departed for the relative tranquillity of Digby to be replaced by Squadron Leader Myles Duke-Woolley's 124 Squadron.

Having lost nearly half of their number since arriving in 11 Group, 401 Squadron at last had something to celebrate on 22 November during an offensive sweep over France with 72 Squadron. Despite losing Flying Officer H.A. Sprague (shot down in AD516 to become a PoW) they went on to claim two Me 109s and two Fw 190s destroyed, with a further 190 as a probable. Pilot Officer Don Blakeslee achieved his first 'kill' in a long career that would eventually see him become a Lieutenant Colonel and leader of the 4th Fighter Group, Eighth Air Force. Flying as Yellow 3 in AD421 YO-H, Blakeslee attacked the leader in a section of four Me 109s from dead astern, his fire producing an explosion in its centre section. His victim was last seen going down on fire and trailing a plume of thick black smoke. Later, as he was returning to the English coast, he spotted two more 109s flying south-east and managed to get into an attacking position on the No.2, seeing several pieces fly off as his fire hit the aircraft's fuselage, aft of the cockpit.

Yellow 2, Pilot Officer I.C. Ormston, dived on two Me 109s at 8,000ft, his first attack producing no visible effect, but on breaking off he was presented with another 109 which was in a left-hand turn above him and exposing nearly all of its underside. Ormston fired the remainder of his ammunition at full deflection and was rewarded by the sight of the Messerschmitt falling away to crash in a field ten miles south of Marck.

In addition to formations of Me 109s, several smaller groups of Fw 190s were seen, some of which were engaged by 401 Squadron's Blue and Yellow sections. Sergeant Omer Levesque (W3178 – Blue 4) saw an Fw 190 lining up behind a Spitfire below him and immediately dived to attack. The 190 attempted to evade by alternately climbing and diving but Levesque stuck to the task and managed to get in a number of short bursts. At around 5,000ft the German aircraft's hood flew off and a partially opened parachute appeared as its pilot attempted to bale out. Shortly afterwards near Devres, Levesque saw another Fw 190 and managed to get within firing range by selecting full boost. A two-second burst produced a series of black explosive puffs of smoke and the aircraft flew on without taking further evasive action, with its starboard wing low. Unfortunately Levesque then had to break off on being attacked by another 190 and could only claim this aircraft as a probable.

Sergeant Don Morrison (P8783 – Yellow 4) also saw action near Devres but only had the use of his machine-guns as his cannons had jammed. A long deflection burst hit the last in a group of three Fw 190s producing a trail of smoke, but as he was now completely alone, he was unable to press home his attack and was forced to head for the coast. As he crossed the Channel at 100ft he saw three more 190s attacking the Spitfire flown by Flight Lieutenant Neil. Closing in on the No.3, he fired a long burst which caused it to roll onto its back and dive into the sea from a height of 500ft.

No.124 Squadron's only success before the end of the year occurred during a defensive patrol on 17 December when Squadron Leader Duke-Woolley, at the head of Red section, was vectored onto a hostile aircraft that was reported to be operating to the north of the Thames estuary. The aircraft was eventually seen and identified as a Junkers Ju 88, which immediately began a desperate climb to seek the sanctuary of cloud at 2,500ft. Return fire was not particularly accurate and Duke-Woolley had little difficulty closing in to fire both cannon and machine-guns at a range of 300 yards, this being enough to prompt three of the crew to bale out. The Ju 88 then lost height and slowly inverted itself before crashing into the sea.

Throughout the year 11 Group's squadrons had endeavoured to engage the *Luftwaffe* fighter units based in the Pas de Calais at every opportunity, but what, if anything, had been achieved? The destructive capability of the small numbers of bombers used on Circus operations proved to be insufficient to worry the defenders, and on most occasions they contented themselves with occupying the high ground, only joining combat when the tactical situation was in their favour. Manoeuvring a thirty-six aircraft wing was not an easy task and put great pressure not only on the Wing Leader, but on individual Squadron and Flight Commanders whose responsibility it was to maintain the correct position of their respective sections to prevent straggling. The consequences were usually dire should a section lose station with the rest of the formation, their fate often being decided before any assistance could be provided.

Although the RAF hoped to become involved in large-scale actions, the incompatibility of the two main protagonists, the Spitfire V and the Me 109F, meant that there was little likelihood of these combats taking place. Although certain parameters of their performance were similar, the Spitfire's manoeuvrability in a turning fight was greatly superior to the Messerschmitt, and pilots of the latter rarely allowed themselves to be drawn into a turning competition. The main advantage of the 109 lay in its performance in the vertical plane, a situation which was aided by its fuel-injected Daimler-Benz DB601 engine. As a result of such inconsistencies the RAF's desire to 'slug it out' with their opposite numbers was largely wishful thinking. Following the German invasion of Russia, JG2 and 26 could muster no more than 150 serviceable fighters at any one time, but by fighting on their own terms, they inflicted much higher casualties on their opponents even though the RAF frequently put up as many as 300 fighters to protect between twelve and eighteen bombers.

Despite the losses that Fighter Command had sustained, by the end of the year it was stronger than ever before and the infrastructure for continued expansion, in terms of aircraft production and pilot training, was already in place. Those fortunate enough to have survived the year's air fighting were, by now, battle-hardened and ready to pass on their expertise to the new boys fresh out of OTU. In terms of their equipment, the Spitfire V had shown itself to be a match for the latest Me 109F (assuming no tactical advantage to either side) and it would continue to be the RAF's premier day fighter until the advent of the Mark IX in mid-1942. However, the combats that had already taken place with the Focke-Wulf Fw 190 had shown it to be a superb fighter. How would the Spitfire V cope with its new adversary when it was in service in large numbers?

FOUR

IBSLEY WING, JANUARY–JUNE 1942

At the beginning of 1942 concern over the performance of the Focke-Wulf Fw 190 was just one of the problems facing the RAF's fighter pilots as they contemplated further operations over northern France. In recent weeks there had been several unexplained structural failures in Spitfires, the cause of these crashes eventually being traced to incorrect loading, as Supermarine test pilot Flight Lieutenant Clive Gosling explains:

> Initially in the Mark V there were problems with longitudinal stability caused by the loading instructions being ignored at the MUs and in the squadrons. This resulted in a number of aircraft breaking up in the air as they were over-controlled on applying G. Although the aircraft were lively, as the CofG was well aft, they could be extremely dangerous. The instability was dealt with by putting a 6½lb weight on an arm in the elevator circuit. The effect of this was that as G was applied, the weight pulled the control column forward to prevent over-control. This was not popular in the squadrons who complained of a loss of manoeuvrability as they had to pull harder on the control column in tight turns, and that the control column jerked to and fro when taxiing, but at least it stopped people being killed.

Subsequently redesigned elevators increased the Spitfire V's longitudinal stability and did away with the need to use weights in the elevator circuit.

There was also increasing concern over the Spitfire's lack of endurance. As was mentioned in Chapter One, the first attempts to increase the range of the Spitfire by the use of overload fuel tanks were not particularly successful, the LR version of the Spitfire II having flying characteristics which were far from ideal. In early 1942 the first examples of the new long-range 'slipper' tank of thirty-gallon capacity came into use. Unlike the previous fixed installation, it was designed to be jettisoned

51

before entering combat, a jettison lever being mounted on the starboard side of the cockpit below the undercarriage control unit. Although of streamlined design, the new overload tanks still knocked approximately 30mph off top speed, so the usual procedure was to take off on internal fuel before switching to the external tank at a safe height. The additional fuel was sufficient to allow the Spitfire V to operate over the Brest peninsula from bases in Cornwall, or along the Dutch coast from airfields in East Anglia. Malfunction of the jettison tank at any stage would lead to the aircraft having to abort.

The need for additional fuel capacity stemmed not only from the need to operate further afield over enemy territory, but also from the requirement to fly at high speed when in the combat area to try to reduce the performance advantage of the Fw 190. Fuel consumption varied enormously depending on throttle setting and at maximum combat boost (+16lb/sq.in and 3,000rpm), it was a staggering 150 gallons per hour. There could also be large variations in fuel consumption at more modest power settings, and the same airspeed could be achieved using different combinations of boost and rpm. The favoured approach was to fly at high speed utilising low revs and high boost which provided the greatest degree of protection from being bounced, while at the same time achieving the lowest fuel consumption. The first squadrons to use the new slipper tanks were those that formed the Kenley and Hornchurch Wings; other units would have to wait a little longer to be similarly equipped.

These tanks were desperately needed in 10 Group, whose squadrons in Hampshire, Devon and Cornwall had to contend with the English Channel at its widest for their offensive sorties over France. Operations carried out in this sector were typified by those of the Ibsley Wing, which comprised 118, 234 and 501 Squadrons commanded by Squadron Leaders J.C. Carver, H.M. Stephen and C.F. Currant respectively. All were stalwarts of the Battle of Britain: Carver had flown Hurricanes with 87 Squadron, while Stephen had received two DFCs and a DSO for service with 74 Squadron. Currant, affectionately known as 'Bunny', was also an 'ace' and had been awarded the DFC for his exploits with 605 Squadron, which included three aircraft destroyed on 15 September, the day generally regarded as the climax of the battle. Ibsley's Wing Leader was another high-scoring pilot, one who had fought with the Air Component of the BEF in France, Wing Commander Ian 'Widge' Gleed DFC.

The airfield at Ibsley was situated just to the west of the New Forest and lay roughly ten miles north of Bournemouth. Opened in February 1941 as a satellite of Middle Wallop, its importance increased appreciably with the arrival of Gleed in November. The wing took part in some notable actions during the eight months of his command, commencing with the support of Halifax, Stirling and Manchester aircraft of Bomber Command during two attacks on the German battlecruisers *Scharnhorst* and *Gneisenau* in Brest harbour in December 1941.

The first operation (code-named Veracity) took place on the 18th when a mixed force of forty-seven bombers attacked the warships in clear, sunny conditions. No.234 Squadron was led by Wing Commander M.V. Blake DSO DFC, Wing Leader at Portreath, as part of the cover for twelve Stirlings, while 118 and 501 Squadrons were joined by the Hurricanes of 615, all led by Ian Gleed as escort to eighteen Halifaxes. Brest was later described as 'boiling' with flak and several yellow-nosed Me 109Es attempted to break up the wing by diving steeply through it, also making a feint attack on one of 501's Spitfires flown by Pilot Officer J. Harrison. In the main such provocation was ignored, although Pilot Officer Barry Denville of 234 Squadron did chase after a 109 and later claimed it as damaged after scoring hits on its fuselage.

Post-raid photography showed that the warships had not sustained serious damage during the attack, as a result of which a second attempt to put them out of action was made on 30 December (Veracity II). The operation got off to a bad start when bad weather conditions over eastern England grounded the Stirlings and Manchesters from Nos. 3 and 5 Groups, which meant that the attack had to be made by just sixteen Halifax aircraft drawn from 10, 35 and 76 Squadrons of No.4 Group. As the bombers took off from their bases in Yorkshire in the late morning, final preparations and briefings were being carried out at the Ibsley Wing's forward operating base at Predannack in Cornwall, 118, 234 and 501 Squadrons eventually departing at 1317 hrs.

As before, the intention was to arrive in the target area and engage defending fighters before the bombers commenced their run in. On this occasion at least it was to be the Spitfires of the Portreath Wing who saw all the action, claims eventually being made for six enemy aircraft destroyed. As top cover at 20,000ft, the Ibsley squadrons were not drawn into the battle raging below, although a single 109 did manage to close in behind AB854 of 234 Squadron, Sergeant R.W. Joyce being shot down to become a PoW. The only other anxious moment for the wing occurred when the Spitfire flown by Sergeant K. Vrtis of 501 Squadron received flak damage to its starboard mainplane, a matter of inches away from its cannon magazine.

The two Veracity missions marked an end to wing operations for a considerable period as bad weather restricted operational flying to convoy patrols and shipping recces, together with occasional scrambles to intercept raids by small numbers of Do 217s and Ju 88s. This situation lasted for much of January, at the end of which 234 Squadron welcomed a new CO, Squadron Leader F.E.W. Birchfield, in place of Harbourne Stephen, who was posted to India.

It is interesting to note that on the last day in January, Flight Lieutenant Dave Glaser of 234 Squadron took off on a test flight in AD180 which had been fitted with one of the first examples of the negative-G carburettor. The trial was not particularly successful and as soon as Glaser pushed the control column forward, the engine coughed and died just as all the previous ones had. Sergeant Sid Watson, who later flew with 234 and 118 Squadrons, also found problems:

> When subjected to negative-G the flow of fuel to the engine was restricted, causing a momentary loss of power and a puff of black smoke. The Germans, with their direct fuel injection, could simply push the stick forward and down they would go in a steep dive. To follow them down it was necessary to perform a half roll to allow centrifugal force to keep the engine from cutting. I have read how a simple little modification solved this problem and all aircraft were so modified, but they must have missed mine, because it always misbehaved.

The first successful action of the new year for the Ibsley Wing took place on 2 February during an attack on the distillery at Eroudeville by 118 Squadron. When fifteen miles north-east of Pointe de Barfleur, Flight Lieutenant Peter Howard-Williams DFC (AA964 – Red 1) was attacked by several Me 109Fs but managed to get on the tail of one, delivering a five-second burst from astern, which was sufficient to cause it to dive into the sea. Almost immediately he was attacked by the others, a cannon shell exploding behind his radio installation and damaging a number of control wires. A bullet also hit the fuselage of his aircraft just above the throttle and ricocheted off. Having taken evasive action, Howard-Williams then played a game of cat and mouse with his adversaries, in and out of cloud, and managed to damage two of them with machine-gun fire, one in particular taking numerous De Wilde (incendiary) hits on its tail and fuselage.

One of the Ibsley Wing's main duties consisted of shipping reconnaissance flights over the Channel, its operational area taking in the Golfe de St Malo and the coastline around the Cherbourg peninsula. If anything was spotted the usual procedure was to call for a homing, the precise wording giving an indication of the type of target. A 'practice homing' meant a relatively small target, such as a minesweeper, whereas an 'emergency homing' referred to something larger.

On 10 February, four aircraft of 234 Squadron reconnoitred the sea around the Channel Islands. They were led by Flight Lieutenant Dave Glaser.

> I followed an oil slick down past Jersey and we came across a [German] destroyer. I told the boys to keep wide and I would do the quick orbit to call for an emergency homing, which I did. As soon as they got that instruction, they plotted the position and called up the Hurri-bombers so that when we landed we put in our report, briefed them, and were off again within the hour. We went down there but it must have gone hell for leather and we never saw it again.

Considering that the German battlecruisers *Scharnhorst* and *Gneisenau* made their audacious breakout along the Channel just two days later (see Chapter Five), it is highly likely that this particular vessel was on its way to Brest to take part in the operation.

With German aircraft still making frequent use of bad weather conditions to carry out nuisance raids, scrambles were a regular feature of operational life at Ibsley, and on 21 February 234 Squadron's Yellow section, comprising Pilot Officer Cameron (AA725) and Sergeant Cam (AA726), were vectored onto six bandits that had been reported to the south of the Isle of Wight. Two aircraft were eventually sighted heading towards the south coast and weaving. Believing them to be Me 109Es, Cameron commenced an attack, but the two aircraft were actually Tomahawks of 268 Squadron which had been flying on a shipping recce with a section of 501's Spitfires. A cannon shell hit the oil cooler of the lead aircraft flown by Flight Lieutenant C.A.V. Hawkins, who was killed when his machine hit a tree during the subsequent force-landing near Corfe Castle. The Tomahawk was not widely used in northern Europe and it is unlikely that Cameron or Cam would have seen the American fighter in the air before. The subsequent investigation revealed that hostile aircraft had in fact been in the area at the time, but at a greater height.

For the rest of the month there was little activity, although an exception occurred on the 26th when a section of four Spitfires of 234 Squadron spotted three minesweepers to the south of Alderney. In the afternoon, 234 and 501 Squadrons flew as escort to four Hurri-bombers which attempted to locate the ships, but they were unable to find them. On return to Ibsley, two of 234's aircraft collided and Sergeant J. Redfern was killed when his aircraft (AB816) lost its tail and crashed in the River Avon at Ringwood.

By early March better weather allowed the resumption of Circus operations, and on the 9th the Ibsley Wing flew to Redhill to participate

234 Squadron pilots at Ibsley, April 1942 (L to R) Thalbitzer, Cam, Fisher, Mileham, Fairburn, Svendson, Gordon (Sqn doctor) Nickless, Watson, Marshall (front). (Watson).

in an attack by six Bostons on oil storage tanks at Mazingarbe. During the raid 501 Squadron saw a gaggle of twelve Me 109s and pursued them down to 4,000ft, Pilot Officer R.A. 'Dickie' Newbery claiming one destroyed, and Squadron Leader Currant a probable. During the exchanges Currant received a bullet graze on his forehead and later required hospital treatment following a crash-landing at Lympne when his aircraft turned over, bullets having punctured both tyres. No.118 Squadron was also engaged on its way back, Pilot Officer R.W.P. MacKenzie's aircraft (BL332) being particularly badly hit. Despite a valiant effort to bring his damaged machine back, he eventually lost control and was killed when it crashed onto the Dover–Canterbury road.

On 13 March the Ibsley squadrons were back on their own patch with a late-afternoon Roadstead when they escorted three Hudsons of 407 Squadron on the lookout for an armed merchant cruiser. Weather conditions were poor which allowed two Ju 88s to make a sneak attack on 118's Red section, tracer rounds passing just above the port wing of the Spitfire flown by Commander Andre Jubelin (Red 4). Breaking into the attack, Jubelin nearly collided with the 88 but managed to get in a quick burst which produced black smoke from its port engine. The

German aircraft was then attacked by Squadron Leader Carver (Red 1) and his wingman, Sergeant V.K. Moody, but return fire hit Carver's Spitfire and he was forced to bale out.

Following this attack, Jubelin moved in once again and caused further damage despite the fact that his CSU was behaving erratically and causing the engine revs to fluctuate. By the time the Ju 88 eventually escaped into cloud both its engines were smoking heavily and the port motor was on fire. It was subsequently claimed as a probable, shared between Jubelin and Moody.

In the meantime the second Ju 88 was under attack by Ian Gleed, together with Pilot Officer R.C. Lynch of 501 Squadron. Gleed used all his cannon ammunition during several short bursts, strikes being seen on the port engine which gave off several small explosions and flame. Lynch then took over and delivered two attacks, first from astern and then abeam, during which all return fire ceased. After his attentions the enemy aircraft slowed considerably, lost height and then commenced a swing to the right, its starboard propeller windmilling. Before it could be damaged further, it too disappeared into cloud. As it seemed to have been severely hit, it was also claimed as a probable.

Nothing was heard of Squadron Leader Carver's fate for over two days, and as time went by everyone began to fear the worst. There was considerable elation therefore when he was pulled from the Channel by the crew of HMS *Tynedale*, a Hunt Class destroyer, having spent fifty-seven hours and thirty minutes in his dinghy. Although weak, he was cheerful and was picked up just fifteen miles off Portland having travelled nearly seventy miles from the position near the Channel Islands where he had baled out. He had managed to survive on Horlicks tablets, Benzedrine and a small amount of chocolate, and had collected rainwater in the apron of his dinghy to drink. Despite his discomfort, he had still managed to get about four to five hours' sleep each night.

On 15 March an incident occurred which highlighted one of the main difficulties of operating in 10 Group's area, flight into deteriorating weather conditions. Depressions often moved in quickly from the Atlantic and the proximity of the sea meant that coastal areas were occasionally shrouded in mist and fog which could descend in a matter of minutes. No.234 Squadron had been escorting five Hudsons on an anti-shipping patrol but ran into low cloud near Dodman Point on their return. Half the squadron managed to get into Exeter, but six aircraft led by Squadron Leader Birchfield were forced to climb up through the overcast, eventually breaking out into bright sunlight at 3,000ft. Birchfield then led the Spitfires back down again but he was unaware that they were now over the relatively high ground of Bodmin Moor. As they descended through cloud, four of the six crashed. Flight Lieutenant Hogg was killed in BL241, Pilot Officer Locke (BL668) and Sergeant Gray (AA726) suffered serious injuries, and only Pilot Officer Cameron (AA725) escaped unhurt.

Half an hour before this unfortunate episode took place, a twin-engined aircraft was seen near Sept Isles which took violent evasive action and was at first thought to be a Ju 88. Dave Glaser led his section to investigate but warned his pilots to hold their fire until a positive identification had been made. The aircraft was eventually recognised as being a Beaufighter, but one member of his section was suffering from an R/T problem and could not be restrained from launching an attack which damaged the Beau before it eventually escaped in cloud.

On his return Glaser reported what had happened and was somewhat surprised to be berated by the squadron Intelligence Officer for not shooting it down. According to the IO it was one that had force-landed in France some time ago and was now being used by the Germans; however, the following day he changed his tune completely when news came through that it had in fact been an RAF example whose crew had told of successfully evading a concerted attack by three Me 109s! (In a sequel to this incident, the basic facts were written up, with a number of embellishments, for the RAF's training manual *Tee Emm*, a monthly magazine which attempted to imbue professional attitudes to flying by highlighting real events, often with a humorous slant.)

Although convoy patrols were generally pretty tedious from the pilot's point of view, they could, on occasion, provide some excitement, as Pilot Officer Wheldon and Sergeant Vendl of 501 Squadron discovered on 19 March. Two bomb-carrying Me 109Fs attacked the ships they were protecting, but both bombs overshot their intended targets and fell harmlessly into the sea. The 109s then headed for France at high speed with the Spitfires in hot pursuit. Wheldon chased them to mid-Channel but was unable to get closer than 700 yards, and Vendl fired a short burst which succeeded only in easing some of his frustration at not being able to get within range.

By now large-scale daylight attacks by the *Luftwaffe* were virtually a thing of the past, so it therefore came as something of a surprise when radar warned of thirty-plus enemy aircraft approaching the Isle of Wight from the direction of Cherbourg in the evening of 23 March. No.118 Squadron scrambled from Ibsley at 1930 hrs and was joined by Ian Gleed, who was flying his regular aircraft, AA742 (IR-G). Climbing to 18,000ft to the east of Portland Bill, Gleed saw a number of Ju 88s in *Schwarm* formation which immediately broke as a Spitfire of 118 commenced its attack. One of the 88s flew to the west which allowed

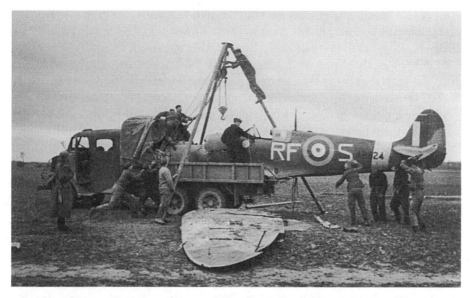

A fate suffered by many Spitfire Vs in mid-1942, AB824 of 303 Sqn is loaded after crash-landing in France following Circus 119 on 4/4/42. (*via Philip Jarrett*)

Gleed the opportunity to move in behind and fire a burst which left its starboard engine on fire. The Ju 88 lost speed so suddenly that he had to break sharply to port to avoid ramming it, and then watched as it went down with flames spreading to the whole of the starboard wing. It was last seen at about 4,000ft diving vertically, completely enveloped in flames.

The Spitfire that Gleed had seen engaging the Ju 88s was that flown by Sergeant Stan Jones DFM, who was later highly commended for breaking up the attack before the target had been reached. Jones fired at one of the Ju 88s with several bursts of up to four seconds and saw strikes on the bomber's fuselage and starboard engine. He was then forced to break away, leaving the German bomber in a steep dive to the west of Portland, and consequently could only claim it as damaged.

For the rest of the month there was little operational flying, 234 Squadron moving to Warmwell on the 23rd to carry out gunnery practice. During the two-week detachment it completed 532 separate details comprising air-to-air, air-to-ground and cannon sorties, all of which produced the prodigious total of 1,550ft of camera-gun film. Back at Ibsley training flights continued, one of 501 Squadron's aircraft being lost on 27 March when Sergeant Childs got into a spin in cloud at 16,000ft during practice interceptions. The forces were so great as his Spitfire plummeted earthwards that he was thrown through the canopy, but he survived with nothing more than bruises and shock. His Spitfire (AB965) crashed on the railway line near Brockenhurst.

Much of early April was blighted by bad weather, and it was not until the 15th that there was an improvement which allowed nine Bostons of 107 Squadron to carry out 10 Group Circus No.1, an attack on Cherbourg docks. Six of 234 Squadron's aircraft were bounced by 109s as they left the target, and Flight Lieutenant D.E. Mileham (AB987) and Pilot Officer M.L. Simon (W3967) did not return. There were further losses the following day during two separate operations when Pilot Officer G.R. Bland (BL889) and Pilot Officer R.S. Woolass (AR374) were shot down near Rauville and Cap de la Hague respectively.

The trend towards increasing losses was arrested, albeit temporarily, on 17 April when the Ibsley Wing flew an early-morning offensive sweep over the Cherbourg peninsula. Squadron Leader Birchfield, Flying Officer Wydrowski and Sergeant Webster of 234 Squadron all fired at a formation of 109s which put in an appearance, but despite their best efforts, only one aircraft was subsequently claimed as damaged. In the meantime, Squadron Leader Currant of 501 was on the tail of another 109 which was seen to stall and drop into a vertical dive with its propeller revolving slowly. It was followed down to 2,000ft by several of 501's pilots who all fired at it, and it was last seen still going straight down, streaming glycol.

In the afternoon the wing again teamed up with the Bostons of 107 Squadron for another attack on shipping in Cherbourg harbour. Flying at the head of 118 Squadron, Ian Gleed initially ordered everyone to stay clear of the flak zone but changed his mind on being told by control that enemy aircraft were climbing to intercept. After bombing, the Bostons turned to the north and Gleed, who was weaving behind and just above them, saw nine 109Fs gaining height to starboard. One of the 109s levelled out and attacked the nearest Boston, but in doing so left itself open to a beam attack. Gleed's fire struck forward of the cockpit and it was later claimed as destroyed following confirmation by the high cover (Polish) wing that its pilot had baled out.

In recent weeks 234 Squadron had seen more than their fair share of bad luck, a situation that was set to continue. On the 18th they carried out a sweep over Cherbourg, together with 118 and 501 Squadrons, but when descending through 8,000ft on their return to Ibsley, two of their aircraft collided. Pilot Officer Cameron, who had survived a crash-landing a month before, had fortune on his side once again when he successfully baled out of BL693, but his No.2 Sergeant, E.A.L. Fairman, (AA938) was killed.

Six days later the squadron took part in a sweep over north-eastern France and came face to face with the much-vaunted Fw 190 for the first time. Sergeant Sid Watson, who had only been with 234 for a short time, should have taken part in this operation but suffered an engine snag shortly after take-off which, ultimately, may have saved his life

On 24 April 234 Squadron moved to Tangmere as a jumping-off point for a sweep to Abbeville, something we really needed! Abbeville [was the] home of the best in the *Luftwaffe* flying some of the new Fw 190s . . . This was to be my first sweep as a new member of 234 (you can see how hard up they were) and I would be tail-end Charlie. After take-off and about ten minutes into the flight, my engine developed a problem and I aborted and landed at the nearest airfield, Ford. Had that problem not occurred, who knows?

Over France, Watson's 'A' Flight colleagues became separated from the rest of the squadron and were badly bounced by Fw 190s of II/JG26. Flight Lieutenant V.E. Watkins (BL831) was shot down and killed, with Flight Sergeant F.C. Fisher (BL623), Pilot Officer N.H. Svendson (BL924) and Sergeant S.H. Machan (AD463) all baling out to become PoWs. Two of these pilots fell to the guns of *Oberleutnant* Kurt Ebersberger, *Staffelkapitän* of the 4th *Staffel*, with the others being claimed by *Oberfeldwebel* Hermann Hoffman, also of the 4th *Staffel*, and *Oberleutnant* Wilhelm-Ferdinand Galland of the 6th.

Sid Watson believes that poor tactics were a contributory factor to such high loss rates:

Because of the formation that was flown by the RAF, i.e. three sections of four in line astern, it was almost impossible to keep a good look out because all one's time was spent trying to play follow the leader. This silly formation stayed with us until 1943 when Wing Commander 'Laddie' Lucas took over the Coltishall Wing. He inaugurated the 'finger four' approach (as used by the Germans) and it was a great improvement. Even then there were still some that resisted, if that can be believed!

Having suffered severely in recent weeks 234 Squadron were withdrawn to Portreath on 27 April to recuperate and were replaced at Ibsley by 66 Squadron the following day. Dave Glaser, who was away on a course at Central Gunnery School, Sutton Bridge, when the move took place, can still recall the shock that he felt on his return, being confronted with a squadron that was virtually unrecognisable from the one he had left just a few weeks before. Glaser considers that poor leadership was the root cause of the squadron's problems at that time, a situation that was not helped by a whole string of Flight Commanders either being lost in action, or allowed to move to other units. His own temporary departure to CGS had also robbed the squadron of valuable operational experience during a difficult period.

During his time at Sutton Bridge, Glaser made sure that he did not spend a day longer than necessary to complete the course. Top students were often retained on the staff and although he achieved above average ratings in the air (where he flew the BBMF's Spitfire IIa P7350), he guaranteed that this would not happen by being sufficiently unimpressive in the classroom. Even the most basic maths seemed to be beyond him and eventually his instructor found it impossible to simplify things any further. At this point another 'student' at the back of the class claimed that he was completely mystified as well. This was none other than Sailor Malan, complete with wry smile, knowing full well what was going on! (After the war Glaser graduated from the Empire Test Pilots School and flew as a production test pilot with Vickers and BAC.)

No.234's replacements at Ibsley, 66 Squadron, were led by thirty-three-year-old Cam Malfroy from Hokitika in New Zealand and had recently received Spitfire Vcs to replace their long-range Mark IIas. The arrival of new aircraft also heralded the first use of the thirty-gallon slipper tank which proved to be much better than the fixed asymmetric installation of the IIa. Pilots reported no noticeable difference in trim and the only change in handling was a feeling of 'heaviness' when the tank was full. There was also general agreement that the Mark V was a big improvement when compared to its predecessor, with much better performance at height and in the climb. The aircraft also appeared to gain speed more quickly in the dive.

Although the pilots were happy, things were not quite as rosy in Engineering. A series of minor snags with the new jet tanks meant that the squadron could not contemplate using them on operations until solutions had been found. The situation became so bad that a representative from Vickers and the designer of the tank itself were brought in to try to unravel some of its 'mysteries'. While the Engineering Officer was tearing his hair out trying to get the new tanks to work, severe problems were also being encountered by the Armament section who were wrestling with the intricacies of the 20mm Hispano cannon. Having been accustomed to the relative simplicity of the 0.303in Browning for so long, the Hispano took some getting used to, and at first gun stoppages were at an unacceptably high level.

Shortly before Ibsley's re-organisation took place, eleven Spitfires of 501 Squadron took off in the afternoon of 25 April to carry out a sweep off Cherbourg. Only six were to return. Flying Officers A. Palmer-

Tomkinson (W3894) and R. Wheldon (BL974) disappeared without trace, while Sergeant K. Vrtis (AB251) crashed in the sea and Sergeant M. Rocovsky plunged to his death when his parachute failed to deploy. This heavy casualty list was the result of an encounter with just six Me 109Fs which made the most of local cloud cover and mist to make repeated hit-and-run attacks. On their return, another aircraft was lost when Sergeant Ian Blair experienced engine trouble in AB179 and crash-landed near Swanage.

Although Fighter Command's policy of taking the initiative over France had been called into question, there was in reality little else that it could do if its operational effectiveness was to be maintained. Losses had already begun to mount once again in 11 Group, and despite the fact that the Fw 190 had not yet been seen in 10 Group's area, it would only be a matter of time before it was encountered here as well.

In the meantime the Ibsley Wing were at least made aware of their new adversary on the occasions when they flew from 11 Group bases on Rodeos over north-eastern France. One such operation occurred on 5 May when 118 and 501 Squadrons flew as top cover for the Tangmere Wing during a sweep of the Pas de Calais. A group of fifteen Fw 190s were seen, but on this occasion they kept their distance and showed no inclination to fight. Ian Gleed, who was leading with 501 Squadron, tried to bring them to combat but all dived away as soon as the Spitfires launched their attack. All, that is, except one which carried on merrily, straight and level, and took no evasive action whatsoever. Gleed attacked from 300 yards on the starboard quarter and hit the 190, which half-rolled as if it was about to dive away. However, it then righted itself and flew on for some time before it slowed suddenly and fell out of the sky streaming grey smoke. On returning to base it was claimed as a probable, Gleed's combat report commenting that its pilot must have been the German equivalent of Pilot Officer Prune!

Four days later the wing was at Tangmere once again, thirty-six Spitfires taking off at 1245 hrs as target support wing for Circus 168, an attack by six Bostons of 226 Squadron on Hazebrouck marshalling yards. The French coast was crossed at Hardelot at 1325 hrs, each unit flying in three sections of three with one section weaving, the weavers being positioned one in front above, one behind above and one below. By the time a report was received from Kenley control of enemy aircraft climbing to the north-east of St Omer, 118 were at 21,000ft with 66 to their right at the same height and 501 at 20,000ft, also on their right. As they approached St Omer, a second gaggle of twenty-five Fw 190s were seen a mile away and the Spitfires wheeled towards them to counter any attack.

During the turn 118 Squadron, who were on the outside, lost about 800 to 1,000 yards and were immediately attacked by the first group of 190s. Outnumbered, and in a poor position, Sergeant M.B. Green soon went down in flames in W3722 and Squadron Leader J.H.B. Walker (BL264) and Sergeants F.W. Hough (AR365) and G. Shepherd (AB791) were dispatched in quick succession. Nos. 66 and 501 circled several times in an attempt to close the gap but were prevented from doing so by the other group of Fw 190s, who made no real effort to attack and were content to contain them. Even so, Pilot Officer E.W. Gillespie (W3845) of 501, who had become detached from the rest of the squadron, proved too tempting a target and was shot down. No.118's suffering was not quite complete as Pilot Officer Thomas crash-landed at Manston having been wounded in combat, and Pilot Officer G.H. Aalpoel (BL580) brought his aircraft down near Tangmere, out of fuel.

The Fw 190s had all come from JG26, much of the damage being caused by *Hauptmann* Joachim Muncheberg's II *Gruppe*, whose pilots were eventually awarded three Spitfires confirmed. 'Pips' Priller's III *Gruppe* eventually got in on the act, Priller himself claiming a Spitfire north of Gravelines. On their return the pilots of the Ibsley Wing did not make any claims, although it appears that an Fw 190 may have been shot down by one of the pilots who failed to return, as *Leutnant* Heinz Reiche of the 5th *Staffel* was killed when his aircraft crashed near the Forêt d'Eperlecques.

This action, and that fought on the 5th, are good indicators of the *Luftwaffe*'s thinking at this stage of the air war over northern Europe. Although they possessed a superior machine in the Fw 190, they were still not prepared to engage RAF fighters unless they held both numerical and tactical advantage. The 11 Group Rodeo to the Pas de Calais saw them decline combat; but for one pilot's incompetence, they would have escaped without loss. In contrast, the operation to Hazebrouck produced a determined response. It showed that they had the benefit of excellent ground control, and once 118 Squadron had become separated from the rest of the wing, the level of tactical awareness and co-operation between the two German formations was of the highest order.

The Ibsley Wing saw little action for the rest of May, although there was a notable exception on the 15th. Nos. 66 and 501 Squadrons took off from Ibsley at 1327 hrs to escort eight Hurri-bombers of 175 Squadron, the intention being to locate a convoy of six cargo vessels which had been seen near Cap de la Hague on a morning shipping reconnaissance. The operation also included 118 Squadron, who took off eight minutes later to provide rear support. The Hurricanes, together with their escort, passed over Bournemouth at 1,000ft ten minutes after take-off, before descending to sea level to avoid radar detection. No.66, which had been designated as close escort and anti-flak squadron, was flying in sections of three, two each side of 175 Squadron, which was in two flights, line astern.

The patrol area between Alderney and Cap de la Hague was reached at 1355 hrs but instead of the expected convoy, three M-class minesweepers were seen steaming at ten knots in line abreast four miles to the north-west of Querqueville. As 501 went up to 1,000ft to act as cover, 66 dived to sea level in sections line astern. They raked the ships with cannon fire which succeeded in suppressing the ship's defences, as 175 Squadron climbed to 500ft to commence their attack. Each Hurricane was carrying two 250lb GP bombs with a three-second delay, and although they had only been operational for a month, their attack proved to be deadly accurate.

The ship nearest land received two direct hits near the stern causing it to burst into flames, and it appeared to be sinking as the squadrons withdrew. There was absolutely no doubt about the middle one of the three which was hit twice amidships and also had two near misses towards its stern. It blew up and sank shortly afterwards. The remaining vessel was damaged by two bombs, one of which burst under its bows while the other exploded close on the port side. The enemy appeared to have been taken completely by surprise by the attack, which took just one minute to carry out. No aircraft were damaged and all returned safely, landing at Ibsley at 1442 hrs.

It was not until 3 June that the Ibsley squadrons ventured over to France in strength once again when they escorted six Bostons of 226 Squadron during a raid on Cherbourg docks (10 Group Circus 6). Bombing height was 14,000ft with 501 as close escort 1,000ft above, 66 and 118 Squadrons 1,000ft higher still. Top cover was provided by Spitfires of the Exeter Wing. Ten miles north-east of Cherbourg three Fw 190s were seen, the first time they had been encountered in this area, but they did not attack. In the meantime the high cover squadrons had been heavily engaged and a running fight was carried out back across the Channel which saw three Spitfires shot down for one enemy aircraft destroyed, with another claimed as a probable.

The following day it was the turn of the Hurri-bombers of 175 Squadron, who attacked the airfield at Maupertus (10 Group Ramrod 21). On this occasion 501 Squadron provided top cover at 17,000ft with 66 and 118 Squadrons accompanying the Hurricanes 2,000ft below. After the bombers and their escorts had dived to 10,000ft to deliver the attack, a group of eight to ten Fw 190s slanted down onto 501 Squadron, unseen due to haze. Sergeant B. Strachan (W3842) was shot down almost immediately, his aircraft being seen to crash in the sea, and Sergeant J.E.A. Potelle's Spitfire (AB381) was badly hit, leaving him no alternative but to bale out. As the dogfight spilled out from the coast Sergeant Jerabek (Red 3) saw an Fw 190 diving down behind Green section and turned towards it. The German pilot had badly misjudged his speed in the dive and, having overshot his intended target, turned his aircraft onto its back to disengage. This only served to expose its belly to Jerabek, however, a short burst at point-blank range being sufficient to send it spinning into the sea.

With 66 Squadron protecting the Hurricanes, 118 joined the battle, Flight Lieutenant 'Dickie' Newbery (Yellow 1) hitting a 190 in a head-on attack before getting on the tail of another. A five-second burst from the rear port quarter caused several large pieces to fall off and it was last seen in a vertical dive, pouring black smoke. Squadron Leader Carver (Red 1) damaged an Fw 190 which flew across his path from right to left and then engaged three others, but, such was the level of confusion, he was unable to make any positive claim.

It is interesting to note that Carver's combat report includes several observations on the relative merits of the Spitfire Vb and the Fw 190. At one point he had chased after a 190 that was leaving the fight and, during a 2,000ft climb, found that he could maintain his position quite easily and

F/L 'Dickie' Newbery of 118 Squadron with EN966 *Fiducia*. (*via Smith*)

66

lost no ground. He also judged that the 190 was only 'slightly superior' in the dive. The average height of the engagements had been 15,000ft.

Carver was not the only pilot to claim that the Spitfire Vb was not markedly inferior to the Fw 190 – several others made similar statements. Flight Lieutenant Gus Daymond, who flew with 71 Squadron, estimated that the two aircraft shared equality in manoeuvrability, although he did admit that the 190 was 'slightly faster'. In contrast to Carver's conclusions, he was of the opinion that it possessed a better rate of climb. Dave Glaser, who encountered Fw 190s on many occasions during his service with 234 Squadron, recalls his impressions of the German aircraft:

> It was good, but we didn't know enough about it. If I had known all the things that they were having to put up with, it would have made a hell of a difference. The major thing was not to be jumped, that's why we did a terrific amount of formation flying during which we practised crossover turns. I found that I had no trouble with the Fw 190s in turning inside them and I adopted the thing of a right turn during which I gained what height I could by side-slipping in the turn. The *Luftwaffe* pilots had to work within limits and if it came down to a dogfight I found that within three turns I could get round onto them. I don't think it was the pilots not getting the most out of their aircraft, I got the impression that they were not all they were cracked up to be.

In fact, the true potential of the Focke-Wulf would be revealed within a matter of days (the relative merits of the 190 and the Spitfire V are discussed further in Chapter Eight).

Maupertus was on the receiving end of another attack by Hurricanes of 175 Squadron on 6 June, during which bombs were seen to fall in the eastern corner of the airfield. On withdrawing, an Fw 190 attacked and damaged one of the Hurricanes and Pilot Officer P.H. Stenger of 118 Squadron engaged another which was subsequently chased by Squadron Leader Carver and his No.2, Sergeant L.H. Jones. The enemy aircraft made off to the south at high speed, but before Carver and Jones could join up with the rest of the squadron, they were bounced by around nine Fw 190s and both were shot down and killed.

With losses beginning to mount once again, the decision was taken on 8 June to patrol in mid-Channel in the somewhat vain hope that the *Luftwaffe* could be drawn into combat under conditions more advantageous to the RAF. Nos. 118 and 501 Squadrons flew at 28,000ft about thirty-five miles south of St Albans Head with 66 Squadron, who had taken off fifteen minutes later, providing rear support. Approximately twenty-five enemy aircraft were seen well to the south, in four separate

118 Squadron. Back row (L to R) ?, Parker, Levinson, Costello, Blackburn, Wootten, I. Jones, Watson, ?, Spencer, de Courcy. Front row (L to R) Buglass, S. Jones, Brown, Stewart, Nickless, Robson, Talalla, Newbery (reclining). (*Wootten*)

formations at heights varying from 20,000 to 33,000ft, but they declined the invitation to attack and no combats took place.

Following the sad loss of Squadron Leader Carver, 118's new CO was Squadron Leader E.W. 'Bertie' Wootten, who took up his new post on the 10th. Twenty-four-year-old Wootten was no stranger to 10 Group operations: his first tour had commenced in August 1940 with 234 Squadron at Middle Wallop and a year later he was awarded the DFC and promoted to Flight Commander. On leaving 234 at the end of November 1941, he had a short spell at No.2 Delivery Flight at Colerne before moving to 10 Group HQ as Squadron Leader, Tactics, his final posting before taking over at 118 Squadron.

It was not until 20 June that the Ibsley Wing next encountered the enemy in any great numbers, and once again they suffered severely. Having flown to Redhill in perfect weather conditions, the wing took off at 1445 hrs to join up with their colleagues from Biggin Hill over Pevensey Bay before heading out over the Channel towards the Pas de Calais. The operation was intended as a diversion for an attack by

Bostons of 88 Squadron on a power station at Le Havre (Circus 193) and the French coast was crossed at Hardelot at 20,000ft from where the formation flew on to St Omer. Here a large force of twenty-five to thirty Fw 190s was seen and again it was 118 Squadron who took the brunt of the attack. Three Dutch pilots, Sergeant C. Van Houten (EP234) together with Pilot Officers J. Veen (EP134) and P.H. Stenger (AR449), lost their lives, and Adjutant R.N. Nioloux (Free French) was shot down in AR455 and taken prisoner.

The destruction of one of these aircraft was witnessed by Sergeant Tommy de Courcy, who had become separated from the rest of his section. He was about to join up with another lone Spitfire when he became aware of cannon shells flashing past him and saw an Fw 190 firing at the other aircraft from astern. Pulling his aircraft around, he managed to get in a one-second burst from the port rear quarter at a range of 250 yards. His fire produced a cloud of white smoke from the Focke-Wulf and it went into a vertical dive which de Courcy was not able to follow. As he went down, however, he caught a fleeting glimpse of the other Spitfire trailing glycol and in a spin. Low on fuel, he set course for home and landed at Gatwick with just five gallons remaining.

While 118 Squadron was fighting for its lives, 501 was also in trouble. Looking behind and to his left, Pilot Officer J.A. Jackson (Yellow 3) saw three Fw 190s diving on Blue section and moved over to attack the leader, who was firing at Pilot Officer Preston (Blue 3). The 190 broke sharply

BM252 *Bombay City* served with 122, 222 and 130 Squadrons before being SOC in September 1945. (*via Philip Jarrett*)

to port and then rolled onto its back, at which point Jackson fired a long burst with no deflection. He saw the German aircraft go into a dive, and just as it did there was a vivid red flash from behind its cockpit. It then flicked into a spin and was last seen trailing white smoke at around 6,000ft.

As for the rest of the squadron, Pilot Officer A.E. Drossaert's Spitfire (EN961) was hit in the fuselage by a cannon shell, and Flight Lieutenant P.J. Stanbury was lucky to get back after losing contact with his section. On his way home he saw a Spitfire in the distance being attacked by an Fw 190, which was probably AB497 flown by Flight Sergeant V. Bauman, who was later confirmed as a PoW. Once again the Ibsley Wing had come up against aircraft of II/JG26, its *Kommandeur*, Joachim Muncheberg, securing his eighty-second and eighty-third victories with *Oberleutnant* Ebersberger, *Unteroffizier* Gerhard Birke and *Oberleutnant* 'Wutz' Galland, brother of Adolf, claiming one apiece.

The day after this operation it was announced that Ian Gleed was to leave the Ibsley Wing for Fighter Command HQ, where he was about to take over the post of Wing Commander, Tactics. Thanks to his dynamic and aggressive leadership, the profile of the wing had been raised considerably during his eight months in charge, a time when offensive operations had been flown at every available opportunity despite increasingly heavy losses. The fact that morale was maintained during this difficult period was largely down to his character and fighting spirit, and it was with great sadness that he took his leave. The disappointment of losing such a popular leader was tempered to a certain extent as his replacement was 'Bunny' Currant, whose command of 501 Squadron passed to Squadron Leader J.W. 'Pancho' Villa DFC and Bar.

In addition to personnel changes it would not be long before there would be further upheavals. Ibsley was taken over by the USAAF in August 1942 and the P-38F Lightnings of the 1st Fighter Group flew in from Goxhill on the 27th, the resident Spitfire squadrons having to move a little further to the north to take up residence at Zeals. Although this situation would only last until December when 66 and 118 Squadrons returned to Ibsley, winter rain and snow ruled out operations for a considerable period, and by the time better weather allowed unrestricted use, the airfield was home to the Czechs of 310, 312 and 313 Squadrons. As the end of an era, it is, perhaps, fitting that the story of the Ibsley Wing be ended in the high summer of 1942, although its involvement in one of the most infamous operations of the war still needs to be told.

CHAPTER FIVE

CHANNEL DASH, FEBRUARY 1942

In the late evening of 11 February 1942 the German battle-cruisers *Scharnhorst* and *Gneisenau* and the heavy cruiser *Prinz Eugen* slipped out of their base at Brest to commence their audacious voyage along the English Channel. The fact that they managed to succeed in sailing within sight of the English coast in broad daylight, without mishap, has gone down in British history as one of the most embarrassing episodes of the entire war. As much has been written about the so-called 'Channel Dash', it is not proposed to re-tell the story in any great detail, but rather to give a brief introduction to the breakout and record the involvement of Fighter Command's Spitfires on that fateful day.

The capability of the *Scharnhorst* and *Gneisenau* to wreak havoc among Naval units and merchant shipping had been uppermost in the minds of the Admiralty ever since the sinking of the aircraft carrier HMS *Glorious* on 9 June 1940 as she sailed back to the UK following the ill-fated landings in Norway. Later, during the early part of 1941, the two capital ships broke out into the Atlantic where they embarked on a two-month cruise sinking twenty-two merchant ships with a combined tonnage of 116,000 tons before finally entering the port of Brest on 22 March. When photographic reconnaissance revealed their presence a week later, the decision was taken to carry out a blockade whereby aircraft of Bomber and Coastal Commands would attempt to cause sufficient damage so that further Atlantic sorties would be out of the question.

Despite the fact that the main objective was to disable the ships permanently, the possibility of their escape and return to a German port had to be addressed. Such a contingency was given the code name Operation Fuller, which fully recognised that any voyage would most likely take the ships along the English Channel, rather than a route around the British Isles, which would be contested by the Royal Navy. In the light of what was to happen subsequently, it was unfortunate that all planning was carried out under the assumption that the ships would

71

leave Brest in daylight so that the most vulnerable part of the journey, the passage through the Straits of Dover, would take place at night.

The actual breakout took place shortly after dark but was delayed by Wellingtons of Bomber Command which raided Brest in the early evening, the ships eventually departing at 2145 hrs. By 0830 hrs the following morning, the battle group were off Le Havre but by a combination of bad luck and ineptitude the British still had no idea of their presence.

The German air operation to protect the ships had been masterminded by *Oberstleutnant* Adolf Galland who had devised an elaborate plan that utilised the single-engined fighters of JG1, 2 and 26, plus Me 110 and Ju 88 night-fighters of NJG2 and 3, a total of approximately 250 aircraft. During daylight hours the plan called for sixteen fighters to be over the ships at all times, patrols lasting for thirty minutes. Relieving aircraft were to take up position ten minutes before the preceding patrol was due to depart so that, for ten minutes out of every half hour, there would be thirty-two fighters in attendance. Stores had been pre-positioned at a number of airfields along the Channel coast so that these aircraft could land away from their normal bases and be back in the air in the minimum amount of time.

Despite jamming, British coastal radar began to report signs of air activity, the movement of which pointed to the fact that it was covering shipping. Shortly afterwards a second radar station reported two large surface vessels off Cap Gris Nez, but it would not be until the return of Spitfires of 91 Squadron an hour later that the level of activity in the Channel would begin to be appreciated.

Throughout the morning of 12 February, 91 Squadron put up several pairs of Spitfire Vbs from its Hawkinge base to carry out 'Jim Crow' reconnaissance sorties over the Channel area. The first aircraft to take off at 0845 hrs was DL-Y, flown by Sergeant Brown who was accompanied by Sergeant Omdahl in DL-R. On reaching the French coast at Boulogne the pair split up, Brown heading south towards Dieppe, while Omdahl flew north towards Zeebrugge. Off Berck, Brown spotted two E-boats, but the largest naval activity was seen by Omdahl who sighted six minesweepers off Zeebrugge with a further eleven to the north of Dunkirk. Diving down, he fired at one of the latter and saw cannon strikes all along its length, subsequently claiming it as destroyed. Unknown to the pilots, the E-boats were in fact heading south to join up with the battle group, who by now were steaming steadily northwards towards the Straits of Dover, and the minesweepers were busy clearing a passage through the eastern Channel area.

The second patrol of the day was flown by 91 Squadron's Commanding Officer, Squadron Leader Bobby Oxspring (DL-J), with Sergeant Beaumont (DL-N) acting as his No.2, the two pilots taking off at 1020 hrs. Oxspring later wrote of their experiences in his book *Spitfire Command* (William Kimber, 1984):

> ... We flew along the cloud base which varied between about 1,200 and 1,800ft. This gave us the opportunity to nip into cloud if we encountered too many German fighters. Following the coast past Le Touquet towards the Somme estuary we suddenly ran into some bursts of heavy flak. Banking into a turn we peered down through the rain and sighted a large oval of destroyers and smaller escorts in the middle of which were three much larger ships in line astern, all leaving creamy wakes indicating that the force was moving fast.
>
> My first reaction that the Royal Navy was a bit off course was soon dispelled when we saw flak guns on the deck firing at us. As we turned across the flotilla we spotted two fighters beneath the cloud, but because of rain on our windscreens we could not immediately identify them. We closed to about 500 yards on their tails and then I saw they were Spitfires. Calling Beaumont to break off we climbed up to the cloud base again. As we did so, we saw the two Spitfires dive down and open up with cannon on some E-Boats in the outer convoy screen. It was obviously imperative that we should get this disturbing information back to Hawkinge and as we set course we eyeballed a big gaggle of German fighters over the French coast which hastened our decision.
>
> There existed a regulation stating that strict radio silence must be maintained in matters concerning reconnaissance intelligence. Not being informed of the code word 'Fuller' and its significance, I decided to break the rule and called in the clear to Bill Igoe at Biggin Hill Ops reporting what we had seen.

The two Spitfires that Oxspring had seen near the ships were flown by the experienced pairing of Group Captain Victor Beamish DSO DFC and Wing Commander Finlay Boyd DFC (Station Commander and Wing Commander Flying respectively at Kenley). Because of his high rank, Beamish should not have been flying anywhere near the French coast, but it had proved impossible to keep him off operations completely. In their reluctant acquiescence to such trips, higher authority decreed that his forays be strictly rationed and the long-suffering Boyd frequently had the responsibility of making sure that he returned safely. During their patrol Beamish and Boyd spotted two Me 109s which dived away towards the coast, the Spitfires following in hot pursuit. The two Battle of Britain veterans then got the shock of their lives when the chase took them directly over the battlecruisers at low level, with more 109s pouring down from above.

As they were beating a hasty retreat, Oxspring and Beaumont arrived safely back at Hawkinge at 1050 hrs. No action had been taken in response to Oxspring's R/T call and there is doubt as to whether it was received at all, even though it was clearly picked up by the German listening service on the French coast. It was not until the arrival of Beamish and Boyd twenty minutes later that the suspicious activity that had been noted on the radar screens was finally confirmed for what it was. Even so, the initial response was one of disbelief, and more time would be lost before the gravity of the situation finally hit home.

The forces that could be sent to do battle were pitifully inadequate and the first attempt to halt the progress of the German fleet came from six 825 Squadron Fairey Swordfish torpedo-bombers of the Fleet Air Arm led by Lieutenant Commander Eugene Esmonde DSO. After departure from Manston at 1225 hrs, the Swordfish should have made rendezvous with the whole of the Biggin Hill Wing, but only 72 Squadron appeared out of the murk over Ramsgate to accompany them on their way.

When fifteen to twenty miles out over the sea, a large warship appeared out of the haze, escorted by numerous smaller vessels, and almost immediately a number of Fw 190s were seen heading straight for the Swordfish. Pilot Officer Eric Bocock (AA914), at the head of Yellow section, dived down in a head-on attack on the leading pair of Focke-Wulfs and then carried on firing at the remaining enemy aircraft strung out behind. Bocock had the pleasure of seeing a cannon strike on the cowling of one of the aircraft before having to break right to avoid a collision. During the attack he had been followed by his wingman, Sergeant J. Garden (W3430), who had moved into echelon port to get a shot at the 190s, one of which pulled up in a climbing turn to starboard in front of him. A three-second burst produced flashes on its belly just aft of the cockpit.

By now the action was taking place very close to the warship, which was later identified as the *Gneisenau*. Bocock got a momentary glimpse of two 'explosions' which were accompanied by large columns of black-looking water 30–40ft high. These were taken as being torpedo strikes but were in fact the result of the battlecruiser's main eleven-inch guns being fired. He was also aware of some of the Swordfish aircraft breaking away and one crashing in the sea in a cloud of spray.

Looking behind, Bocock saw another Fw 190 closing in behind Sergeant Garden and called out to his No.2 to break. The 190 pulled up into a steep right-hand turn but Bocock found that he was able to hold it easily and fired a six-second burst during which his cannon ammunition ran out. Bits of debris began to fly past him and the German aircraft began to stream black smoke. Suddenly the 190 shuddered and fell away as if its pilot had lost control, disappearing beneath the Spitfire's wing in a dive beyond the vertical. As the combat had taken place only 150ft above the sea, it appeared certain that it would have dived straight in, and all that could be seen afterwards was an oil-streaked patch of foam. Bocock fired at and damaged another Fw 190 before returning to base with his ammunition completely expended.

The other members of Yellow section, Pilot Officers J. Rutherford and F. de Naeyer (Yellow 3 and 4), also saw action, the former closing to fifty yards on an Fw 190, observing hits on its wing-roots, engine and cowling. The 190 was last seen skimming the waves and was claimed as damaged. Later, Rutherford spotted three crew members from a Swordfish clinging to a half-submerged dinghy and climbed to 3,000ft to give Mayday calls.

During the combat de Naeyer had become separated from his leader and subsequently climbed to around 4,000ft where he was able to observe the water spouts as the *Gneisenau* fired its guns in the direction of the attack, and large numbers of E-boats and MTBs weaving violently. Suddenly he became aware of an Fw 190 heading at high speed towards the North Foreland and set off in pursuit. When in sight of the English coast the 190 carried out a strafing attack on a surface craft and then climbed steeply, before stall turning and flying on a reciprocal course. De Naeyer kept up the chase but, due to the high speed of his opponent, was unable to close below 350 yards. More or less as a last resort he fired a four-second burst at long range which produced a vivid flash just behind the cockpit on the port side and the 190 immediately reared up and turned to starboard. Maintaining his fire, de Naeyer watched as the German aircraft continued its turn, eventually hitting the sea in a huge cloud of spray. Content with his work, he returned to base together with Squadron Leader Brian Kingcome (AB150 RN-J), who had followed him all the way.

Although Yellow section had had the most success, Blue section's leader, Pilot Officer B. Ingham (AB848), added to the squadron's score when he went to the assistance of a Swordfish that was coming under attack by a pair of Fw 190s. Sadly, he was too late to save the biplane, its petrol tank exploding just before he was able to bring his guns to bear on the second of the 190s. His fire severely damaged the German aircraft and Flight Sergeant Robillard (AB258 – Blue 3) reported that he saw it dive into the sea after Ingham had broken away.

Despite the best attentions of 72 Squadron, the attack by the six Swordfish torpedo-bombers had been carried out against overwhelming odds and all were hacked down, either by marauding German fighters or the seemingly impenetrable wall of flak thrown up by the ships themselves. The gallantry of the Fleet Air Arm crews was of the highest order, none more so than their leader, Lieutenant Commander Esmonde, who was posthumously awarded the Victoria Cross. The Focke-Wulfs had come from III/JG26, which lost three pilots in this action, all from the 9th *Staffel.*

Unable to make the rendezvous with the Swordfish in time, the other Biggin Hill squadrons (124 and 401) led by Squadron Leader Myles Duke-Woolley were vectored on a more southerly course, arriving over the German fleet as 72 were busy down below. No.124 Squadron had moderate success, claiming two Me 109s damaged by Flight Lieutenant J. Kulhanek, plus an Fw 190 damaged by Pilot Officer M.P. 'Slim' Kilburn, but it was to be the Canadians of 401 who saw more in the way of action.

As the squadron was patrolling in sections, Pilot Officer I.C. Ormston (AA926 – Yellow 3) selected one of two Me 109s which had appeared on his left-hand side and closed to 150 yards, firing a long five-second burst with cannon and machine-guns. Flames immediately erupted from the enemy aircraft's engine and it fell away in a vertical dive and was lost to view. At the same time, a second 109 had been engaged by Pilot Officer A.E. Harley (AD232 – Yellow 1) and his wingman, Sergeant Don Morrison (P8783). As the two manoeuvred to get into a firing position behind the Messerschmitt, they were joined by Ormston, who had regained height after his previous combat, and the three went into a rough line abreast formation. The 109 then crossed in front of them at a range of around 250 yards, allowing each pilot to fire in turn as it obligingly flew through their sights. Hits were registered in each case and it was last seen plummeting vertically down through cloud.

The other members of the squadron to put in claims were Pilot Officer Geoffrey Northcott (AD418) and Flight Sergeant Harry MacDonald (AA973), of whom each damaged Me 109s. MacDonald was accompanied by Pilot Officer Omer Levesque (W3131), both pilots crossing over the coast near Mardyck in pursuit of enemy aircraft. Levesque was last seen chasing inland after yet another 109, his pursuit eventually taking him back over the sea where he was shot down (he was rescued and spent the rest of the war in *Stalag Luft III*).

In contrast to the Biggin Hill squadrons, the Hornchurch Wing, comprising 64 and 411 Squadrons, saw little in the way of action mainly due to the fact that they were ordered to patrol off Calais, the battle fleet by now having moved further to the north. A few Me 109s were still in the area and one was claimed as probably destroyed by Group Captain Harry Broadhurst, who was leading the wing. The rest of the patrol was

Line-up of 485 Squadron Spitfire Vbs, AB918 OU-Y 'Wellington I' in foreground. (*via Philip Jarrett*)

spent 'stoozing' up and down, being fired on by a number of flak ships. All aircraft returned safely by 1415 hrs.

The next Fighter Command units to be committed were 452, 485 and 602 Squadrons of the Kenley Wing, who were airborne at 1320 hrs to escort Beauforts of 217 Squadron from Thorney Island. Arriving over Manston at 1330 hrs there was no sign of the Beauforts, so the wing flew to the north-east on a report of forty-plus enemy aircraft over the Channel. Part of the German flotilla was sighted two miles off Mardyck and, as there appeared to be no air cover, 452 Squadron, led by Squadron Leader Keith Truscott, dived down in line astern to strafe a destroyer. Flak was intense at first, but the last two pilots to attack experienced no return fire and the decks appeared to be clear of personnel. Black smoke was seen issuing from the rear of the bridge as the Spitfires retired.

After his direct involvement during the morning, there was no way that Group Captain Victor Beamish was not going to take part in the action that followed. He and Wing Commander Finlay Boyd formed a separate section in the wing and also carried out an attack on a destroyer, raking it from stem to stern. Seven pilots of 602 Squadron carried out an attack on a flak ship which formed part of the outer escort screen.

No.485 Squadron, in the meantime, had maintained their height and eventually encountered part of the air umbrella which was still attempting to retain air superiority over the German fleet. Led by Squadron Leader E.P. 'Hawkeye' Wells DFC and Bar (AA732 – Red 1),

485's Blue and Yellow sections were committed to the battle to counter numerous small formations of Me 109s which attempted to lure their opponents towards the coast and into a range of anti-aircraft gun batteries.

Flight Lieutenant Bill Crawford-Compton (W3747 – Blue 1) led his section after a *Schwarm* of Me 109s and managed to get a shot at the No.4 which caused a large piece to detach from the port wing. It was last seen trailing thin black smoke and was claimed as damaged. Later, he fired at the last in a group of three 109Fs and although he observed no apparent damage, he saw the aircraft hit the beach about five miles west of Ostend. While all this was going on Pilot Officer Harvey Sweetman (AB860 – Blue 3), who had temporarily lost his position in the section, had a 109F on his tail which was being fired at by Pilot Officer David Clouston (W3577 – Blue 4). Sweetman later managed to get in a burst himself and the aircraft's destruction was confirmed by Crawford-Compton.

Yellow section, led by Flight Lieutenant G.H. Francis (BL385), chased after four 109Fs which flew off towards the convoy at 600ft to try to entice them into the flak. As Francis broke away he saw a mixed formation of approximately twenty enemy aircraft, Me 109s and Fw 190s, flying up and down at 700ft. Turning towards them he got onto the tail of an Fw 190 and had no difficulty in closing from 200 yards down to 75 yards. A long burst of fire sent it down with black smoke pouring from its engine, and as it was last seen going straight down at only 300ft, it was later claimed as destroyed. Pilot Officer Reg Grant (W3528) also claimed the destruction of an Me 109F, while Sergeant J.D. Rae (AD114) damaged another. In addition, Squadron Leader Wells led his section in an attack on an E-boat which was hit by all and claimed as damaged.

Efforts to attack the battlecruisers by Coastal Command Beauforts and Hudsons were generally hampered by poor serviceability and mis-understandings as to the exact positions of the capital ships. Each attack formation was intended to fly out with fighter protection but there were a number of confusions at rendezvous points caused by late arrivals, poor weather and the fact that the fighters were unable to talk to the bombers by radio. Worsening weather over the Channel was making the situation even more chaotic, and the relative speed with which the German ships were making good their flight towards safety meant that there was very little time left to mount a successful operation.

Before the aircraft of Bomber Command could make their contribution, three squadrons of Hurricane fighter-bombers (Nos. 1, 3 and 607) were thrown into the increasingly desperate attempts to inflict serious damage on the German flotilla. At 1315 hrs the Spitfire Vbs of 313 (Czech) Squadron joined up with eight Hurricanes of 607 Squadron and flew to a point five miles off the French coast to the north-east of Calais. Visibility was very bad, but two flak ships were seen and attacked, one receiving a direct hit. The other ship was strafed by six pilots of 313, together with two of the Hurricanes, and a number of those taking part, including Squadron Leader K. Mrazek DFC (AA869 – Red 1), reported hits. Another flak ship was shot up by Flight Lieutenant Fejfar and Sergeant Dohnal.

Over at Westhampnett, 129 (Mysore) Squadron finally got into the action when it escorted six Hurricanes of 1 Squadron on the lookout for enemy ships to the north of Dunkirk. Three destroyers were eventually seen in line astern and each was attacked by a pair of Hurricanes with cover being provided by a section of four Spitfires. All of the ships were damaged, but one of the Hurricanes was shot down in flames and another was badly hit, its pilot surviving to become a PoW. No.129 did not come through unscathed as Pilot Officer G.J. Davis (AA921) was lost to flak and Sergeant Wilson (W3800) had a considerable portion of his starboard wing shot away but managed to make it back, baling out successfully over Martlesham Heath. The only other casualty was Flight Sergeant McPhie, who was attacked by three 109s shortly after setting course for home, the subsequent engagement damaging his aircraft and wounding him in the heel. Flight Lieutenant H.C.F. Bowman succeeded in levelling the score, however, by damaging one of the Messerschmitts.

Also based at Westhampnett, 41 Squadron had been at readiness since 1127 hrs and had flown two uneventful defensive patrols before it was eventually sent on its first offensive sorties over the Channel. Taking off at 1350 hrs it encountered twenty Me 109Fs five miles from the Belgian coast and in the ensuing dogfight claimed three destroyed, one each to Squadron Leader P.H. 'Dutch' Hugo (BL248 – Red 1), Pilot Officer F.R. Cambridge (BL477 – Blue 2) and Sergeant R.E. Green (AA931 – Blue 3). Sergeant B.P. Dunstan (W3565 – Green 4), who had turned back early with technical trouble, failed to return.

Nos. 65 and 111 Squadrons, who had also been kicking their heels since 1130 hrs, finally took off from Debden just after 1400 hrs, the wing being led by Group Captain J.R.A. Peel DSO DFC. Shortly afterwards they joined up with 222 and 403 Squadrons from North Weald and proceeded to the North Foreland before heading out to sea. Weather conditions remained poor with cloud base down to sea level in places. By the time the Spitfires arrived over their designated patrol area to the north of Dunkirk they were at around 1–2,000ft and immediately ran into large numbers of Me 109s and Fw 190s, the squadrons rapidly splitting up into sections and pairs as combat was joined.

During the mêlée three of 111's pilots fired their guns, all with excellent

S/L C.N.S. Campbell of 403 Squadron with (L to R) Parr, Walker and Lodge (I.O). (*Parr*)

results. Pilot Officer Prihoda attacked an Me 109F which was attempting to get behind another Spitfire and his three short bursts were sufficient to cause its pilot to bale out. He later used up the rest of his ammunition on another Me 109 which seemed to 'flutter' in its flight as though its pilot had lost control, but as he was coming under attack himself he was forced to break away and could only claim it as damaged. Another Czech, Flight Sergeant Hruby (W3310), fired a short burst with cannon at a 109 and saw debris fall from it before it escaped in cloud.

Not far away Sergeant Peter Durnford spotted a 109 being chased by another Spitfire which was well out of range. He executed a tight left-hand turn which positioned his aircraft about 300 yards behind the Messerschmitt and fired a maximum deflection shot as it tried to out-turn him. By now the other Spitfire was very close and Durnford was forced to break away to avoid colliding with it. As he did so, he was aware of the 109 going down in an inverted dive at no more than 1,000ft. He later claimed it as probably destroyed.

No.65 Squadron also had good fortune, thanks to its CO, Squadron Leader H.T. Gilbert (BL372), who made a total of seven separate attacks, the second of which was delivered from 200 yards on an Me 109F. A three-second burst from dead astern resulted in black smoke and flames erupting from the Messerschmitt's engine and it pulled up sharply before turning onto its back and diving into the sea. Gilbert's final attack involved a five-minute chase after another 109F during which he achieved numerous machine-gun hits before his ammunition finally ran out. His No.2, Sergeant T.D. Tinsey (BL349), then took over and caused further damage before he was forced to break away. Four other pilots fired their guns, but only Pilot Officer Colin Hewlett (AB133 – Yellow 1) put in a claim for an Me 109F damaged.

Of the North Weald units, Squadron Leader C.N.S. Campbell DFC of 403 successfully prevented an attack on a pair of Hudsons by three Me 109s but in doing so lost contact with the rest of the squadron. In the target area he saw what appeared to be a ship ablaze, and two flak ships putting up a curtain of fire to the level of the cloud base. After circling for approximately fifteen minutes, during which time he was joined by two of his section together with three aircraft from another unit, Campbell returned to the south coast, flying as close escort for eight Wellingtons which were also returning home.

As a relative newcomer to operational flying, Pilot Officer Charles Magwood recalls his impressions:

> Just six weeks after being posted to 403 Squadron, this was my 'Baptism of Fire', although I saw very little other than my leader's tailwheel! We flew through a multi-layered cake of cloud cover and as soon as we popped through the bottom layer we were subjected to the most horrendous ack-ack from the cruisers. The squadron was split up into twos by the supporting yellow-nosed 109s and for protection we would pop back up into the upper cloud layer. Despite the conditions, Flight Sergeant Ryckman destroyed one and damaged another.

Sergeant Eric Crist (AA967 KH-B) also has clear memories of the day:

> We were stationed at North Weald and, except for two pilots on readiness, most of us had left the dispersal area for lunch at the mess. It was a typical winter day with low scudding clouds at about 1,200ft giving 8/10 cover. The height of the cloud tops ranged from 6–8,000ft. We had just settled down to lunch when the CO received an urgent call from ops to scramble 403 Squadron with operational orders to be given when the wing was airborne. Urgent indeed!
>
> We were airborne in record time and directed to establish air cover for bombers attacking the German battleships breaking out along the Channel, in the vicinity of Calais. We flew above cloud until the Wingco decided we were there, and then we spiralled down through a hole in the cloud from bright sunlight into a rather gloomy overcast. We were not alone. It looked as though every aircraft that was flyable was heading for the same location, Swordfish, Hudsons and Wellington bombers, all bravely attempting what was basically a suicidally hopeless task.
>
> As for the battle itself, it quickly became an almost individual

Sgt Eric Crist in front of AD258 KH-E. (*Parr*)

affair as our squadron, following a head-on attack by Me 109s, was soon operating in sections of four or two. Jack Ryckman and I, while loosely aware of where the others were, operated as a unit of two most of the time. The low cloud ceiling which compressed and intensified the activity was both a help and a hindrance. A help when hard-pressed, you could use the cloud for cover, and a hindrance when your foe did likewise. Jack shot down a 109 during one of the many skirmishes, and he and I both fired on another 109, pretty well destroying the tail section before it disappeared in the murk. One hour and forty minutes after take-off we landed at Southend to re-fuel before returning to our home base.

My only comment on the whole operation would be that if bravery alone could have carried the day, then surely the crews of the Swordfish would have prevailed. Such was not the case and one by one they fell into the sea.

The combats referred to by Crist took place off Gravelines at around 2–3,000ft. Ryckman, who was flying W3426 KH-D, attacked an Me 109F, his initial burst causing it to stop its manoeuvring, allowing a second, and longer, burst, one that produced multiple hits on wings and fuselage. Heavy black smoke and flames then shot from its engine and it disappeared in cloud going straight down. Flight Sergeants Crawford and

Sgt G.A.J. Ryckman (right) with F/L Brad Walker. (*Parr*)

Somers (Blue 2 and 3) also fired, but neither made any claim. (Flight Sergeant G.A.J. Ryckman was shot down and killed on 20 April 1942, his 22nd birthday, when serving with 126 Squadron in Malta).

The other North Weald squadron, 222, led by Squadron Leader 'Dickie' Milne, stayed up to protect the others and saw action only briefly. A pair of 109s made something of a half-hearted attack on them only to be shot at by Milne, but his fire did not appear to have any effect and he made no claim. Sergeant R. Wood (BL768) later managed to fire at an Fw 190 and claimed it as damaged.

Although the *Scharnhorst* had come to a temporary halt at 1415 hrs having hit a mine, the progress of the German battlecruisers had been brisk, having averaged a good twenty-five knots. By the time the final fighter sorties were carried out in mid-afternoon, the flotilla was off the Dutch coast and steaming north at full speed from the Hook of Holland. Having already seen considerable action, 11 Group's squadrons got airborne again as soon as possible, but as many aircraft had been forced to land at forward airfields virtually out of fuel, it had taken time for everyone to make it back to their home airfields. By the time they got away again the activity had shifted further to the north-east and, in general, their patrols yielded little of note.

The final fighter actions of the day involved 118, 234 and 501 Squadrons of the Ibsley Wing from 10 Group. Having been released for training in the morning, the call to readiness went out at 1155 hrs and all three squadrons were airborne an hour later, heading for West Malling. Due to a hitch with the refuelling arrangements, a section of 118 Squadron, led by Wing Commander Ian Gleed, took off again at 1410 hrs, the rest of the wing departing twenty minutes later.

The first four aircraft, which also included 118's CO Squadron Leader Carver, located the battle-cruisers and escorting craft fifteen miles north-north-east of Ostend and proceeded to circle them. By now Bomber Command had been committed to the battle and numerous friendly bombers were seen heading for home, but at first there was little to be seen of the *Luftwaffe*, only one Me 109 appearing, which was chased off. Large numbers of 109s did eventually appear but by this time fuel was low and the section returned to West Malling, landing at 1600 hrs.

The remainder of the wing took off at 1430 hrs and located two destroyers, together with two flak ships, sixteen minutes after crossing the coast at Dover. Weather conditions were still extremely poor and several sections became split up. Sergeant Thomas (AD204) and Pilot Officer I.S. Stone (AD239) of 118 Squadron were attacked by large numbers of Me 109s, which resulted in Stone being shot down and Thomas's aircraft suffering Cat. B damage.

Another of 118's pilots, Commander Andre Jubelin of the Free French Navy, became separated from Pilot Officer MacKenzie when the latter chased after an Me 109. He later wrote of his experiences in *The Flying Sailor*, a personal account that gives a good indication of conditions over the Channel:

> The swell was very noticeable, with high, spray-crested waves. Here and there squalls blended sea and clouds. A hundred feet above the surface I turned west-north-west. I opened the glass roof of the cockpit, for the windscreen was misted and prevented good vision ahead. It was raining. On emerging from the squall I came suddenly upon a whole fleet. It was an amazing picture. Some miles to the south, clearly outlined against the strip of sky between sea and ceiling, the three great ships the *Scharnhorst*, *Gneisenau* and *Prinz Eugen*, were steaming east. Their grey masses were flecked with the brief flashes of their medium-calibre guns.
>
> Turning south, I came down to low level, twenty feet above the white wave crests. To my right a destroyer was firing at me. One of its automatic weapons, as the vessel rolled, made an avenue of fragile columns of spray along the water. As I passed, I took aim at

the bridge and gave it a burst. Men dropped down behind the bulwarks and my bullets caused little grey clouds to rise. Diving back into a hollow in the swell I came . . . abeam of the rear ship in the line, the *Prinz Eugen*. An aircraft spiralled across my field of vision, struck the water and disappeared. The column it sent up was whipped away by the wind into a thin curtain of foam. I did not have the audacity to open fire on the bridge of the heavy cruiser. I took evasive action by spiralling up to the right and held my breath during the few seconds that my aircraft showed its belly to the entire armament of the *Prinz Eugen*. I don't even know whether I was fired on.

I descended below the ceiling again. This time the German squadron lay to port. The leading ship, the *Scharnhorst*, had broken alignment . . . signal flags came fluttering along her yards, it looked as if something had gone wrong down there. I should have liked to stay, I had got into the mood of a spectator and knew all about dodging round among those excellent well-placed nimbus clouds, but, it was now half past three.

Grazing the clouds, I took leave of the ships which hardly seemed to trouble themselves with my insignificant person. Thirty minutes later, in poor visibility, I crossed an unknown coast. I tried vainly to get into communication with some base. The ether was thick with a thousand conversations, among which my defective English did not succeed in arousing the interest of any of the speakers. My petrol level was low. I eventually came upon the lofty spires of Canterbury, Maidstone (West Malling) was only five minutes away.

I am not, I confess, very proud of my sortie. But being what I am, a professional sailor turned airman, the encounter with this redoubtable squadron making its escape at thirty knots through angry seas, under a sky of menace, made too strong an appeal to my senses to allow me to be anything but a spectator.

Due to such weather conditions most squadrons had found it virtually impossible to stay together for very long while in the target area. Such a situation also produced something of a lottery when it came to engaging the enemy or, in turn, being engaged. During its patrol, 234 Squadron was attacked twice out of cloud without even knowing that danger existed. Pilot Officer D.E. Pike (AA727) disappeared without trace, and AA722 (AZ-B) was last seen over the Channel pouring black smoke. Its pilot, Pilot Officer D.N. McLeod, managed to make it to the French coast where he carried out a successful crash-landing. Back over the Channel, Flight Lieutenant D.A.S. McKay (BL241 AZ-E) descended through cloud to see three Me 109s to his right and 1,000ft below. Turning in behind the machine on the right-hand side of the formation, he fired a burst from 200 yards which caused it to rear up and collide with the lead aircraft. Both 109s were subsequently claimed as destroyed although, as McKay was alone at the time, neither could be confirmed.

By now the German fleet was within range of 12 Group's squadrons based in East Anglia. These included 19 Squadron, whose ten Spitfire Vbs lifted off from their base at Ludham at 1526 hrs led by Flight Lieutenant Lloyd Chadburn in BL380. They were soon down to nine, however, as Sergeant D.T.E. Reid (AD332) lost contact in cloud shortly after take-off, the remaining aircraft carrying out an uneventful forty-minute patrol before returning at 1655 hrs. A second patrol was carried out half an hour later but, once again, no enemy aircraft were encountered. The body of Sergeant Reid was later discovered by a trawler off Great Yarmouth.

The return of the 12 Group squadrons marked the culmination of a maximum effort which resulted in seventeen enemy aircraft being claimed as destroyed (plus three probables) for the loss of eight Spitfires. In reality only seven German aircraft had been lost, and four pilots, all from JG26, had been killed. Although the fighter conflicts had resulted

No.403 Squadron pilots (L to R) P/O J.F. Parr, P/O D. Colvin, Sgt E.A. Crist, Sgt F.H. Belcher, Sgt Monserez (front). (*Parr*)

in something of a stalemate, elsewhere the story was one of unmitigated disaster with Bomber Command losing sixteen aircraft and Coastal Command five. In addition, six Hurricanes and four Whirlwinds were shot down during low-level fighter-bomber operations. When the six Fleet Air Arm Swordfish are taken into consideration, a grand total of forty-three aircraft had been lost for little gain.

Despite all the effort, which had also included attacks by Royal Navy destroyers, the two battlecruisers *Scharnhorst* and *Gneisenau* and the *Prinz Eugen* had been successfully shielded and sustained no damage during the day's operations. That is not to say, however, that they got through unharmed. Reference has already been made to the *Scharnhorst* hitting a mine, and although this did not delay its progress very long, a similar incident later in the evening caused severe damage. The *Gneisenau* also hit a mine off Terschelling and the pair finally limped into Kiel the following day. Thus, indirect action by Bomber Command had succeeded where the rather belated implementation of Operation Fuller had failed.

SIX

FOCKE-WULF SUMMER

By the middle of 1942, JG2 *Richthofen* and JG26 *Schlageter* had completed their conversion onto the Fw 190A and had approximately 200 machines serviceable at any one time. The technical snags which had caused problems shortly after the Focke-Wulf's introduction to operational service had largely been overcome and the benefits of standardisation could now be exploited to the full. In comparison with the Me 109F, the new fighter offered its pilots much greater freedom when it came to engaging enemy formations, an advantage that could not be grasped fully as long as the 109 was still fighting alongside it.

It also took time for *Luftwaffe* pilots to adjust to their new mount. Before its arrival they had contented themselves by fighting defensively, only joining combat when the tactical situation was in their favour. Actions had usually consisted of short, sharp encounters on the fringes of the RAF's incursions into northern France and only when the 109s achieved local superiority did they consider coming down in any strength to indulge in a dogfight. Although still not in the same league as the Spitfire, the Fw 190's performance in the horizontal plane was better than the 109F which allowed its pilots to be much more aggressive in combat. As confidence grew with increased experience, they were able to take the initiative on many more occasions. The actions that had already been fought in the skies over France had shown the Fw 190 to be a formidable adversary, but the level of dominance that it was capable of achieving was underlined during operations that were carried out on the first two days in June 1942.

Situated three miles to the south-east of Saffron Walden in Essex, Debden was one of 11 Group's most important stations and had been in the forefront of the desperate actions fought during the Battle of Britain. In the early war years it was associated mainly with the Hawker Hurricane, but by mid-1942 these had been replaced by the Spitfire Vbs of 71, 111 and 350 Squadrons.

No.71 had re-formed in September 1940, its pilots being drawn from American volunteers who thus formed the first of the so-called 'Eagle' squadrons. It had been flying Spitfire Vbs since September 1941 and was commanded by Squadron Leader Chesley Peterson DFC from Salt Lake City, Utah. No.111 Squadron was one of the most famous units in the RAF and had flown some of the classic inter-war biplane fighters including the Gloster Grebe, Armstrong Whitworth Siskin and Bristol Bulldog. It was now led by Squadron Leader Peter Wickham DFC whose first combat 'kills' had been achieved in Gladiators in the Middle East. The wing was completed by 350 Squadron, which had formed with Belgian personnel in November 1941 and was commanded by Squadron Leader D.A. Guillaume DFC, and 65 Squadron, which was based at Debden's satellite at Great Sampford.

On 1 June eight Hurricane fighter-bombers carried out an attack on a target near Bruges in Belgium (Circus 178). Direct protection was provided by the Spitfire Vbs of the Hornchurch and Biggin Hill Wings, the Debden squadrons being required to contribute target support. No. 65 Squadron was first away from Great Sampford at 1245 hrs with the Wing Leader, Wing Commander J.A.G. Gordon, in the lead, 71, 111 and 350 Squadrons lifting off from Debden ten minutes later. Having crossed the English coast at Deal at 1312 hrs, the wing climbed over the Channel so that it crossed into occupied Europe at Thourout with 65 in the low position at 20,000ft and 111, 71 and 350 stepped up above and behind at 22, 23 and 25,000ft respectively. Weather conditions were ideal with excellent visibility.

As the Spitfires curved towards Bruges, condensation trails could be seen a few thousand feet above and to the south as a large force of Fw 190s from I and III/JG26 watched and waited. The attack did not materialise until the wing was on its way out near Blankenberge, but when it came, it was timed to perfection and delivered with devastating effect. The German formation was led by *Major* Gerhard Schopfel who launched a feint attack by part of his force which succeeded in drawing 111 Squadron out of position. Within seconds, all squadrons were heavily engaged and the action that followed emphasised the fact that the *Luftwaffe* could now seize the initiative and press home its advantage, if it so desired.

Looking down and to his left, Squadron Leader Peterson (BL449 – White 1) saw six 190s diving on 111 Squadron and immediately went to its assistance. The Germans were aware of the threat and turned towards him, but by closing his throttle completely and pulling hard, Peterson found that he was able to get behind one at around 100 yards' range. Two bursts of cannon and machine-gun fire struck the wing-root and cockpit area of the 190 and it spun away trailing white petrol smoke.

Pulling back up to 20,000ft, Peterson attempted to help four Spitfires of 350 Squadron which were being attacked by a Focke-Wulf formation twice its size. By the time he arrived it was already too late and six of the 190s transferred their attention to him. Despite carrying out a series of violent evasive manoeuvres, his aircraft suffered a cannon strike in its wing but was not further damaged, even though all six of the enemy aircraft were, by now, very close. During a hectic dogfight, Peterson even managed to achieve a few De Wilde strikes on one of the 190s before diving for home.

No.71 Squadron's Red Section, led by Flight Lieutenant Gus Daymond DFC (BL583), was also attacked and began a hard turn to the left in an effort to get into a favourable position. During the turn Daymond became aware that his No.2, Pilot Officer E.G. Teicheira (BM386), was not turning as steeply as the rest of the section and he was not seen again. By now more 190s had arrived and the action had turned into general free-for-all. As he was endeavouring to help a Spitfire that was coming under attack, Daymond was set upon by no fewer than five 190s. Wringing every ounce of performance from his aircraft, he was able to foil their attacks which were kept up right from the Dutch coast to a point ten miles off the North Foreland. Like his CO, he managed to get off some snap shots and one of the 190s suffered minor damage to its rear fuselage. Most of 71 Squadron's pilots fired their guns and Pilot Officer Eugene M. Potter (W3761 – Red 3), Pilot Officer Robert S. Sprague (W3368 – White 3) and Sergeant Morgan (W3957 – White 2) all put in claims for Fw 190s damaged.

The initial attack on 111 Squadron as witnessed by Chesley Peterson was carried out by *Hauptmann* Johannes Seifert's I *Gruppe* which shot down Rhodesian Sergeant R.C. Bryson (AB938 – White 2) and Sergeant W.H. Cumming (BL728 – Blue 4). Several other aircraft were hit, including Flight Lieutenant R.C. Brown (AB905), Sergeant G.C. Heighington (BM629) and Sergeant H.D. Christian (AR281), but all managed to return to base without further mishap.

Continuing his dive, Seifert then attacked 65 Squadron. Almost immediately Wing Commander Gordon (BL936 – White 1) was heard giving a Mayday call and both he and his No.2, Sergeant R.E. Parrack (BL647), were shot down and killed. As Blue section were trying to fight their way home they came under accurate fire from the heavy gun batteries situated along the coast, but this did not deter *Oberleutnant* Johannes Schmidt of the 3rd *Staffel* who shot down Pilot Officer J.R. Richards (AR391 – Blue 3). As Richards took to his parachute, his wingman, Sergeant V. Kopacek (AB133), also came under attack, but he managed to break free and landed a few minutes later at Manston with a shrapnel wound in his right thigh. His Spitfire was later classified Cat. Ac although he resolutely maintained that the damage had been caused by flak and not by enemy aircraft. Thanks to the efforts of the rescue services, Pilot Officer Richards was picked up by motor launch after spending two and a half hours in his dinghy and was brought safely back to Manston.

The top cover squadron, No. 350, was attacked by around twenty Fw 190s of *Hauptmann* Josef 'Pips' Priller's III *Gruppe*, which had maintained its height as Seifert had dived through the lower squadrons. Blue section soon became separated and Flight Sergeant G.G.A.J. Livyns (BL822 – Blue 4) was shot down near Ostend having lost touch with his leader. In the meantime, White section was also in trouble as its No.3 had been forced to return early with engine trouble, and Sergeant L.J.A. Hansez (W3626 – White 4) was shot down before he could close the gap with the two remaining aircraft.

Two other members of Blue section, Flight Lieutenant Du Monceau (BL540 – Blue 1) and Flying Officer R.J.L. Laumans (AB173 – Blue 3), found themselves quite alone and, as they were crossing out over the coast, witnessed a Spitfire go into the sea near Ostend. The aircraft came down close to a fleet of fishing boats but there was no sign of a parachute. Not long after another Spitfire was seen being attacked by an Fw 190, its pilot baling out into the sea. As Du Monceau sent out a Mayday call, his No.2 chased inland after the 190 which was soon joined by four others. Robert Laumans takes up the story:

> Between each engagement I tried to fly a few miles towards England as it was obvious that I couldn't shoot down all of the Germans. It was also obvious that they wouldn't let me go! My petrol was going down fast but I was ready to do battle to the finish. It was no good trying to flee as the Fw 190 was faster than the Spitfire V so I faced them each time they attacked. Finally, when I was firing at one of the enemy in front of me, two of his comrades attacked from astern, one left, one right. A shell suddenly entered my cockpit from the left-hand side, pierced the dashboard and exploded in the petrol tank in front. My aircraft was immediately set on fire and the only thing I could do was to bale out. The combat had started at around 25,000ft and I abandoned the aircraft at 900ft, more than enough time to deploy the parachute. I ended up in the sea somewhere between Ostend and Dover, successfully opened my dinghy, and remained drifting for sixty-three hours. On the third day, in late afternoon, I was picked up by the Germans a couple of miles outside Nieuport (Belgium). I spent three days at Coxyde airfield with high fever (exposure) and was eventually sent to *Stalag Luft III* at Sagen.

One of the most worrying aspects of this operation was the fact that a formation comprising forty-six Spitfires had been badly mauled and had

Blast pens at North Weald with W/C David Scott-Malden's AB202 S-M in foreground. (*Aitken*)

suffered losses approaching 20%. There had been several occasions in recent weeks when large numbers of Fw 190s had been encountered, but this was one of the first actions that the Germans had been confident enough to take on a complete wing. Up until now they had been content to pick off individual squadrons or sections which had become detached from the main wing formation, surplus aircraft being used to contain the remaining RAF fighters rather than engage them. Thanks to the fighting qualities of the Fw 190, such reservations could now be swept aside.

The events of 1 June highlighted the difficulties Fighter Command now had to contend with over northern Europe. The battle to win the technological war has often been likened to a pendulum swinging to and fro, with the advantage going to one side and then the other. For the time being at least, it was abundantly clear that this effect had moved decisively in favour of the *Luftwaffe*. As far as the RAF was concerned, worse was to follow.

By the beginning of June, 403 (RCAF) Squadron was based at Rochford having moved the short distance from North Weald in early May. Originally formed in March 1941 as an Army Co-operation squadron with Tomahawks, its role had been changed shortly afterwards and it had begun operational flying with Spitfire Vbs the following August. The unit was commanded by New Zealander Squadron Leader Al Deere DFC and Bar, who had been posted in on 1 May to pick up the pieces following the loss of Squadron Leader C.N.S. Campbell and Flight Lieutenant H.P. Duval on 27 April. During a wing sweep near Le Touquet, intense and accurate flak had caused Duval's aircraft (AA834) to collide with that flown by Campbell (BM123), the impact violent enough to break off the latter's port wing. Both machines dived out of control and only Campbell succeeded in baling out, Duval's aircraft going straight into the sea about half a mile offshore.

On 2 June, the day after Debden's misfortune, 403 Squadron flew an uneventful early morning Rodeo over northern France, one that was in marked contrast to a similar operation carried out shortly afterwards. At briefing the squadron was informed that it was to rendezvous with the rest of the North Weald Wing (222 and 331 Squadrons) over Chatham before setting course for Hastings, where it would meet up with the Spitfire Vbs of the Hornchurch Wing. Having formed up at zero feet, it would then climb over the Channel so as to cross the French coast at Cap Gris Nez at 20–25,000ft. The route over France would see them sweep east to St Omer, before turning right to come out at Le Touquet. The squadron's composition was as follows:

Blue Section	Red Section	Yellow Section
F/L E.V. Darling	S/L A.C. Deere	F/L B. Walker
W/O D.G. Campbell	Sgt Murphy	P/O J.E. Gardiner
F/O J.F. Parr	P/O D.S. Hurst	P/O L.J. Somers
F/Sgt G.D. Aitken	P/O R. Wozniak	Sgt N.E. Hunt

The operation passed off without incident until the withdrawal was being made with 403 Squadron bringing up the rear at 24,000ft. A formation of twelve to fifteen Fw 190s was seen closing from behind, and when it got within range Deere called the break which immediately sent Red and Blue sections pulling hard to the left to meet the attack, while Yellow section turned in the opposite direction, climbing as it did so. During his turn Deere looked to his left towards Yellow section and was horrified to see another formation of Fw 190s coming out of a thin layer of cirrostratus, 2,000ft above. By now the first group of 190s was almost upon them and there was just time for a short head-on burst, the enemy aircraft pulling up to cut off 403's line of retreat.

Al Deere was heavily attacked from all sides and exhausted all of his ammunition in short bursts at close range, engaging numerous individual aircraft from head-on, astern and full deflection. Because he was continually having to break as other aircraft attempted to get on his tail, he was unable to observe the results of his fire. About ten miles to the west of Le Touquet he saw two aircraft hit the sea, one of which was positively identified as being a Spitfire. This particular machine broke up in mid-air, but its pilot appeared to bale out successfully. Although he was chased until mid-Channel, he managed to avoid further combat.

F/L Brad Walker, S/L Al Deere, F/L Francis (Eng Off) and F/L 'Mitzi' Darling with Deere's fiancée Joan. (*via Wozniak*)

About fifteen miles south-west of Dungeness, Deere witnessed the pilot of a second Spitfire bale out, and shortly afterwards another went into the sea about three miles away to his left, its pilot also baling out, but at very low level. After sending a Mayday call for the first pilot, who by now was in his dinghy, he flew towards the position where the second aircraft had gone in. Conditions were hazy, but eventually he saw an oily patch on the water and soon after located the pilot who was also safely in his dinghy. After sending another Mayday, Deere flew low over the downed airman and saw him wave back, but as he was getting low on fuel, he was forced to land at nearby Lympne before returning to Rochford.

Deere's wingman, Sergeant Murphy, was attacked at the same time as his leader and fired a two-second burst of cannon and machine-gun at an Fw 190 which flew through his sights. He saw it stall-turn onto its back before spinning away and at first thought that he had caused some damage until he saw another enemy aircraft carry out the same manoeuvre without being fired upon. He then managed to get on the tail of another 190 but was reduced to firing with machine-guns only after his cannons jammed. He was then attacked by several 190s and had to take violent evasive action at the end of which his height was down to 3,000ft. In his confusion he headed for France instead of England and passed over

P/O Roy Wozniak (right) relaxes with F/L Terry O'Leary (left) and P/O Doug Hurst. (*Wozniak*)

many small villages, all of which seemed to have anti-aircraft batteries positioned nearby, which opened fire on him. Realising his error, he quickly got onto the correct course for home but freely admitted later that he never expected to make it back. After crossing the English coast he landed at Manston to refuel before returning to Rochford.

Pilot Officer Roy Wozniak (Red 4) also made it back, but only just.

> We did not encounter any action until we were turning back when we were told to get out, as there were too many enemy fighters to handle. The other squadrons dived for home as instructed, but being top cover, it was too late for 403 Squadron. The Germans dove in from behind and from the sides and we had to fight it out in spite of being outnumbered three or four to one.
>
> As we were breaking into the aircraft behind us, I was hit in the fuselage from the side by an explosive cannon shell which knocked me into a spin. Fortunately I was protected from the shrapnel by the

95

armour plate behind my seat (later I found a piece of shrapnel imbedded in the heel of my shoe that had passed under the armour). We were instructed to stay in spins until we were well away from the action, since coming out you don't have flying speed and are a sitting pigeon for the enemy. However, as I did not know the extent of my damage, I decided to pull out of the spin. Fortunately the aircraft came out, but unfortunately there was a German fighter with two wingmen on my tail.

When I saw bullet holes appearing in my wings, I broke sharply into the attacking aircraft. They pulled up for another go and were soon on my tail again. This time I throttled back and waited until they were closer and even more bullet holes were appearing. I then broke around sharply and almost collided head-on with the leader. That seemed to be enough for them and I was able to proceed home on my own. However, this was not the end of my problems.

When I reached base and tried to lower my wheels, they wouldn't lock in the down position. Fortunately I decided to rock the aircraft with rudder instead of snapping the aircraft out of a dive. This did the trick, and the wheels locked down. I did not realise that, of the two cables to the elevator, one was sheared, and the other partially sheared and stretched. Had I dived the aircraft, the cable could have snapped and I would have dove right into the ground.

Since I had a great deal of play in my stick (due to the stretched cable) I felt I was susceptible to a high-speed stall. I came in for a high-speed landing and as my aircraft floated down the airfield, I thought I was going to overshoot and hit an aircraft at the end of the field. I tried to go around again but the motor was dead. When I touched down I applied left rudder, but the aircraft pulled to the right and came to a quick stop. This was the result of my tyre being punctured by a bullet passing through the wing. When I got out of the aircraft the Medical Officer asked me if I was OK. I said 'just a moment', and looked up my pant legs to see if it was blood or sweat. Thank goodness, it was sweat!

They hauled the aircraft away and later, the Engineering Officer told me that I had a cylinder knocked out of the motor – no wonder I had such confidence in the Spitfire and particularly the Rolls-Royce Merlin engine.

Yellow section leader, Flight Lieutenant 'Brad' Walker, who was followed throughout by his No.2 Pilot Officer Ed Gardiner, saw twenty-plus enemy aircraft coming in from the south and at first turned to meet the attack, but on seeing four Fw 190s come out of cloud directly behind

Damage to Roy Wozniak's AD114 KH-W. (*Wozniak*)

Red and Blue sections, turned his attentions to this new threat instead. Firing a short burst from 400 yards he succeeded in making the section break off but then had to go to the assistance of Pilot Officer Gardiner, who was coming under attack from an Fw 190 on his port beam. The two chased it as it spiralled upwards into cloud, but on coming out could find no trace of the rest of the squadron. Although they saw many more 190s in the distance as they returned, they were not attacked and landed at Southend at 1130 hrs. (Gardiner was the son of the Hon. James Gardiner who was Minister of Agriculture in the Canadian government. Sadly, he was one of three 403 Squadron pilots shot down and killed on 19 August 1942 during the Dieppe Raid.)

For Sergeant Norris Hunt (Yellow 4), the two Rodeos flown on 2 June were to be his first (and last) operational sorties over enemy territory. He recalls:

> This date will forever be imprinted deeply in my memory which, through the years, has become somewhat clouded and misty – due partly to a subconscious desire to keep an unpleasant period of my life under wraps. That was the day my life changed quite suddenly and dramatically and remained so for the next three years – the day I was ignominiously shot out of the skies over France!

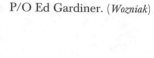

P/O Ed Gardiner. (*Wozniak*)

I remember it was a lovely spring morning when, upon reporting to the flight room before breakfast, S/L Deere called me aside and asked, 'Hunt, do you feel ready for an operation over the French coast?' This was the moment for which I had been training for the past twelve months and, although deep down in my heart I knew that I really did not possess the skills, tactical knowledge or experience that was needed to take on the Hun, I confidently and enthusiastically replied, 'Yes sir'. Evidently I was to replace Pilot Officer 'Chuck' Magwood who was 'under the weather'.

It was to be a fighter sweep over the French coast in the area of Cap Gris Nez and the object of the exercise was to entice the enemy up for a scrap. I was to take up the No.4 position in Yellow section which was on the right flank ('ass-end Charlie' as it was colloquially called). I thought this was a bit odd because it was generally customary to start a 'new boy' off as No.2 to the CO, to be nicely tucked away in the middle of the squadron. I remember taking off in formation and flying low, just above the roof tops of the cottages and villages. The English countryside looked so soft and peaceful that morning and one could see villagers trudging off to work for the day. It seemed so incongruous – that we were going off to do battle!

The thing that stands out in my mind about that first sweep was that my attention and concentration was almost entirely taken up by trying to keep up with my No.1. Just imagine a squadron weaving madly about the skies – No.4 has to travel twice as far with each turn as No.1, and the 'new boy' generally gets the oldest kite which is often not as fast. Fortunately the first sweep was entirely uneventful and we all landed safely approximately one hour and fifteen minutes later. I remember saying to myself, 'What a piece of cake!'

After breakfast we were assembled again for another briefing with pretty much the same 'gen' as before, but this time, as we were climbing steeply above the Channel, repeated warnings came from control over the R/T regarding big concentrations of bandits. These warnings grew in intensity until they estimated that the enemy had numerical superiority as well as height advantage. By this time we were well over French territory and Wing Commander Scott Malden's voice came over the R/T ordering the wing to turn sharply right and dive for home. All squadrons did precisely that, except 403! Either Squadron Leader Deere did not hear the order, or disobeyed it. Our squadron was left all alone to be pounced on by a swarm of Fw 190s – there must have been forty of them, or more. The sky was literally full of black swastikas in all directions.

By the time Deere gave the order to break, tracer bullets were flying by and some crashed into my fuselage behind me. I could not just keep tailing my No.1 (that would have been utter suicide) but had to make a violent evasive turn into the oncoming enemy aircraft. By this time I was well separated and found myself completely surrounded. As I was all alone in unfriendly skies it did not take long for me to decide to get the hell out of there – and quick! I suddenly remembered that an aircraft that is doing diving turns is hard to hit, so I did precisely that from 27,000ft on a course for England. I finally reached the French coast at sea level but tracers again came flying by, awfully close to my aircraft. More defensive manoeuvres were called for and in the process of doing so I found to my dismay that three Fw 190s had followed me down.

I pushed the throttle 'through the gate' for extra boost from the Merlin engine but that increased my fuel consumption and I began to worry about running out of petrol over the Channel. My situation was getting rather desperate and the thought suddenly came to me that my final moments on this planet were drawing to a close. It may sound strange but the thought that flashed through my mind at that time was a vision of the 'Sky Line Trail' in the Gatineau Hills, north of Ottawa, which was my favourite place to hike in the fall. I was so desperate I said to myself, 'let's make a real fight of it', so the next time they came at me I got one in my sights and pressed the button to fire my guns. I wasn't going to swerve and if he hadn't blinked we would have crashed head-on. I don't see how I could have missed him, but in my situation I could not look about for results!

In the meantime they had got smart and left one of the three out in front of me so that when I turned, I presented a nice target. I felt the impact of bullets hitting my engine and another whizzed by my head through the Plexiglas of the canopy. I guess it is a subconscious movement, but during a steep turn you turn your head towards the direction of the turn. If I had not done so, the bullet would have gone through my head! Smoke began billowing from the engine and as it began spluttering, I could feel the loss of power. I was too low to bale out and I did not relish the thought of ditching in the Channel. As I was not far from the French coast, I elected to try to make it ashore. Suddenly, I became aware of two Fw 190s flying in formation with me as a sort of escort. It was touching that there still remained some 'esprit de corps' in the German *Luftwaffe*.

I tried desperately to open my canopy but the bullets that had pierced it must have caused it to jam. I also tried feverishly to lower my flaps to slow my approach down, but the hydraulics must have been damaged too and they would not respond. The next instant I was heading for a field adjacent to the beach. I tried to keep the nose up so that I would 'pancake' in, but there was not enough airspeed. On impact with the ground, the nose of my aircraft dug in and I did a nice somersault, landing upside down in the mud. With the canopy closed and the aircraft literally lying on top of me, it was impossible for me to extricate myself from it. I could hear the engine hissing and smell the glycol leaking all about me. The terrifying thought of being burned alive in this coffin struck and I started screaming for help – silence, nothing but dead silence!

I waited for the flames to start but thanked God that they never did. It seemed like an eternity, but I suppose it may have been about an hour, when I heard the guttural sounds of Germans speaking nearby. Soon they managed to heave up on a wing and stuck the barrel of a Luger at my head. I thought they were going to shoot me, but instead they hauled me out. I suffer from claustrophobia and was nearing the point of hysteria when this assistance arrived.

Never did I appreciate so much the ecstasy of filling my lungs with sweet, cool air and standing upright on my own two feet!

Afterwards, I remember feeling very humiliated, lowly and humble – that I was where I was because of my own inadequacy. I also felt angry, both with myself and with S/L Deere. It has only been in recent years that I have been able to discuss the events of that fateful 2 June and analyse just what happened.

Hunt was to spend the rest of the war in *Stalag Luft III* at Sagen, but before that he followed a route similar to thousands of other airmen who had the misfortune to be taken prisoner.

I believe I must have been in some degree of shock after the ordeal I had been through, and the exact details of the next day or so remain rather hazy. The next thing I remember was gazing westward through the bars of a prison cell in Frankfurt. This was '*Dulag Luft*' which was a sort of receiving centre for captured Allied aircrew and was run by the *Luftwaffe*. Each PoW was held in solitary confinement for several days during which time he was systematically interrogated. It was strange to hear uniformed Germans speaking perfect English, some even with the distinctive 'upper crust' accent. I remembered being told by our Intelligence Officers back home that if we ever got ourselves in this situation, we were required to state only our name, rank and regimental number. This is all they got from me. However, I could not hold back my reaction of amazement when one of my interrogators said, 'Oh, you

F/Sgt George Aitken. (*Aitken*)

must be a new member of 403 Squadron – we haven't heard about you!'

Hunt's opposite number in Blue section, Flight Sergeant George Aitken, fared a little better, although his fate could quite easily have been the same. Following the initial attack, Aitken fired at an Fw 190 that was on the tail of Flying Officer Jack Parr, but as he did so he felt machine-gun bullets thudding into the armour plating behind his seat. His radio was smashed and some bullets also perforated his cockpit cover. After several steep turns he levelled out but could not see any sign of his section. What he did see were Fw 190s to his left and right, with a group a little further away and behind. The 190 to his right dropped its wing to attack, but his evasive action caused its tracer to pass harmlessly underneath. By now Aitken was down to 10,000ft, but another enemy aircraft had manoeuvred onto his tail without being seen. The first indication of his predicament came as cannon strikes appeared on both wings and again he threw his Spitfire into a steep descending turn to the left, only pulling out at around 5,000ft.

With the danger apparently gone, he set course over the Channel, but found that he had to wind on full forward trim to maintain the correct attitude in pitch. His engine was sounding increasingly rough, with puffs of white smoke and flames coming out of the exhaust, and an additional hazard was caused by petrol leaking into the cockpit. Unable to maintain height, he decided that it was about time he got out. Having removed his straps, he slid the hood back and opened the side door, at the same time throttling back and pulling on the control column to raise the nose. Putting his left leg on the wing, he pulled the ripcord, but was flung perilously close to the tailplane as his parachute billowed open.

Aitken had baled out at no more than 1,000ft and as he floated down he watched his aircraft plunge into the sea, sinking immediately. As a non-swimmer, the prospect of being immersed in the English Channel was not particularly appealing, so he made sure that he carried out his drill to the letter. After inflating his Mae West, he turned his quick release buckle and, shortly afterwards, hit the water. Although he was pulled for a short distance on his back by his parachute, he soon freed himself, inflated his dinghy and climbed in.

Not long after, he saw Al Deere's Spitfire, which was soon replaced by several others, one of which carried the code letters S-M, the personal markings of Wing Commander David Scott-Malden, leader of the North Weald Wing. After thirty minutes in the water, Aitken was picked up by a motor launch from Newhaven, treated to a large Scotch and put to bed while an unsuccessful search was made for the pilot of the second Spitfire which had been seen to crash in the Channel. He was then transferred to RAF rescue launch No.147 and taken to Dover. As he remarked fifty-seven years later, 'Just one of my lucky days!'

Flying Officer Jack Parr (Blue 3), whom Aitken had tried to help, recalls his experiences:

Mid-morning on 2 June 1942 was bright and sunny, and our wing of Spitfires was roaming the French skies for the second time that day. Banjo, our ground control, was continuously warning us that the Germans were up in considerable strength and eventually our Wing Commander gave the order to turn right and dive for home. At the 26,000ft level there should have been no problem in outrunning the Fw 190s but at this moment our Squadron Commander gave the order 'Sherry squadron, break left – sharp left'. Our twelve Spitfire Vbs were immediately engaged by about forty enemy 190s.

I was in Blue 3 position, and as I tightened into my turn shells smashed through the hood and into my instrument panel. Glass or a metal shard cut me above the right eye, which was superficial, but bled freely. A moment later, as I straightened out for a quick burst of cannon and machine-gun fire at a 190, I was hit from below by cannon fire. My Spit lost power and I had the choice of baling out or a belly landing. I chose the silk.

I had only a few seconds in which to bale out, not an easy procedure in a Spitfire. I pulled the pin on the Sutton harness that held me in my seat, then jettisoned the hood. The helmet and its radio and oxygen cords were removed. I raised the seat as high as possible, trying to get the nose of the aircraft up to establish level flight, then shoved the stick forward hard. The idea was that the aircraft would go straight down and the pilot straight out.

It worked, and I landed in a ploughed field where I immediately tried to dispose of my parachute. I tried to bury it, but until you've tried you have no appreciation of the immense amount of material in a parachute. As I was kicking away at the dirt two German soldiers arrived, their rifles at the ready. They were on bicycles and had been watching my descent. Looking back, it would seem to me that the order to head home was too late in coming and Al Deere had no alternative to the action he ordered.

Parr was taken to a military headquarters in a nearby village before being moved to the *Luftwaffe* airfield at Abbeville where he met and lunched with some of the resident pilots who showed him the utmost courtesy. At least half spoke excellent English and the conversation naturally turned to the course of the war. When asked if Germany would win the war in the west his hosts, surprisingly, answered in the negative; for them the real conflict was that taking place in the east, and they were all firmly convinced that Britain would eventually join forces with Germany against the Russians. After being given a chance to examine one of their prized Fw 190s, the aircraft that had shot him down, Parr was driven away to begin three years of captivity.

Another member of Blue section, Warrant Officer Don Campbell (Blue 2), also found trouble:

> It was a complete shambles as our squadron became separated from the rest of the wing. I was following my leader (Flight Lieutenant Darling) when I was suddenly hit and my plane burst into flames. I got out at about 20,000ft and landed in the Channel about two miles from Le Touquet. The Germans came out in a small boat and said to me those famous words: 'For you the war is over. You try to escape and we will shoot you.'
>
> I was taken to the same hospital at St Omer that had attended to Douglas Bader nearly a year before. Here I was treated for a small wound and facial burns. Pilot Officer Larry Somers (Yellow 3) was

P/O Larry Somers inspects flak damage to his aircraft after a low-level Rhubarb. (*Aitken*)

in the same hospital, he was in a bad way and had very severe burns to his face. Afterwards, I was the only one from my squadron to be sent to *Stalag* 8B in Upper Silesia but, as I was an NCO, after a year and a half I was transferred to a camp known as *Marlag und Milag Nord.* I was one of twelve Warrant Officers who were sent to this camp between Bremen and Hamburg.

To complete 403 Squadron's misery, Pilot Officer Doug Hurst (Red 3) was also shot down and taken prisoner.

In all, this unprecedented action had resulted in the loss of six pilots and eight aircraft. As only George Aitken had been rescued from the Channel, it appears that the other pilot seen in the water was 'Mitzi' Darling. A Battle of Britain ace, he was second only to Al Deere in terms of operational experience and was a highly gifted Flight Commander who had been awarded a well-deserved DFC towards the end of his first tour. He had only been with 403 for a month having been specifically requested as replacement for Flight Lieutenant Duval. There is, however, considerable confusion in the 403 Squadron ORB regarding the Spitfires used on this operation but thanks to research carried out by George Aitken, who recorded serial numbers and code letters in his logbook, the identities of the aircraft lost or DBR can be confirmed as: F/S Aitken – W3564 KH-K; P/O Wozniak – AD114 KH-W; P/O Hurst – BM162 KH-T; Sgt Hunt – AB799 KH-J; W/O Campbell – AD208 KH-L; F/O Parr – W3324 KH-E; F/L Darling – AR389 KH-D; P/O Somers – BL707 KH-Y.

The combined strength of the enemy formations was later estimated at forty to fifty and once again the damage had been done by elements of JG26. The Fw 190s that had trailed 403's Spitfires were 1st *Gruppe* machines led by its CO, Johannes Seifert, who claimed his thirty-sixth victory during the battle, while the flank attack was carried out by aircraft of the 2nd *Gruppe* led by *Hauptmann* Joachim Muncheberg, who shot down two to bring his score to eighty-one.

For the RAF such serious losses were reminiscent of the worst days of 1940, although Pilot Officer Amor, 403 Squadron's Engineering Officer, did his best by obtaining the delivery of nine new Spitfire Vbs by 1730 hrs. By working all night, he and his staff had thirteen aircraft on the flight line the following morning. Although aircraft could be replaced quickly, experienced pilots could not, and during the afternoon of the 3rd, 403 moved to Martlesham Heath to recuperate. From here they carried out defensive operations until 18 June when they were withdrawn to Catterick, their replacements being 332 (Norwegian) Squadron which moved in the opposite direction on the same day.

One of 332 Squadron's Spitfire Vbs seen at Catterick in early 1942. (*via Philip Jarrett*)

For some, the blame for 403 Squadron's débâcle lies squarely with Al Deere; it is certainly true that he lacked current operational experience and had seen little of the Fw 190, but equally, there are those who say that the call for the wing to dive for home was too late in coming which resulted in 403, as the last squadron, being placed in an impossible position. Whatever the reason, it was now clear that an advanced aircraft, when used in small, well co-ordinated formations, could inflict serious losses on a numerically superior foe. Despite such setbacks, Fighter Command still sought to bring the *Luftwaffe* to battle over northern France, but its pilots rarely held the upper hand and usually fought at a disadvantage. This was brought about, in part, by their use of large, unwieldy wing formations which allowed German ground controllers plenty of time to manoeuvre defending fighters into the most advantageous position to attack. Close radar control was often unnecessary as the opposition was visible from many miles away.

Despite the use of overload fuel tanks, worries over the Spitfire's lack of range persisted and it was no coincidence that the Focke-Wulfs had launched their attacks as the RAF fighters were coming towards the end of their respective sweeps. The German pilots knew that their counterparts would be casting anxious glances at their petrol gauges and that combat at this stage would seriously erode precious fuel reserves.

Although a number of RAF fighter squadrons now flew with each section in 'finger four' formation, many others still retained the outdated four in line astern, a factor which also contributed to high loss rates.

The level of casualties sustained in the summer of 1942 caused considerable disquiet within Fighter Command and the Air Ministry, and Air Chief Marshal Sholto Douglas had to concede that the Fw 190 was now 'the best all-round fighter in the world'. Despite such an assertion, a few short weeks later the Spitfire V was to be pitched into the largest single-day battle of the entire war, one in which it was hoped to inflict a decisive defeat on its principal adversary.

SEVEN

THE DIEPPE RAID

Operation Jubilee, the assault on Dieppe devised by Vice-Admiral Lord Louis Mountbatten, Chief of Combined Operations, was carried out by elements of the 2nd Canadian Army on 19 August 1942. One of the critical factors of any invasion of northern France would be the re-supply of ground forces when ashore, and at first it was thought that the best way to achieve this would be to capture an existing harbour. The raid was purely exploratory, and was designed to test the feasibility of amphibious forces being able to seize a port facility. Objectives were limited, and all forces were to be withdrawn within the day having created as much damage to installations as possible.

As things turned out, the choice of Dieppe was unfortunate as it was well defended and had steep cliffs overlooking the beaches where the

AD194 of 118 Squadron also flew with 111, 403 and 222 Squadrons before being delivered to Russia. (*Watson*)

landings were to take place. This provided an important strategic advantage to the defending forces who were able to deliver withering crossfire onto the Canadian troops below. Other painful lessons were learnt, in particular the need for intensive supporting fire to suppress local defences, the assistance that was actually provided comprising several squadrons of Hurricane fighter-bombers, three squadrons of Bostons from 2 Group and eight Navy destroyers proving to be totally inadequate. In the event the Canadian forces suffered severe losses with over 1,000 killed, and a further 2,000 soldiers taken prisoner. None of the objectives was achieved.

Fighter Command's hierarchy viewed the Dieppe operation as a golden opportunity to bring the enemy to action, Leigh-Mallory in particular looking forward to inflicting defeat on the locally based fighters of JG2 and 26. Mainly thanks to the cover provided by forty-two squadrons of Spitfire Vs from 10, 11 and 12 Groups, a situation of air superiority was created in the immediate area of Dieppe and throughout the day the RAF flew a total of nearly 3,000 sorties. Most pilots flew virtually round the clock, and thanks to their efforts the *Luftwaffe* were largely prevented from adding to the Canadians' problems. There were numerous clashes from first to last, but despite optimism at the time, German records show that, in terms of air-to-air combat, the RAF was out-scored by almost two to one.

There would be little point in discussing the numerous actions that took place over Dieppe in any great depth as these are more than covered in Norman Franks's comprehensive study *The Greatest Air Battle* (Grub Street). The experiences of the Ibsley Wing (66, 118 and 501 Squadrons) were, however, typical and serve to illustrate the fighter operations carried out during the day.

Preparations for the Ibsley Wing's participation in Operation Jubilee commenced at midday on 16 August when the various road parties left for their forward operating base at Tangmere. On arrival, squadron personnel were not particularly pleased to discover that they would be living in a large tented encampment on the perimeter of the airfield, but very soon everyone knuckled down and got on with the job. The Dieppe operation had originally been scheduled for early July (under the code name Rutter), but bad weather had forced its cancellation. On that occasion the Ibsley squadrons had made the move to Tangmere only to do nothing for four days. Everyone hoped that this would not be another wasted trip.

The following day ground crews ensured that all aircraft were in top line condition and stripped out any unnecessary weight to maximise performance. Servicing work was carried out until dusk although in the evening the Ibsley squadrons had to return to their home base to carry out a diversionary sweep over the Cherbourg peninsula, together with the Spitfire Vbs of the Exeter Wing. It was important for the Germans not to suspect that a large-scale operation was imminent and this patrol, together with similar ops carried out elsewhere, was an effort to maintain 'business as normal'. Although eight Fw 190s were seen 3,000ft above, they made no attempt to attack and all aircraft returned safely to base.

Preparations for the big day continued on 18 August with the few remaining aircraft being seen to by the maintenance crews, and in the evening all personnel paraded at dispersals at 1830 hrs to be briefed. One of those who attended was Sergeant Sid Watson of 118 Squadron.

> We were all confined to the base and on the evening of 18 August a full-scale briefing took place and the harbour town of Dieppe was the designated target. We now knew that it was to be a combined operation of all three services and the air force would be called upon to play a major role. Until that time, we at squadron level never realised just how many fighters were being committed and it was awesome to think that forty-six Spitfire squadrons alone were taking part [this figure includes four Spitfire IX squadrons].
>
> The briefings by the army liaison officers were very self-assured, describing how their first people ashore would silence the batteries of heavy guns defending the beach. The tanks would forge ahead through the town to achieve their objectives. After a period of time they would all return to the beach and board their landing craft for the trip back to the UK. So assured was one army type that he claimed if any pilot was shot up he should make for a race-track that was just south of Dieppe and force-land – 'There will be a NAAFI truck there and you can get a cup of tea and a cake.'

Most air and ground crews were at their positions by 0345 hrs the next morning to be greeted by a thick ground mist which persisted until dawn. Then, the almost continuous sound of aircraft taking off proclaimed that the attack on Dieppe had started. In fact the first aircraft away from Tangmere departed before the first streaks of light appeared when the Hurricanes of 43 Squadron led by Squadron Leader 'Dan' Du Vivier DFC took off at 0425 hrs to attack gun positions overlooking the landing beaches. In contrast, the Spitfires of the Ibsley Wing had to wait until 0750 hrs to join the action, the intervening period being enlivened by two air raid alerts, the second of which warned of six enemy aircraft approaching from the south, although none was seen.

Much to 66 Squadron's dismay, only 118 and 501 Squadrons were required for the first operation of the day which consisted of escorting three Blenheims of 614 Squadron, who were to add to the smoke screen that had already been laid over the gun batteries situated on the headland to the east of the main landing beaches. When twenty-five miles south of Selsey Bill, however, the operation was called off, both squadrons returning to Tangmere. On their way back 118 spotted an empty bomber dinghy in the sea and circled it to give a fix, before signalling to two ships which were in the vicinity. They then encountered an Army Co-operation Mustang whose violent evasive action at first led them to believe it was an Fw 190. Pilot Officer B.J. Blackburn (EN926) was tempted to make a pass at it, but its true identity was established at around 800 yards' range and it was left to go on its way.

Having taxied back to their dispersals, 501 Squadron's pilots were informed that they could go for a second breakfast, but shortly after ordering bacon and egg, they had to dash back to their aircraft to escort the Hurricanes of 87 Squadron, who had been detailed to attack gun positions pinning down the Canadians attempting to secure the eastern beaches. So 501 took off again at 1025 hrs, together with 66 Squadron, who were led by their CO, Squadron Leader R.D. Yule DFC, on their first patrol of the day.

The Spitfires crossed the Channel at 500ft before pulling up to cover the Hurricanes as they dived down to strafe gun posts on the eastern headland. No.501 Squadron's pilots saw a 'pall of thick, yellow, evil-smelling smoke' hanging over Dieppe and as they flew over they noted that much damage appeared to have been done. Intense light flak was experienced from the east of the town which damaged the tailwheel of EN974 (SD-D) flown by Canadian Flight Sergeant A.R. MacDonald. One ship just offshore was seen to be on fire, and another small ship near the east headland blew up as 501's aircraft approached, leaving 'a flicker of burning oil on the water'.

As soon as they landed back at Tangmere at 1155 hrs 66 Squadron's armourers dashed out to see if the pilots had fired their guns, but on discovering that they had not, were sadly disillusioned and trudged dejectedly back to their dens. During their debrief, the pilots commented on the effectiveness of the smoke screens which were so thick in places that little on the ground could be seen. They also reported that two Dornier Do 217s had been seen trying to dive-bomb shipping, and that one of these had been shot down. Although six Fw 190s had approached at one point, they made no attempt to engage.

While 66 and 501 Squadrons had been airborne, 118 Squadron took off at 1120 hrs for their second escort mission, providing top cover for two squadrons of Hurricanes (32 and 174) whose objective, once again, was to suppress the fire coming from the headlands either side of the harbour. Although he was scheduled to take part, Sid Watson never made it.

> We had spare pilots (in case of losses) and everyone was keen to take part in operations. I was fortunate to be included in the second sortie but encountered a problem on take-off. On airfields with runways it was normal for four Spitfires to take off in formation. At Tangmere the runway wasn't wide enough to accommodate four aircraft so one machine had to use the grass beside the runway – in this case, that was me. Tangmere had experienced many bombing attacks from time to time and the craters had been filled with anything available such as rubble of all sorts. For whatever cause on the take-off run, just before lift-off, my port tyre blew out. The port wingtip touched the ground and the aircraft commenced a great circle route across the runway at about 90mph. The next four aircraft were already barrelling down the runway and for a while I was heading straight for them. The ultimate collapse of the starboard undercarriage leg straightened me out and I finally came to rest on the grass on the opposite side of the runway. Spitfire EN964 Cat. B damage.

The eleven remaining pilots of 118 Squadron, led by Squadron Leader 'Bertie' Wootten, found a similar situation over Dieppe to that witnessed by 66 and 501 half an hour before. Although they saw the gun flashes of the Hurricanes as they fired, the pall of smoke along the beaches prevented them from seeing the results. Pilots were also unsure as to whether ships seen in the harbour were on fire, or merely adding to the smoke screen. Wootten later recorded in his logbook that there must have been a 'hell of a battle' going on above the overcast as bits of debris and complete aircraft were falling all around them. One of the aircraft was recognised as being a Spitfire, but the other machines could not be identified. Very little could be seen around Dieppe itself due to smoke and haze.

Even by mid-morning it had become apparent that the Canadian troops carrying out the assault on Dieppe were in serious trouble. Despite the attacks on local defences by Hurricanes and Boston bombers, the many gunposts situated on the cliffs on either side of the beaches were still able to direct their fire on the exposed troops below. Although precise details of what was happening were difficult to come by, enough was known for the decision to be made to bring forward the time for the withdrawal of the troops by two hours to 1100 hrs.

Back at Tangmere, the military liaison officers were making every effort to keep all pilots informed of what little information was coming

No.118 Squadron pilots relax at Tangmere prior to Operation Jubilee. (*Wootten*)

out of Dieppe, although some of the phrasing was deliberately vague. No.501 Squadron were told that the landings had been a 'partial success' but from the manner of the briefing, and the pilots' own observations and experiences over the scene of the action, it was clear that the operation had been far from the straightforward setpiece alluded to a couple of days before. As Sid Watson later put it, 'So much for our tea and cakes!'

Having taken a light lunch which had been delivered to dispersals, some pilots managed to snatch a little sleep before they were called once again. No.66 Squadron was first away at 1425 hrs, its task being to provide cover for four Bostons who were to lay a smoke screen to protect the last of the vessels leaving Dieppe. The Boston was the fastest of 2 Group's twin-engined medium bombers, and as they commenced their run in to the target area at maximum speed, 66 Squadron had extreme difficulty in providing adequate cover. It proved to be impossible to escort the Bostons in squadron strength so a section of four aircraft was detached to stay with the bombers while the rest orbited to regain some semblance of order before returning to base.

During the approach to the harbour one of the Bostons (AL680 of 226 Squadron) was shot down by flak, its crew of three surviving the subsequent ditching to become PoWs. As they were turning to begin their homeward journey the four Spitfires which had stayed with the Bostons were attacked by four Fw 190s which succeeded in shooting down Lieutenant V.R.E. Nissen (AB514) and Sergeant R.N. Loyns (AB517), both of whom were killed. As if to emphasise the cosmopolitan nature of

Fighter Command, Nissen was twenty-one years of age and came from the Transvaal, South Africa, while Ron Loyns was a Canadian from Saskatoon in Saskatchewan, and was just twenty. Again the squadron landed without having fired its guns.

While 66 Squadron was busy off Dieppe, 118 and 501 took off once again at 1500 hrs, together with the Tangmere Wing, to take their place over the returning convoy to protect it from air attack. Both squadrons would be in for an extremely busy afternoon. By the time they arrived, the ships were approximately eight miles from the coast and were being severely harassed by Do 217 and Ju 88 dive-bombers, all escorted by Fw 190s.

No.501 Squadron, led by Wing Commander Pat Gibbs, reached the convoy at 1520 hrs, split up into loose fours and was in combat almost immediately. A group of eight to ten Fw 190s were seen and one was damaged by Blue section's leader, Flight Lieutenant P.J. Stanbury (EP538 SD-A), who found that he could out-manoeuvre the enemy aircraft at will and gain on it even in the climb. Unfortunately weather conditions were beginning to close in rapidly by this time and the combat proved to be inconclusive, the 190 disappearing into thick cloud at 5,000ft having suffered hits to its fuselage and tail.

Wing Commander Gibbs (EP120 – Whitewash Red 1) sighted several formations of Fw 190s and, having taken evasive action, found himself alone when three Do 217s broke cloud to the south of the convoy to carry out a largely ineffectual dive-bombing attack. Joining in with several other Spitfires, he chased after a Dornier as it made a desperate attempt to seek the protection offered by the French coast.

Gibbs continued to close on the Dornier as the other aircraft in front of him attacked and then broke away. He eventually opened fire at 500 yards with a three-second burst but was not aware of having inflicted any damage. On closing to 300 yards, he saw strikes on the fuselage and mainplanes whereupon the Do 217 suddenly lost speed, which allowed him to fire again from point-blank range using up the remainder of his ammunition. A large cloud of black smoke was seen to erupt from the starboard motor, the propeller coming to a sudden stop as the engine seized. Before he could determine the aircraft's fate, Gibbs was attacked from behind by an Fw 190 and received two hits, one on the port aileron, the other in the starboard mainplane. Turning into the attack, he got away by diving to sea level and eventually joined up with 501 Squadron's Yellow section.

Flight Sergeant G.A. Mawer (EP191 SD-P) chased after two more Dorniers that were seen heading to the south and damaged one of them. Just as he was breaking away a cannon shell burst above his canopy which momentarily stunned him and caused a slight cut on his head. There was no sign of his attacker, and after some difficulty he jettisoned what remained on his hood and returned to base without further mishap.

Pilot Officer W.R. Lightbourne (AB402 SD-K) also had an eventful trip, the full details of which only emerged eighteen hours later when he was delivered to hospital at Gosport. Having been attacked from behind by an unseen enemy, he was forced to bale out of his stricken aircraft, but in doing so his parachute caught in the cockpit and he found himself draped around the tailplane. The buffeting he received badly fractured his right leg and also paralysed his right arm. Despite his injuries, he managed to free himself and floated down to land in the sea whereupon he endured what he subsequently described as 'a nightmare of a dinghy drill'. Luckily he had descended close to some of the ships that were evacuating what remained of the Canadian troops, and he was quickly hauled aboard. After two hours with no proper splint, he was painfully unloaded onto a larger ship where at last he was able to receive some treatment for his shattered leg.

As 501 Squadron returned to the English coast it found that the weather conditions had deteriorated considerably in the one and a quarter hours that it had been away. At Tangmere visibility was down to 600 yards and cloud base was around 300ft. Wing Commander Gibbs led six aircraft into Shoreham, but despite the conditions another four Spitfires made it safely into Tangmere. The remaining member of the squadron, Sergeant A. Lee (EN963 SD-E), was unable to locate his home base and the wreckage of his aircraft was eventually located on a hillside near Billingshurst, twelve miles north of the airfield. The rescue party found Lee dead in the cockpit, the impact with the ground having been severe enough to break his safety straps.

No.118 Squadron had also been heavily engaged over the convoy with Yellow section, led by Flight Lieutenant J.B. Shepherd (AR453), in the forefront of the action. Shepherd latched onto a Do 217 as it commenced its dive to bomb the convoy but had to break away as another Spitfire cut in front of him. After it had broken away he moved in once again, firing many short bursts which severely damaged the bomber and set it on fire. The Spitfire that had got in Shepherd's way was that flown by Flying Officer J.G. Stewart (EP206 – Red 3), whose attack from the starboard rear quarter scored hits all along the enemy aircraft's fuselage. Next in line was Flight Sergeant Sid Watson (EN953 – Yellow 4), who used up all of his ammunition in two quarter and two stern attacks. By now the Dornier was well alight and it was seen to crash into the sea with yet more Spitfires firing at it. The 'kill' was officially shared between Shepherd, Stewart and Watson.

Having got in a 'consolation burst' at the Do 217 just before it went into the sea, Sergeant Tommy de Courcy (EP130 – Red 4) attacked another, firing a number of bursts as close as 100 yards. The German bomber appeared capable of withstanding considerable punishment and de Courcy's only reward for having used all of his ammunition was to have seen a few pieces of debris fly off. He need not have worried unduly as to the fate of the Dornier as this was the aircraft that was subsequently attacked and crippled by Wing Commander Gibbs. It was later claimed as destroyed following a report from Squadron Leader J.E.J. Sing of 501 Squadron, who saw it crash into the sea six miles north of Dieppe.

While at Shoreham, three of 501 Squadron's aircraft were scrambled on a report of intruders, but these were not sighted and they returned to Tangmere at the end of their patrol. Wing Commander Gibbs also flew back, but the weather was now so bad that two less experienced pilots were forced to travel by road. In the evening, reports were received that a number of unidentified aircraft were approaching the Tangmere area and six Spitfires of 118 Squadron, led by 'Bertie' Wootten, scrambled to intercept. With a cloud base estimated at 400ft and in conditions of heavy rain, nothing was seen, and all pilots were happy to be back on the ground again within half an hour.

Although the Tangmere guns, and some other batteries nearby, fired a few more rounds, they eventually fell silent and the hectic activity which had commenced in the early hours of the morning came to a close. Initially it was thought that the air battles over Dieppe had gone well and congratulations were received from sector control on the successful day's score. The defenders had indeed suffered severely, and if the Dieppe Raid had been part of a concentrated attack on the northern coast of France, JG2 and 26 would have been hard-pressed to cope. Although nearly 100 aircraft were claimed by RAF pilots, post-war research shows that Axis losses were forty-eight, of which only twenty-three were fighters, a figure that represents approximately 10% of the available fighter strength.

RAF losses for the day from all causes included sixty-two Spitfires, as a result of which twenty-nine pilots had been killed, with a further eleven becoming PoWs. It was hardly the decisive defeat that Leigh-Mallory had been longing for, and it was only Fighter Command's numerical strength that allowed it to withstand the day's events without serious harm. Even so, ten pilots ranked Flight Lieutenant or over had either been killed or taken prisoner, the most senior being Wing Commander 'Mindy' Blake, leader of the Portreath Wing, who was shot down and captured in his personal Spitfire Vb W3561 (M-B) when flying with 130 Squadron.

With three pilots killed, the Ibsley squadrons had suffered more than most, but despite this, morale remained at an extremely high level and

Tangmere and Ibsley senior pilots, S/L 'Dan' Du Vivier in cockpit then (L to R) W/C
P.R. 'Johnnie' Walker, W/C Pat Gibbs, G/C Charles Appleton, S/L Bertie Wootten
and S/L Bobby Yule. (*Wootten*)

everyone was cheered to have been involved in an operation that had hit
the enemy hard. From a very early start all personnel had worked flat
out, 66 Squadron's ORB noting the 'zeal and enthusiasm' with which
their ground crews had maintained a maximum effort throughout the
day.

'Bertie' Wootten recalled the day as one of high drama, one in which
his squadron had performed well, although he was ultimately disap-
pointed not to have been more successful with his own shooting, having
to be content with a few full deflection shots at Fw 190s. Despite the fact
that his No.2 told him that he had hit one of them, he did not bother to
put in a claim. Two of his pilots, Flight Lieutenant John Shepherd and
Pilot Officer Frank Brown, later received the Distinguished Flying Cross
in recognition of their exploits during the Dieppe Raid.

There is little that can be said to commend the events of 19 August,
although some valuable lessons were learnt for the future. The capture
and subsequent use of an existing port facility was seen to be unfeasible,
but perhaps the most important conclusions to be drawn were that there

had to be much greater co-ordination between air and ground forces, and that air power also had to be used much more widely to destroy airfield and communication targets well away from the scene of the landings.

In a little over twenty-one months' time the next venture into France would see the Allies initiate an offensive that would last not just for one day, but for weeks and months until the European war was brought to a successful conclusion. Against all the odds, the Spitfire V would still be around to play its part.

EIGHT

A Present from the Enemy

Before we leave the year 1942, we must turn the clock back nearly two months to discuss an action that took place over the West Country, one that finally led to the secrets of the celebrated Focke-Wulf Fw 190 being revealed. No.10 Group Ramrod 23 was carried out on 23 June and consisted of an attack by Bostons of 107 Squadron on the airfield at Morlaix, with escort provided by the Spitfire Vs of the Czech Wing, comprising 310, 312 and 313 Squadrons. In addition, the Portreath Wing (19, 130 and 234 Squadrons) was tasked with contributing withdrawal support.

Having flown to Exeter from their base at Great Massingham earlier in the day, six Bostons led by Wing Commander L.A. Lynn made rendezvous with the Czech squadrons over Exeter before setting course from Start Point at 1830 hrs. The formation flew at sea level for twenty minutes and then started to climb so that they crossed the French coast at Plestin at 9,000ft. No.310 Squadron, led by Squadron Leader F. Dolezal, were flying as close escort, with 312 (Wing Commander A. Vasatko) to port at 10,000ft and 313 (Squadron Leader K. Mrazek) to starboard at 11,000ft. No opposition was met before the target was reached, but one of the Bostons, AL747 flown by Pilot Officer R.A. Bance, was hit by flak during the bombing run which put its starboard engine out of action. The attack itself was carried out from the east during which twelve 500lb bombs, together with the contents of twelve 40lb bomb containers, were deposited on hangars and buildings on the west side of the airfield.

Shortly after the attack two Fw 190s were seen approaching from the south-west and were engaged by 313 Squadron, one being damaged by Squadron Leader Mrazek (BM419 – Red 1). A few minutes later, as the force was approaching the Ile de Batz, two more put in an appearance, one of which was attacked by Pilot Officer Josef Prihoda (BM295 – Blue 3), whose fire caused it to dive vertically into the sea. In a separate engagement another 190 managed to get through to the Bostons and damaged Z2262 flown by Pilot Officer P.K. Burley. It was quickly engaged by Squadron Leader Dolezal without result, but Flight Lieutenant E. Foit

(AD542) had better luck, achieving a number of strikes on the forward fuselage.

By this time the damaged AL747 was losing height and Dolezal detached his section from the rest of the squadron to provide cover. Shortly after, it was joined by 130 Squadron, which had recently arrived with the rest of the Portreath Wing. The remainder of the return journey was uneventful until about ten miles from Start Point when control warned of enemy aircraft in the vicinity. The bombers had in fact been chased back by a number of Fw 190s of JG2, even though they were under strict instructions, from no less a person than *Reichsmarschall* Hermann Goering, that they were not to venture more than halfway across the Channel.

As the English coast was being approached, 312 Squadron was still flying to port of the Bostons in three sections of four, line astern. Although no enemy aircraft had been sighted, the starboard section began an orbit to the right, while the other two sections turned in the opposite direction. During the turn, Sergeant J. Mayer became separated from his leader, Wing Commander Vasatko, which allowed the Fw 190 of *Unteroffizier* Wilhelm Reushling to close in and blast the Czech Wing Leader from the sky. The German pilot's moment of glory was to be short-lived however, as his aircraft was damaged by debris from Vasatko's Spitfire and he was forced to bale out. He was rescued from the sea five miles south-east of Brixham, but despite an extensive search, the Czech was never found. Flight Lieutenant Kasal and Sergeant V. Ruprecht were also attacked, Kasal being slightly wounded in the right leg by a shell splinter when a bullet exploded in his cockpit.

Of the units that formed the Portreath Wing, 130 Squadron did not see any action at all, and 234 Squadron managed only a single desultory combat when Squadron Leader Birchfield fired without effect on an Fw 190. In contrast, Squadron Leader P.R.G. Davies, at the head of 19 Squadron, witnessed several large splashes in the sea and decided to take his section down to investigate. As he was orbiting the scene he fired at an Fw 190 which passed through his sights, subsequently claiming it as damaged, but at the same time his No.2, Sergeant A.L. Ridings, was shot down and killed. Flight Sergeant R. Royer's aircraft was also hit and he was forced to make an emergency landing at Roborough.

As the action continued off the south coast, four Spitfires were scrambled from Bolt Head, but only two managed to get airborne. Pilot Officer J. Strihavka of 310 Squadron was about to take off in BL265 (NN-L) when he was hit by Flight Sergeant F. Mares of 312 Squadron in BL512. Both pilots escaped without injury but Strihavka's aircraft was written off in the collision. This left Flight Sergeant Frantisek Trejtnar (BL517 NN-E)

BL479 of 316 Squadron. (*via Philip Jarrett*)

and Flight Sergeant T. Motycka, who took off to patrol over Exeter at 4,000ft.

Looking down, Trejtnar saw the Czech Wing circling over Exeter prior to landing, but then spotted a solitary Fw 190 about 10,000ft above him. It was flying north and continued to do so as he climbed to cut off its line of retreat. The Focke-Wulf was lost from view for a while but at 18,000ft he saw it again, still 1,000ft above. It was an A-3 variant and was being flown by *Oberleutnant* Arnim Faber of 7/JG2, who had watched Trejtnar carefully as he attempted to get into an attacking position. Choosing the right moment to strike, Faber dived to attack head-on, his fire hitting the Spitfire's starboard wing and wounding its pilot in the right arm. Severely damaged, Trejtnar's aircraft was pitched into a spin which had still not been recovered at 5,000ft, at which point he baled out. As the combat had taken place near Black Dog village, approximately twelve miles north-west of Exeter, the extent to which Goering's edict had been broken is clear.

Having circled his victim as he descended on his parachute, Faber then made the elementary mistake of flying a reciprocal course which took him north instead of south. Eventually a coastline appeared which he assumed to be that along the English Channel but in fact was the north coast of Devon. When land reappeared after an appropriate amount of time, he was confident that he was back over northern France but in reality he was flying along the south coast of Wales. Selecting the first airfield that presented itself, he performed an immaculate victory roll prior to landing which was watched with amazement by RAF personnel at Pembrey, a training station near Llanelli. To complete a comedy of errors, no one could locate any guns to carry out an arrest and after a certain amount of indecision, Faber was eventually marched off to captivity by an officer brandishing a Verey pistol!

Not surprisingly, news of the Fw 190's arrival got around extremely quickly and Flight Lieutenant Dave Glaser of 234 Squadron recalls flying to Pembrey the following morning with Wing Commander 'Mindy' Blake to have a look at it. Security was tight and it was probably only Blake's seniority that saved the day. Another interested party who arrived shortly afterwards was promptly arrested and placed behind bars, pending proof of identity. Faber was still around and, according to Glaser, offered to fly the Focke-Wulf in mock combat against any number of Spitfires. To prove he was not trying to escape, his scheme proposed taking off with minimal fuel, but it was obvious to everyone that he would take to his parachute at the earliest opportunity, thereby denying the RAF its prized possession. For the time being at least, the Fw 190 remained firmly on the ground.

Having been given the RAF serial number MP499, it was flown at RAE Farnborough the following month before being delivered to the Air Fighting Development Unit (AFDU) at Duxford for comparative tests which confirmed Fighter Command's worst fears. The 190 proved to be 20–30mph faster than the Spitfire V at all heights and its climb rate was approximately 450ft/min better. It was markedly superior in the dive and also excelled in terms of rate of roll, thanks to its large, well-balanced ailerons. The only crumb of comfort for Spitfire pilots was that the Mark V still had the edge when it came to turning circles, although even this advantage could be reduced by selecting ten degrees of flap on the Focke-Wulf and utilising the power of the BMW radial to overcome increased drag.

With such an apparent superiority, how is it that many combat reports filed by Fighter Command pilots rate the Fw 190 as being only marginally better? The 190's greatest asset was its speed, which allowed it to close rapidly on the opposition, and undoubtedly many Spitfire pilots were shot down without knowing what had hit them. If a general dogfight ensued, however, both height and speed would tend to be reduced as each aircraft tried to out-manoeuvre the other, factors which would serve to reduce the German aircraft's advantage. If the combat became a turning competition, the Spitfire's superior performance in this respect might even give it the upper hand.

AA937 flew with 64 Squadron before undergoing performance trials at AFDU. (*via Philip Jarrett*)

For the Spitfire V to stand any chance of survival over northern France, it was clear that it had to be flown at high speed, conducive with reasonable fuel economy. The most effective evasive manoeuvre was found to be a high-speed shallow dive, but this pre-supposed that the 190s had been seen well before they were within firing range. Even when they were seen in good time, they could still spring a surprise as Dave Glaser recalls:

> We were out over France one day when ops called up and said, 'Watch out, fighters are up.' We were just coming up to the coast on the way home, hedge hopping, right down low. They went across us from left to right going east, and everybody thought that they hadn't seen us, but they b — well had! We were going down a valley and they came round the other side of it and the first thing I knew was 'Wiggy' Webster [Sergeant J.B. Webster – 234 Squadron] yelling at me, 'For God's sake break, there's one behind you.' I looked in the mirror and all I could see was a prop practically taking my rudder off. I didn't even have time to see whether he was shooting or what was happening, but then he broke away and it was all over. Their thing was to come in very fast and right up close – it was all over so quickly, but on this occasion we got away with it.

On another trip Glaser witnessed a variation on a standard *Luftwaffe* tactic when a single Fw 190 was seen below his formation, seemingly oblivious to the fact that a large number of Spitfires were a few thousand feet above him. Such decoys had been used for a long time, but the difference this time was that it was seen to be flying with one undercarriage leg extended as though it had suffered battle damage. Glaser was about to go after it when he looked behind, saw its friends up-sun and quickly changed his mind. When Faber's machine was examined it was found that the 190 could easily be turned into a 'lame duck' as it had an electrically operated undercarriage, and by pulling a circuit breaker it was possible to bring one leg up, while the other stayed down.

At the same time as the Fw 190 was tested against the Spitfire V, the AFDU compared the German aircraft with an early example of the Spitfire IX. Here the results were much more favourable and showed that the performance gap had been closed; indeed, at medium levels and above 25,000ft, the Mark IX was superior. As the Spitfire IX would not be available in appreciable numbers for some time to come, there remained the problem of how best to use the Spitfire V. As was mentioned in Chapter Four, the use of overload fuel tanks allowed the Mark V squadrons to use high power settings on offensive sorties to reduce the chances of being 'bounced', but it was to be the work of the engineers at Rolls-Royce that would provide a solution, although in doing so, operational use would be severely restricted.

Of all the major powerplants that were used in fighter aircraft during World War Two, the Rolls-Royce Merlin was one of the smallest: its capacity of 27 litres compared with the 33.9 litres of the Daimler-Benz DB601N which powered the Messerschmitt Me 109F-1 and the 41.8 litres of the BMW 801 fourteen-cylinder radial as fitted in the Focke-Wulf Fw 190A. Whereas other manufacturers tended to favour the use of large, moderately supercharged engines to develop the necessary power, Rolls-Royce chose to utilise their expertise in the field of supercharging to a much higher degree. As the Spitfire V was to remain in service until the end of the war largely thanks to a re-design of its Merlin supercharger, it is necessary to look at the basic theory behind these devices and to appreciate why they were so important to the piston-engined fighters of the period.

The power that is developed by a petrol-driven piston-engine is proportional to the weight of the fuel–air mix that is burnt in a given period, which is dependent on the capacity of the cylinder and manifold air pressure (MAP). With a normally aspirated engine (i.e. non-supercharger-driven) MAP is determined mainly by atmospheric pressure, which decreases with altitude so that power will also reduce at the rate of approximately 3.5% per 1,000ft. Perversely, altitude performance was one of the key service requirements for fighter aircraft of the time. In addition to the need to gain height quickly, it was imperative that they then have sufficient speed advantage to catch and shoot down high-flying bombers. Without a supercharged engine, this was just not possible.

In effect, superchargers are compressors which maintain sea-level conditions up to a certain altitude. Most from the early war period were of the centrifugal type whereby the fuel–air mix was drawn into the eye of an impeller or rotor which rotated at a speed around nine times that of the crankshaft. The rotor caused the charge to be flung outwards under centrifugal force, increasing its kinetic energy. As the rotor blades were also divergent, the charge was subjected to an increase in pressure. After being thrown out by the impeller, the air then entered the diffuser where divergent stator blades caused a further increase in pressure before it was finally introduced to the cylinders. Depending on the level of compression, the air may also have been passed through an aftercooler to reduce its temperature and reduce the risk of detonation.

Supercharger technology advanced rapidly throughout the late 1930s with the result that power levels were maintained to much greater heights. Some superchargers were of the two-speed type which allowed the pilot effectively to 'change gear' as the aircraft climbed so that the blower rotated faster in relation to engine rpm. In some installations an auxiliary blower was installed upstream of the main supercharger to increase pressure levels further.

With such high levels of boost available, the problem of over-boosting at low altitude had to be addressed as this could easily lead to the engine suffering structural damage. Such disastrous happenings were prevented as boost pressure could easily be regulated by the position of the throttle butterfly valve. As height was gained the throttle would be gradually opened to maintain a constant value of MAP so that at a certain altitude the throttle butterfly would be fully open. When this point was reached the aircraft was said to be at its 'full-throttle altitude', above which the supercharger could not maintain constant boost pressure. Trials with the Rolls-Royce Merlin 61, which featured two-speed, two-stage supercharging, showed that its full-throttle altitude was just below 30,000ft, which was 10,000ft more than the figure achieved with the Merlin 45.

Just as larger-capacity superchargers increased power at altitude, reducing or 'cropping' the diameter of the impeller allowed full power to be delivered at much lower heights. Rolls-Royce found that by using a rotor of only 9.5in diameter on the Merlin 45, full-throttle altitude was achieved at a relatively low 5,900ft. Known as the M-Series Merlin, boost pressure was raised to a maximum of +18lb/sq.in, and although this had the effect of increasing top speed low down, there was a dramatic fall-off in performance above 12,000ft. Use of the new engine would ultimately lead to the Spitfire LFV (LF for low-altitude fighter), which would be introduced from mid-1943.

Having had the benefit of testing Faber's Fw 190, the performance that was needed from the Spitfire V for it to be able to compete on more or less equal terms was now known. In early January 1943 Spitfire LFVb W3228 was tested at the Aeroplane and Armament Experimental Establishment (A&AEE) at Boscombe Down fitted with a Rolls-Royce Merlin 50M complete with negative-G carburettor and producing 1,585hp. Its top speed was measured at 350.5mph at 5,900ft, which brought its performance at that height very much in line with that of the Focke-Wulf Fw 190, and was marginally better than the top speed achieved at that height by the latest Messerschmitt 109, the *Gustav*.

Shortly before these trials, the AFDU tested a Spitfire Vb featuring clipped wings whereby the outer portions of the wings were removed and replaced by streamlined fairings. This reduced wing span by 4ft 4in to 32ft 6in, and reduced wing area by 11 sq.ft to 231 sq.ft. The main aim was to increase the Spitfire's rate of roll which had previously been

Another view of AA937 of AFDU. (*via Philip Jarrett*)

markedly inferior to that of the Fw 190. This was found to have been achieved, but at the expense of a small increase in the minimum turning circle. Other benefits included a 5mph increase in top speed at all heights up to 10,000ft, and there was also a modest improvement in diving performance.

Although the benefits from clipping the wings were considerable, this modification would not be adopted universally and many LFVs would retain their wingtips throughout their subsequent careers. Even individual squadrons did not standardise one way or the other and were likely to operate a mix of clipped and unclipped examples at any one time. One modification that they all featured, however, was a strengthening of the wing structure to cater for the increased loads that the aircraft would have to contend with in the denser air at low level. Evidence of this work could be seen in the two longitudinal strakes on the upper surfaces of each wing over the wheel wells.

Further modifications were carried out to allow the Spitfire V to operate in the fighter-bomber role with 250lb or 500lb bombs. With its strengthened 'universal' wing, the Mark Vc was capable of carrying two 250lb bombs in the under-wing position and achieved considerable success in the ground attack role in the Mediterranean and Middle East theatres. The Type 'B' wing, as fitted to the Mark Vb, was not stressed for carrying under-wing stores, instead, provision was made for the carriage of a 500lb bomb on the fuselage centreline, although this meant that the overload fuel tank could not be fitted, which inevitably restricted combat radius. The pilot's bomb release button was situated on the throttle control lever on the port side of the cockpit.

Flight Lieutenant Clive Gosling flew the Spitfire LFV as a production test pilot with Supermarine.

> The LFV was an exhilarating aircraft to fly at low level and you would see 340–350mph on the ASI. Its rate of climb was also very good. I remember flying the Mark XII prototype, DP845, against Jeffrey Quill flying an LFV and at full power we reached 15,000ft together. However, due to the greater power of the Griffon, I was able to gain on JKQ in a turn and when he rolled under and dived away I was able to catch him easily in the dive.

From the tests carried out it was clear that the modified Spitfire V would be able to hold its own against the opposition for the foreseeable future, but only as long as it was operated within its restricted height band. With the Spitfire IX fulfilling the classic air superiority role, Mark V pilots would have to be content with the close escort of medium bombers, variety being added by ground attack work, shipping reconnaissance

Spitfire Vbs of 243 Squadron. (*via Philip Jarrett*)

sorties and occasional offensive sweeps. Despite such limited scope there would still be plenty of opportunities for them to achieve glory.

By early 1943 the general war situation was looking much more promising. In North Africa German forces were in headlong retreat, and on the eastern front the turning point had been reached in the shattered streets of Stalingrad. With the gradual build-up of American forces in the UK, there was at last genuine hope for the setting up of a second front, and from the experiences of combined operations in the desert the need for air superiority over and around the front line and for the co-ordinated use of tactical air power was overwhelming.

As the new year dawned, however, the specialised low-altitude variant of the Spitfire V was still some months away from squadron service, and the pilots in 12 Group, like many others in Fighter Command, would have to make do with their old aircraft for a little longer. Despite this they were to prove that the Mark V was still an aircraft to be feared.

NINE

COLTISHALL WING, JANUARY–JUNE 1943

Although well known for its proliferation of bomber airfields during World War Two, East Anglia was also home to a number of fighter stations of which Coltishall was, and still is, the best known. Ironically it was built during the final stages of the RAF's pre-war expansion as yet another bomber base, but the German *Blitzkrieg* in May 1940 and the occupation of Holland and Belgium led to a sudden change of role. Situated ten miles to the north-east of Norwich, its location proved to be ideal for operations over the Low Countries and against enemy shipping in the North Sea.

By early 1943 Coltishall had two satellite airfields, Ludham (167 Squadron – Spitfire Vbs) and Matlaske (56 Squadron – Typhoon Ibs), these squadrons being joined on 17 January by 118 Squadron, which flew in to the parent airfield from Wittering. No.118 was still commanded by Squadron Leader 'Bertie' Wootten, and over the next eight months would see considerable action along the Dutch coast, often as escort to Coastal Command Beaufighters of the North Coates Wing. There would also be frequent close escort missions with 2 Group Venturas and Bostons, and Rhubarbs would be carried out over Holland whenever weather conditions were suitable.

Early operations were disappointing, however. Several shipping recces were flown by sections of four aircraft, but apart from the Dutch fishing fleet going about its business, little was seen. The squadron's first Boston escort on 21 January was not a resounding success either. No.118 arrived at the rendezvous point over Orfordness at the appointed time, only to be informed that the bombers had joined up with 167 Squadron out to sea and had already left. The Bostons were eventually located off the Dutch coast as they made their way back from an attack on Flushing.

Action was not long in coming, but as far as 118 Squadron was concerned, it involved the wrong people. On 28 January Coltishall was visited by the King and Queen, who then moved on to inspect 167 Squadron at Ludham. It was during this second visit that a Junkers Ju 88

P/O S.A. Watson, Sgt C. Anderton, F/L J.B. Shepherd and
F/Sgt A. Buglass of 118 Squadron. (*Watson*)

of KG6 appeared off Lowestoft looking for shipping targets. No.118 Squadron, who had put up a standing patrol for just such an eventuality, was told to hold off and two of 167's Spitfires were scrambled from Ludham instead. This resulted in a victory for Pilot Officer C.T.K. Cody, which greatly impressed the King, but not 118 Squadron's diarist, who later wrote resentfully 'this bird should have been ours'!

Any feelings of injustice were short-lived as 118's first 'kill' in 12 Group occurred during an attack on the coke ovens at Ijmuiden by twelve Venturas of 21 Squadron the very next day. The bombers flew inland for ten miles before turning to commence their run up to the target, by which time a group of Fw 190s had been seen preparing to attack. Before they could do so they were engaged, Sergeant Les Lack (EN926) firing at one which was seen to crash into the sea two miles from the target. Squadron Leader Wootten and Sergeant Joe Hollingworth both damaged Fw 190s, although Hollingworth's aircraft (EP646) was itself hit by a cannon shell. Sadly, Flight Sergeant A.L. Cross (EN932) failed to return.

On 30 January Pilot Officer Frank Brown (EP227) and Sergeant Tony Smith (EP413) carried out a Rhubarb to the north of Haarlem and succeeded in destroying a locomotive and damaging a number of trucks on the Uitgeest–Castricum railway. Some Fw 190s were seen on the way back near Ijmuiden, but, as very little ammunition remained after the attack on the train, the pilots wisely decided to head straight home.

Although daylight attacks by German bombers had virtually ended, coastal towns suffered frequent nuisance raids by Fw 190 fighter-bombers which flew in at high speed to deliver a 500kg bomb before heading back over the North Sea. There was little that could be done to combat these hit-and-run attacks as the 190s invariably came in extremely low to avoid radar detection. This meant that the only defence against them was to fly standing patrols in the hope that the Spitfires and Typhoons would pick them up. On 2 February 118 Squadron flew a number of these so-called 'anti-Rhubarb' patrols with aircraft stepped up from sea level to 1,000ft, but nothing was seen. Their efforts smacked of a certain desperation; even the faster Typhoons were hard-pressed to bring the 190s to combat when they were lucky enough to see them.

Activity for the rest of the month centred mainly on the escort of 21 Squadron Venturas during two attacks on the coke works at Ijmuiden on 13 February and a raid against the torpedo workshops at Den Helder on the 19th (12 Group Ramrods 9, 10 and 11 respectively). Ramrod 10 produced a reaction from a total of twelve Fw 190s, some of whom carried out a head-on attack on the bombers as they approached the target. Nos. 118 and 167 Squadrons were involved in a number of brief exchanges, but little damage was inflicted by either side. The operation to Den Helder appeared to catch the German defences off guard: no enemy aircraft were seen and flak was of only moderate intensity from Texel. Taking full advantage, the Venturas produced excellent bombing results with one huge explosion, the shock wave from which was felt by the pilots of 118 Squadron's Spitfires flying top cover at 10,000ft.

Although Rhubarb sorties could on occasion produce useful results, they also added substantially to Fighter Command's losses, and many pilots and aircraft were to be lost for little gain. On 24 February Flight Sergeant Angus Buglass (EN969) and Flight Sergeant George Croall (EP123) took off to seek out railway and barge traffic in the Bergen area. Just before the Dutch coast was reached, Buglass decided that it was too risky to continue as there was insufficient cloud cover, but before they could return to base, his aircraft was hit in the spinner by flak. His windscreen immediately became coated in oil and his airspeed fell away so rapidly that the best he could manage was around 140kt.

In an attempt to ascertain the damage to his leader's aircraft, Croall flew underneath, but as he did so his aircraft's starboard wing touched the sea which caused it to turn on its back and dive straight in. There could be little doubt that Croall died instantly. With his engine giving every sign that it would not last much longer, Buglass decided to head for the Dutch coast so that he could bale out, but could not get his aircraft to climb above 400ft. After being shot at by a number of German soldiers, he chose to make one final attempt to get home and eventually made it to the Newark lightship where he carried out a successful ditching and was rescued after fifteen minutes in the water by a Walrus of 278 Squadron.

During the first two weeks of March no major bombing operations were carried out as the Ventura squadrons were detached to take part in Exercise Spartan. This was a large-scale tactical exercise designed to test the ability of units to operate effectively in a rapidly changing ground environment, such as would be experienced in any invasion of north-western Europe. No.167 Squadron also took part, operating from Kidlington and Fowlmere, its aircraft painted in distinctive white markings to differentiate between friend and foe. For the duration of the exercise pilots lived under canvas and survived on field rations. At the end of the day the official observers decreed that the friendly 'invading' forces had triumphed over the defending 'enemy' fighters.

While the other units participated in Spartan, 118 Squadron remained on operational duties at Coltishall and on 11 March a section of four Spitfires led by Flight Lieutenant 'Dickie' Newbery carried out a reconnaissance to the west of Ijmuiden where they encountered a pair of Fw 190s. Newbery (Red 1) ordered the break and, together with Pilot Officer Stan Jones (Red 2), attacked the leading 190 causing damage to its fuselage. In the meantime Flying Officer Frank Brown (Red 3) was involved in a head-on attack on the second enemy aircraft, return fire seriously damaging his Spitfire's starboard wing. His No.2, Pilot Officer C.L.F. Talalla (Red 4), immediately climbed above the 190 which appeared to be manoeuvring to renew its attack on Brown. Diving down from 500ft, he opened fire closing to 100 yards, at which point he saw an explosion near its cockpit. The German aircraft slowed appreciably and soon after dived into the sea. Concern over Brown's damaged machine led to an immediate return, but all aircraft landed safely.

No.167 Squadron returned to the action on 18 March when it joined forces with 118 as close escort for twelve Venturas of 464 Squadron during an attack on Maassluis. Having made rendezvous over Orfordness at 1500 hrs, the force set out over the North Sea and proceeded to the target without interference. The Venturas bombed from 12,000ft but were attacked by eight Fw 190s on their way out. Coltishall's Wing Leader, Wing Commander H.P. Blatchford DFC, who was flying with 167 Squadron, dived on four 190s that were seen heading towards the bombers. There was a considerable gap between each pair and Blatchford used his height advantage to close on the No.2 of the leading *Rotte*, opening fire at a distance of 200 yards. The 190 was hit on its fuselage and rolled into a flat inverted spin which was not recovered

The Netherlands

Terschelling   Ameland

Vlieland

Texel

• Den Helder

North
Sea

• Bergen
Egmond •
Castricum •
Ijmuiden •
• Haarlem
Zandvoort •   • Amsterdam

• The Hague   • Utrecht
Hook of   • Gouda
Holland
Maasluis •   • Schoonhoven   • Arnhem
Rotterdam
                                • Nijmegen
Overflakkee
Schouwen

Walcheren   Woensdrecht
• Flushing
• Breskens
Zeebrugge • Knokke   • Eindhoven
Blankenberge
Ostend Bruges   • Antwerp

• Ghent

before it entered cloud. Blatchford then used his momentum to get behind the leader and delivered three short bursts which blew several pieces off the German aircraft's wing. It rolled left-handed onto its back, at which point the wing detached, its pilot having just enough time to bale out before his aircraft went into the sea.

No.118 Squadron's Blue section also saw action. Flight Lieutenant

Newbery (Blue 1) fastened onto the tail of an Fw 190 and delivered two long bursts which used up all of his ammunition. He was then warned by his No.4, Sergeant Roy Flight, that a pair of 190s were coming in from behind so he immediately half-rolled out of the combat, losing sight of his opponent as he did so. This engagement was witnessed by Sergeant Hollingworth (Blue 3), who later reported that as soon as Newbery broke away, the entire tail unit of the 190 broke off. Squadron Leader Wootten (Red 1), who had remained with the bombers along with the rest of the squadron, saw a large splash in the vicinity of Newbery's combat, which took place about three miles away from that involving Wing Commander Blatchford.

After his warning to Newbery, Sergeant Flight attacked the second of the Fw 190s he had seen and fired a two-and-a-half-second burst with cannon and machine-guns from around 400 yards. The German aircraft gave off a dense cloud of black smoke and commenced a series of erratic manoeuvres which culminated in a vertical dive. Flight followed it down but was set upon by another 190 as he descended through 2,000ft. He managed to evade its attack but nearly misjudged his speed in the dive and pulled out with only 100ft to spare above the sea. Considering his own close call, he felt certain that the Fw 190 he had fired at would have gone straight in, and subsequently claimed it as probably destroyed.

The Venturas, with the remaining sections of their escort, returned to the English coast where they were shot at by a flak ship off Felixstowe which mistook the formation for an enemy raid. For once the gunners' aim was deadly accurate and EP228, flown by Sergeant Les Lack of 118 Squadron, crashed into the sea, killing its pilot.

At the end of March the Ventura squadrons carried out three attacks on the docks at Rotterdam in the space of two days. On the 28th twenty-four Venturas of 464 and 487 Squadrons mounted an extremely effective attack which saw direct hits on two merchant ships moored in the harbour. A number of Fw 190s were seen, but no combats took place. Two further attacks were carried out on the following day; results on the first were difficult to assess due to haze, but the second produced numerous hits within the docks area and there were several near misses on oil storage tanks. Two Fw 190s from a group of ten made a half-hearted attack on 167 Squadron's Yellow section, but quickly departed when 118 Squadron moved over in support.

On 4 April, the target was Rotterdam once again, the attack comprising twenty-four Venturas with escort provided by fifty-six Spitfires drawn from 118, 167, 302, 306 and 317 Squadrons, together with eight Typhoons of 56 Squadron. The German response on this occasion was determined and many combats took place.

The Venturas bombed in four boxes of six on a wide front, but as they turned to withdraw, one box lost position with the rest of the formation. Near the Dutch coast Squadron Leader Wootten (Red 1) saw four Fw 190s coming in rapidly from behind and turned his section to meet them, but at the same time noticed more Focke-Wulfs coming up from below. He was then involved in a number of combats from 9,000ft down to sea level before he saw a lone Ventura without protection. Moving over to provide cover, he was attacked from behind by two Fw 190s and a general dogfight ensued. As he twisted and turned he managed to get behind one of the enemy aircraft and fired a short burst which hit its engine. Oil from the 190 obscured his windscreen, but he then had to take violent evasive action as tracer shells passed close by. With the danger apparently over, Wootten headed for home and noticed four Fw 190s milling around an aircraft burning in the sea, which he assumed was the Ventura he had attempted to protect. On his way back Wootten was set upon by another Fw 190, narrowly avoiding a head-on collision as he broke into its attack. He eventually managed to get onto its tail, securing cannon strikes on its wing and rear fuselage.

Another member of Wootten's section, Flight Lieutenant Simmonds (Red 3), went to the aid of a Ventura which was pouring smoke from its port engine. A pair of Fw 190s were driven away, but were quickly replaced by two more. Simmonds carried out a head-on attack on one of the enemy aircraft without effect, but had more success on breaking to the right when he was able to get onto its tail to fire a number of short bursts

F/O F.T. Brown, Sgt S.A. Jones, Sgt J. Hollingworth and F/O P.S. Dunning of 118 Squadron. (*via Smith*)

with minimal deflection. Hits were seen on the starboard wing-root but the 190 quickly dived away out of range. By this time Simmonds had been joined by Sergeant Hollingworth (Red 2), who turned in behind the other 190 and fired a burst thirty degrees from astern which sent it down to crash in the sea. Hollingworth later attacked another Fw 190 and claimed it as damaged.

In the meantime 118 Squadron's Yellow and Blue sections had also been busy. Sergeant C. Anderton (Yellow 2) had not been able to jettison his long-range fuel tank and was straggling when he was attacked from behind by four Fw 190s. Turning into them he opened fire but did not see any results. Climbing vertically, he stalled off the top whereupon another 190 approached head-on. He fired a long burst, and as the 190 shot past he saw its cockpit hood fly off. The only other pilot to make a claim was Flying Officer Brown (Blue 3) for an Fw 190 damaged.

Several of 167 Squadron's aircraft fired during the engagement including those flown by Wing Commander Blatchford, Squadron Leader Stewart and Flight Lieutenant Healy, but no claims resulted. Blatchford's Spitfire was hit by cannon and machine-gun fire during the mêlée, the offending Fw 190 then being attacked and damaged by his wingman, Sergeant Nash. During the action, the Venturas lost two aircraft, AJ169 of 464 Squadron and AE957 of 487 Squadron, while Flying Officer H.B. Levinson (EN926) of 118 Squadron and Sergeant G.J. Cassidy (EP608) of 167 Squadron were both shot down and killed.

Poor weather over the next few days allowed a certain freedom when it came to planning offensive sorties and on 10 April four Spitfires of 118 Squadron took off from Coltishall in mid-morning to look for potential targets near the Dutch coast. The operation got off to an inauspicious start when Flight Sergeant de Courcy's aircraft was damaged by light flak just after landfall had been made, but worse was to come. During an attack on several barges and tugs on the canal near Zand, another gunpost opened up with extremely accurate fire which hit W3429, flown by Australian Pilot Officer Alan Beer, as it flew low over the lock gates. Announcing over the radio that he had been hit, Beer attempted a crash-landing but lost control and his aircraft was seen to hit the ground and blow up, leaving no hope that he could have survived. During the attack, all of the barges were damaged, and one was left on fire. Sergeant Anderton (Blue 4) flew so low that his aircraft was splattered by mud and water thrown up by exploding cannon shells.

During low-level sorties, pilots had to endure the perils of ground fire on numerous occasions. Known flak concentrations were avoided wherever possible, but 20mm anti-aircraft guns were highly mobile and could

P/O Alan Beer. (*Watson*)

crop up almost anywhere, as Pilot Officer Sid Watson of 118 Squadron explains:

> We had reason to respect the formidable German flak capability, there was so much of it and it was deadly effective. Of course they had plenty of targets to perfect their skills and there was no way to know where it was, even after taking a hit. What you thought was a haystack was in fact a battery, a dugout in the side of a hill, a church steeple, a tower, a railway wagon with flip down sides, any inno- cent-looking target could offer quite a surprise! We lost far more pilots to flak than to enemy aircraft, and as the war went on, after the invasion, this fact became very evident.

For the rest of April 118 and 167 Squadrons flew the usual routine of Ventura and Beaufighter escorts, largely without incident. By way of a change, on the 17th their charges were B-17 Flying Fortresses of the 91st and 306th Bomb Groups, Eighth Air Force, who were returning from a raid on Bremen. The B-17s had been heavily engaged over Germany and sixteen of their number shot down. The relatively short range of the Spitfires, even with overload tanks fitted, meant that they were of limited use as escort fighters, but the sight of them at least provided some relief for the weary American crews who had endured flak and fighters over Germany.

On 3 May Coltishall's Spitfires took part in an operation that would go down as one of the most ill-fated of the entire war. They were detailed to provide close escort to a force of Venturas from 487 (New Zealand) Squadron during 12 Group Ramrod 16, an attack on a power station in Amsterdam. Quite by chance the raid coincided with a conference on air defence that was being held at Schiphol aerodrome, and many of the top *Luftwaffe* pilots in the area had flown in to attend. In addition the German Governor of Holland was also paying a visit to the town of Haarlem, which lay on the bombers' route to the target, so there was already a high state of alert. If this were not enough, thirteen squadrons of 11 Group who were to carry out a diversionary sweep in the Flushing area (Rodeo 212) took off thirty minutes too early, a miscalculation which only served to stir up what the 118 Squadron ORB later referred to as a 'hornets' nest'.

The twelve Venturas took off from their base at Methwold at 1643 hrs, although one had to return shortly afterwards having lost an escape hatch. Rendezvous was made over Coltishall with 118 and 167 Squadrons, together with 504 Squadron, which had been drafted in from Ibsley in 10 Group. Having made the usual low-level approach over the North Sea, the bombers began their battle climb at 1735 hrs so that they crossed the Dutch coast at 12,000ft. Not long after the first German fighters were seen and it soon became clear that on this occasion the opposition was ready and waiting, and in much greater numbers than usual. No.167 Squadron's ORB describes what happened next:

> Before reaching bombing height, the escort was heavily engaged by about 50+ enemy aircraft. Many dogfights ensued. It was obvious that after the first attack on 167 Squadron by 20+ enemy aircraft, who came down very fast from 6 o'clock and dived down below pulling up under the bombers, that the other 30+ enemy aircraft had been detailed to stop us getting to the bombers. Every manoeuvre was made by the Squadron commander and section leaders after each break to return to the bombers. Each section which tried to do so was immediately jumped by 4–6 enemy aircraft who kept about 4,000ft above and eventually succeeded in breaking up the squadron by repeated attacks from three or four different directions at the same time. They did not seem willing to

mix it at our height and came down fast, had a shot and immediately pulled up and regained their height.

No.504 Squadron were at 14–15,000ft but were approximately three miles behind the bombers when the attacks began and found it impossible to make up lost ground. They too estimated the enemy force at fifty-plus and again the policy towards the top cover Spitfires was one of containment rather than confrontation. This was achieved by II/JG27, together with elements of JG26. In the meantime the Fw 190s of II/JG1, led by *Gruppenkommandeur Hauptmann* Dietrich Wickop, were hacking down the Venturas one by one so that as the target was reached, only one aircraft remained, that of Squadron Leader Leonard Trent. Shortly after bombing he too was shot down and miraculously survived being thrown from his aircraft as it plummeted earthwards (Trent was subsequently awarded the Victoria Cross).

No.118 Squadron's pilots found themselves completely overwhelmed by the large numbers of *Luftwaffe* fighters sweeping into attack. Pilot Officer Sid Watson was among them:

It is hard to imagine any aircraft less suited than the Ventura to a daylight operation against a heavily defended target such as Amsterdam. We crossed the North Sea on the deck until the Dutch coast became apparent then started to climb to the bombing height which was to be 12,000ft. Because of the poor performance of the Ventura it was a slow climb and the Spitfires had problems maintaining position. The bombers tightened up their formation with a box of six leading and directly behind a box of five. 'A' Flight of 118 was on the port side with four aircraft in battle formation, 'B' Flight was on the starboard side and to the rear was Red section led by Wing Commander Peter 'Cowboy' Blatchford. I was the Wingco's No.2.

The formation finally reached bombing height and set course for Amsterdam. At that moment control called, 'Hello Cowboy, there are seventy-plus bandits approaching you from the south. Keep your eyes open.' Moments later someone spotted the enemy about 5,000ft above us and said, 'They're coming down.' With their height advantage and great speed, they came right through the top cover [167 and 504] without pause, down beneath us and up into the bombers. Everything happened so terribly fast. The bombers were being decimated.

The close escort had a duty to turn into the attack and endeavour to have the enemy veer away, but with the numbers we had to contend with we were in a jam. I stuck with the Wingco until he made a fatal mistake and went down under the bombers after an Fw 190 and, of course, a following Fw 190 was lining up on him. I shouted a warning to break right, which I did, as I was also under attack. That was the last I saw of him.

Amid the carnage, the performance of another 118 Squadron pilot was to provide the RAF's only real success in an otherwise disastrous day. Sergeant Roy Flight from Romford in Essex had joined the squadron in September 1942 to commence operational flying when still only eighteen years of age, a feat he had achieved by lying about his age when presenting himself for selection. Flying EP413 as 'Blue 4', he was flying to the left of the bombers and had crossed about seven miles into enemy territory when he was attacked from behind. His combat report recalls subsequent events:

I was attacked by an Fw 190 from astern and was forced to break towards him. He made a head-on attack at me and . . . I opened fire at 200 yards with a one-second burst of cannon and machine gun. Pieces fell off the enemy aircraft, he broke to my right, firing as he did so, scoring machine-gun hits on my leading edge (starboard wing). I pulled round sharply onto his tail and saw he was on fire below the cockpit. I gave a two-second burst of cannon and machine gun from 400 yards nearly dead astern. Pieces fell off the enemy aircraft and the pilot baled out. His aircraft crashed about five miles NNE of Haarlem.

I could not find my own section or the bombers although I got to within a mile or two of the target. I recrossed the Dutch coast just south of Ijmuiden weaving violently. About five miles off the coast I saw an Fw 190 ahead and slightly below. Before I could attack, I was attacked myself from above and behind by another 190 but I broke in time. After a few violent turns I got inside him in a right hand turn giving two short bursts from 250 yards allowing one then two rings of deflection. There was an explosion in the enemy aircraft's cockpit, he caught fire and straightened out. I closed dead astern 150 yards and fired, during which my ammunition gave out. The enemy aircraft's undercarriage partly dropped and he turned over and went straight into the sea five miles off the coast.

Flight then set course for the English coast and about forty miles out over the sea came upon two Bostons being attacked by another Fw 190. These were 107 Squadron aircraft that had been involved in a simultaneous raid on the steel works at Ijmuiden. Diving almost vertically, he closed to about 400 yards and fired several short bursts with machine-guns, noting numerous De Wilde strikes on the 190's wing-roots. Eventually his machine-guns gave out as well and Flight was forced to break away and head for home. The squadron ORB later described his camera gun film as 'magnificent' and there could be little doubt that his claim for two destroyed and one damaged was fully justified. The only other claims to be made were by 167 Squadron with one Fw 190 destroyed by Flying Officer Cody, a probable to Flying Officer F.J. Reahill, with two others damaged by Flying Officer J. van Arkel and Squadron Leader A.C. Stewart.

Ten out of eleven Venturas failed to return, the only one to survive having turned back early with its hydraulics shot away and both engines damaged. Wing Commander Blatchford's Spitfire (EN971) was seen to ditch in the sea about forty miles east of Mundesley, but despite an extensive air-sea rescue operation, he was not found. Post-war research indicates that he was most likely shot down by *Oberfeldwebel* Hans Ehlers of II/JG1.

Blatchford's wingman, Sid Watson, was fortunate to survive as he later became involved in combat with another Fw 190, a duel that had certain comic overtones.

For one to understand the speed with which events occur in an air battle, they must of necessity have experienced it. The sky at one moment is filled with aircraft, wheeling, diving, flashing past, over and under. Then, suddenly, you are all alone, where did they go? The sky is empty!

I turned westward to head for home and immediately an Fw 190 is coming at me head-on. The vast majority of the German attackers were only interested in the bombers; they made their high-speed hits then dived away – the successful fighter pilot's credo: Go in fast, get close, hit hard, get out! Here was one German that did not dive away. He thought maybe he could pick off a straggler, mainly me. I estimate our closing speed at about 500mph and we both opened fire at the same time. I rammed the control column forward and passed under him with about three feet to spare.

I had loosened the harness straps so I had more freedom to twist around to look behind, because that is where the unpleasantness usually arrives. Because the harness was extra loose, when I pushed the stick forward the negative-G forced me up out of the bucket seat and the dinghy pack attached to the parachute pack came up on its edge and I suddenly became about a foot or more higher than my 5ft 7in. All this time the Fw 190 is turning again to have another go and I haven't got time to sort out my seating arrangement.

141

My major thought at that moment was to try and lose some height where hopefully I could get some improved performance out of the aircraft, and here is this Hun harassing me. At that time, facing instant death, I couldn't help but think how funny it was sitting up so high, jammed against the canopy. In all, we had three head-on attacks and why we couldn't score with no deflection shots is a puzzle. The German obviously became bored with the whole thing and dived away, as I did, for home. I had visions later of this German pilot recounting to his mates how he had seen the tallest Spitfire pilot in the RAF!

Blatchford was replaced as Wing Leader by Wing Commander A.C. 'Sandy' Rabagliati DFC who had seen considerable action during the Battle of Britain with 46 Squadron, and later in Malta, where he was leader of the Takali Wing. Rabagliati would regularly fly with 118 Squadron during the coming weeks but occasionally opted to join the Typhoons of 56 Squadron, which were based at Matlaske and also came under his command.

The menace of hit-and-run raids by Fw 190 *Jabos* came to a head on 12 May when a low-level attack was made on Lowestoft which left twenty-three people dead and twenty-nine seriously wounded. No.118 Squadron flew anti-Rhubarb patrols up to sixty miles out over the sea but as the

P/O Sid Watson. (*Watson*)

raiders always approached their target fast and low, the chances of being able to carry out a successful interception were remote. Generally the best that could be hoped was for the Spitfires to act as a deterrent, and this was achieved during a patrol by four aircraft led by Flight Lieutenant Newbery in EP646. Three Fw 190s were seen approaching the English coast at 600ft but as soon as they saw the Spitfires, they immediately turned for home at high speed. Newbery led the chase, but even flat out they made no impression and eventually had to give up. The RAF's response to these attacks was to increase the number of Typhoon squadrons in the area with 245 arriving to join 56 at Matlaske, and 195 Squadron moving into Ludham in place of 167 Squadron's Spitfire Vbs.

Equally frustrating were intrusions by high-flying German aircraft. On 15 May a two-aircraft patrol, comprising Sergeant Norman Brown (AR433) and Sergeant Roy Flight (EP413), spotted enemy aircraft at around 25,000ft over Yarmouth. The aircraft were identified as Messerschmitt Me 210s which were chased back over the North Sea for fifty miles despite the fact that there was little chance of being able to get within firing range.

For the rest of the month 118 Squadron's attention returned mainly to reconnaissance work along the Dutch coast together with the escort of a Coastal Command shipping strike on the 17th. A convoy of around fifteen ships was attacked in mid-afternoon by Beaufighters equipped with torpedoes, while others in the flak suppression role took on the escorting minesweepers and flak ships. Two Fw 190s were seen by the escorting Spitfires but they made no attempt to intervene.

This operation was the first to be undertaken in the area by the Canadians of 402 Squadron, who had been at Digby since 21 March. Two months of training had seen numerous sector recces being carried out, together with cine gun and formation flying, as the squadron settled down to life in 12 Group under the command of Squadron Leader Lloyd Chadburn DFC. For the rest of the year the Coltishall and Digby Wings would be closely associated and would fly together on many occasions.

Operations for the first part of June consisted mainly of 'Roadsteads' and shipping 'Lagoons', commencing on the 2nd when eight aircraft of 118 Squadron (including Wing Commander Rabagliati) attacked four armed trawlers near the south-east tip of Terschelling. One trawler was left on fire and sinking, with another in flames and listing badly. The two remaining vessels also suffered a number of hits. A similar operation carried out on 10 June, however, resulted in a lucky escape for Warrant Officer Faulkner. Flying AR450, he was hit by a shell which holed the hood and front screen, wrecked his blind flying panel and also damaged a fuel line. It was considered improbable that the damage had been

143

caused by the trawlers' defences, more likely that it had come about due to the activities of the shore batteries situated on the nearby island of Texel.

During the next few weeks most of the Spitfire V squadrons in 12 Group sent their aircraft to 3501 Servicing Unit at Cranfield so that they could be re-engined with the M-series Merlin 45. No.118 Squadron was temporarily out of the firing line from 14 to 19 June while this work was carried out with 402 Squadron's Spitfires following in early July. When the aircraft returned, most pilots were pleasantly surprised by the additional power that the 'cropped blower' Merlin produced, and more than one squadron diarist recorded increased confidence in the re-worked aircraft and a desire to try them out operationally. They would not have long to wait.

TEN

COLTISHALL/DIGBY WINGS, JULY–DECEMBER 1943

B efore the summer fighting season got under way in earnest, several personnel changes took place in 12 Group which saw the departure of 'Bertie' Wootten to Fairwood Common, and the arrival of Squadron Leader Johnny Freeborn DFC to take over 118 Squadron. At Digby, Lloyd Chadburn became Wing Leader on 13 June, his place as commander of 402 Squadron being taken by Squadron Leader Geoff Northcott, and the recently arrived 416 Squadron also had a new CO in Squadron Leader F.E. 'Bitsy' Grant.

Both Freeborn and Northcott were leaders who possessed a wealth of combat experience. Having previously flown with 401 Squadron (see Chapter Four), Northcott was involved in the battle to save Malta in the summer of 1942, a period in which he made several claims with 603 and 229 Squadrons. During service with 74 Squadron, Freeborn shot down at least twelve aircraft, a figure that does not include the Hurricane that he dispatched during the infamous 'Battle of Barking Creek' shortly after the war started! Like most new appointees, Freeborn found good and bad points with his new squadron:

> 118 Squadron was a happy squadron but lacked discipline. When I took over I found I had a largely tour-expired crew and the two Flight Commanders were not good enough to cope with a highly experienced Yorkshireman, so they went rapidly. I got two new Flight Commanders who had both returned from a tour of duty in Malta at the time of the siege. They provided a firm base for the squadron to build on. The NCO pilots were demoralised as the old Flight Commanders had little or no time for them. I quickly changed this outlook. There was to be no scruffy dress, and neat and tidiness was the order of the day. I also had two stroppy Australians who were quickly kicked into shape and soon I had a good squadron.

The promotion of Lloyd Chadburn to command the Digby Wing was to have a similar effect to that achieved by Ian Gleed at Ibsley a year before. Previously, Digby had been regarded mainly as a station where squadrons could recuperate after a spell in 11 Group, but Chadburn was determined that his boys would be in the forefront of any action going. By sheer force of personality, he inspired everyone around him, and once in the air his calm manner and expert leadership encouraged everyone to give of their best, as Flying Officer Dan Noonan recalls:

> Chad was a very special guy, a great leader, a friend to all, and fun to be with. Once when the wing was returning from Scotland to Digby, we landed at an RAF base to refuel and have lunch. A bunch of us were gathered in the bar and Chad looked in and said, 'OK boys – just one to sharpen the eye!' Another time, returning across the Channel, we were under low cloud at about 1,000ft, nothing to see but sea and cloud, when a sweet gal's voice came over the R/T, 'Wing Leader, what is your position?' Those of us close to Chad's

F/O Dan Noonan of 416 Squadron. (*Noonan*)

kite saw him suck the tip of his finger, then hold it up, with a big grin!

With Chadburn at the helm, it would not be long before the Digby Wing was one of Fighter Command's top-scoring outfits.

Having had their old aircraft given a new lease of life, 118 Squadron were back in business on 21 June when a section of four aircraft led by Pilot Officer Sid Watson successfully attacked a group of 8–10 armed trawlers ten miles west of The Hague. The following morning half the squadron took off from Coltishall for a shipping strike, although Squadron Leader Freeborn and Flying Officer Peter Dunning had to return early due to engine trouble. The remaining six aircraft led by 'Dickie' Newbery located and attacked a number of M-Class minesweepers and escort vessels seven miles south-west of Texel, damaging two of the former. Return fire was intense and accurate, hitting the aircraft flown by Flying Officer H.G. Handley, who was killed when his parachute failed to open, and that flown by Flight Sergeant Croxton-Davies (W3901), which was set on fire and crashed into the sea.

The German flak ships and minesweepers which operated along the Dutch coast were all heavily armed and could throw up a considerable weight of fire. Some vessels were equipped with the 20mm *Flakvierling* 38, a quadruple barrelled weapon capable of firing 720 rounds per minute. By now Sid Watson was one of the most experienced pilots in 118 Squadron. He recalls some of the techniques used on anti-shipping operations:

> Three or four times a week we would be dispatched in a four-aircraft section to cross the North Sea to the Hook of Holland and proceed northward up the coast to Texel or Terschelling on a shipping recce at zero feet. More often than not we would encounter a Dutch fishing fleet of maybe forty or fifty fishing trawlers escorted by a few armed trawlers. Normally we wouldn't bother them, but on the odd occasion the armed trawlers started shooting at us. In that event, at least when I was leading, we would retaliate. Some pilots preferred to attack a ship in a dive, but I liked to go in about ten feet off the water. We often discussed these tactics among ourselves, all I can say is that I'm still here and a lot of others are not!
>
> The guns were fired by pressure on a 'button' on the control column. This wasn't really a button but a strip of metal about three inches long by three quarters of an inch wide with three indentations. The top indent, if pressed, would fire the machine-guns, the middle indent would fire both the machine-guns and the cannon, and of course the bottom indent would activate the cannon only.

One could remember which was which by thinking of the BBC – i.e. Brownings – Both – Cannons. Attacking from maybe 400 yards I would select machine-guns only and use the rudder left and right to spray the ship from stem to stern for a second or so. Now a switch to the central button and let fly with the works, keeping low on the water until the last second. Then comes the tricky part of getting over the ship with all its masts, antennae etc. On one occasion I attacked and had just cleared the ship when it blew up! My No.2 following me thought I had been hit and had dived straight into the ship.

With their aircraft modified for low-altitude work, the duties of 12 Group's Spitfire V squadrons were now widened to include frequent operations over northern France from 11 Group bases, this to be carried out in addition to their existing duties along the Dutch coast. On 23 June 118, 402 and 416 Squadrons took part in Ramrod 100 which involved escorting twelve Bostons during a diversionary raid on Meaulte. Having flown to West Malling to be refuelled, the escort fighters made rendezvous with the bombers over Dungeness before setting course for the objective. On their return from the target six Fw 190s attacked the Bostons near Abbeville and were immediately engaged by 118 Squadron. 'Dickie' Newbery fired at one, which he later claimed as damaged, and Norwegian Second Lieutenant S.K. Liby attacked a second which had been driven off by the combined attentions of 402 and 416 Squadrons. Opening fire at 600 yards, cannon strikes were seen behind the cockpit area and a second burst from 300 yards damaged the mainplane. The 190 then dived steeply out of control in a succession of quick spirals and was last seen at around 3–4,000ft.

Three days later 118 Squadron, together with the Digby Wing, flew from Hurn as withdrawal cover for B-17s returning from a bombing raid on Le Mans (11 Group Ramrod 108). As the Spitfires crossed the French coast they had to contend with heavy flak which was extremely accurate, although Pilot Officer Stan Jones DFM of 118 Squadron was already in trouble, as he recalls:

During my regular practice of checking engine and other controls, I found my engine showing a drop in oil pressure and immediately waggled my wings and turned back (we were very close to Cherbourg). I radioed an SOS stating my problem and position and said I was proposing to bale out. The engine was still turning so I decided to stay with her hoping to get a bit nearer to home.

I decided I would bale out at 2,000ft but when I reached that level the engine seized solid and I could do no more than keep the speed

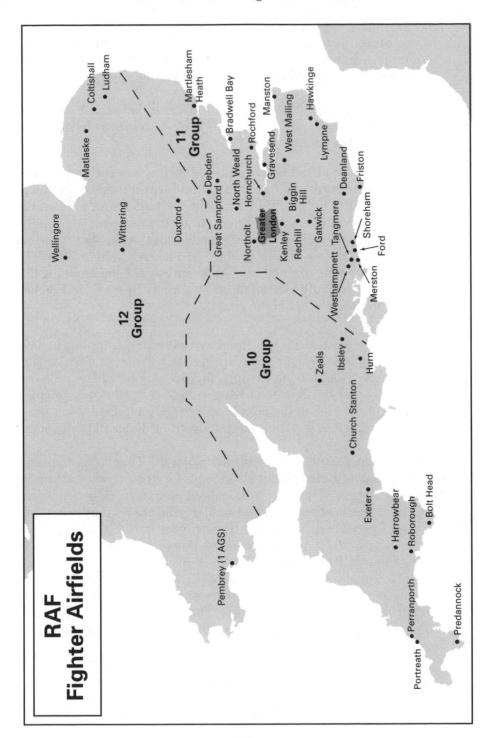

up by putting the nose down and heading back to France. I had to think pretty fast and decided, as I recovered control, I would continue towards France and keep the aircraft on a level keel, although flying speed had to remain about 100mph plus.

By now Jones was losing height rapidly and it soon became clear that he would not be able to make it to the coast. Too low to bale out, he prepared to ditch his aircraft.

I put my arm and head on the gunsight [to act] as a cushion! I know nothing of the crash and woke up to find I was still in the cockpit in very deep water judging by the colour. I climbed out, inflated my Mae West and after an age burst out of the sea with my dinghy which I inflated and succeeded in mounting. After that my right knee froze, as did my left arm, which had taken a hefty wallop. The rest was something of a novelty; there had never been anything like this! I was eventually located at seven a.m. by Spitfires and picked up after fourteen hours in the water.

When all things are considered, Jones was extremely fortunate to have survived. Although low-wing aircraft are generally better in ditching situations than mid- or high-wing layouts, the positioning of the radiators towards the rear of the Spitfire's wing caused a nose-down pitching moment which often led to the aircraft submerging rapidly. Many other pilots who attempted to put their aircraft down on water did not get out in time.

On 27 June operations were resumed along the Dutch coast, a large force of twenty-one Beaufighters attacking a German convoy steaming south off The Hague. The convoy consisted of sixteen ships, including six M-Class minesweepers, and had fighter protection comprising four Fw 190s and two Me 109s. As the Beaus went into the attack, Geoff Northcott swung 402 Squadron behind the ships and succeeded in separating the two 109s from the Focke-Wulfs which were engaged by 118 and 416 Squadrons. Selecting one of the Messerschmitts, Northcott fired a long burst which literally 'shredded' its wing-root and fuselage, producing a plume of black smoke. The enemy aircraft was then temporarily lost from view, but a large splash near the convoy marked its final moment.

In the meantime 118 Squadron's 'Dickie' Newbery (Blue 1) had got into a good position behind an Fw 190 and fired a four-second burst from 150 yards which led to the German machine disintegrating completely, before it fell into the sea. His wingman, Sergeant Hollingworth, damaged another but was then forced to break sharply due to an R/T warning that he was about to come under attack.

The Focke-Wulfs were hopelessly out-numbered and the remaining pair were attacked by 416 Squadron led by Lloyd Chadburn, whose fire struck the leader around the wing-roots and cockpit. It was last seen diving erratically towards the coast but could only be claimed as a probable as Chadburn had to break off due to the attentions of flak batteries situated along the coast. The other 190 was quickly dispatched by Flight Lieutenant J.A. Rae and Pilot Officer R.D. Phillip.

Over the next few days a number of Rhubarb sorties were flown and on 3 July four Spitfires of 118 Squadron led by Flight Lieutenant John Shepherd reconnoitred the area around Castricum, destroying a locomotive and damaging a barge. Light flak was experienced and three aircraft returned with minor damage. Two days later, during a Roadstead operation off Den Helder, a 500-ton armed trawler was attacked and left on fire.

On 2 July 611 Squadron took up residence at Matlaske to commence what would be a lengthy stay in 12 Group. They settled in quickly and a few days later their Spitfire Vbs were sent to Cranfield to be fitted with Merlin 45Ms to boost performance. Their first action occurred on 5 July when a four-aircraft reconnaissance near Egmond led to an encounter with Me 109s which saw two of the German aircraft damaged by Squadron Leader E.F.J. 'Jack' Charles DFC and Flight Lieutenant F.F. Colloredo-Mansfield.

With the loss of Wing Commander Blatchford still fresh in everyone's minds, Coltishall suffered further sadness on 6 July when his replacement, Sandy Rabagliati, was shot down into the North Sea when leading an attack on German M-Class minesweepers at the head of 56 Squadron's Typhoons. His aircraft was seen to go into the water about sixty miles from the English coast and, like his predecessor, a massive search of the area by all available aircraft failed to find any trace of him. He was replaced as Wing Leader by Wing Commander P.B. 'Laddie' Lucas DFC, who arrived at Coltishall on 10 July. Flight Lieutenant Tony Cooper, who would fly with Lucas on many occasions later in the year, recalls his impressions:

Lucas was very well known, of course, in the RAF and he was as cool, calm and collected a leader as you could wish for. Everyone liked him immensely and would have followed him anywhere, and he seemed to make no mistakes at all. When you're flying a Spitfire you are not only the pilot, but you're also the navigator, you're also the bomb aimer, if you're carrying a bomb, and the gunner as well, and you have to do all these things at the same time in a very tiny cockpit. The leader has to do exactly the same thing plus he's got the responsibility of twenty-four to thirty-six aeroplanes behind him, so frankly Laddie Lucas was a bit of a hero to me, he was one of the best, a terrific guy and a wonderful leader.

Lucas was somewhat taken aback to discover that his new squadrons were still flying with each section in line astern, the formation first flown by the Biggin Hill Wing over two years before. An ardent believer in the advantages of the open finger four, he quickly used his Malta experience to win over his Squadron and Flight Commanders, and within a matter of days the benefits of the new system were clear for all to see. Under his leadership morale quickly began to rise and he was to provide the direction and stability that transformed the Coltishall Wing into a first-class unit.

By the middle of July the poor weather experienced in the first half of the month had improved considerably and on the 18th a report was received from Army Co-operation Mustangs of a large convoy heading south near Den Helder. The Mustangs had not gone unseen however, and the Germans knew full well what to expect. By the time a strike force of Beaufighters arrived in mid-afternoon they found that the ships had taken refuge in the gap between Den Helder and Texel, and the attack had to be called off.

In the evening twelve Beaufighters (six each from 143 and 236 Squadrons) set out for a second attempt, close escort being provided by 118 and 402 Squadrons, with 416 Squadron as top cover. This time they found the convoy in open waters with a fighter screen of six Me 109Gs to protect them. As the Beaufighters commenced their attack on the ships, the 109s were engaged by the Spitfires of 118 Squadron with Flight Lieutenant Shepherd firing three short bursts at one which blew up and fell into the sea. Shepherd and his wingman, Flight Sergeant Anderton, then attacked another, Anderton firing a seven-second burst with his machine-guns, during which the 109 hit the sea and broke up. On the other side of the convoy 'Dickie' Newbery's section were dealing with a third 109 which eventually fell to their combined fire, the 'kill' officially credited to Newbery himself.

A few thousand feet above, the Canadians of 416 Squadron, led by Lloyd Chadburn, were looking down somewhat enviously, hoping that some trade would come their way. Chadburn saw one of 118 Squadron's victims crash into the sea and almost immediately an Me 109 passed under his squadron. Leading his section into the attack, he fired a two-second burst at approximately 200 yards which produced strikes all over the 109's wing-roots, cockpit and engine cowling. As he broke away, the attack was taken up by Flight Lieutenant Rae (EP206), who fired a three-second burst which caused further damage, the Messerschmitt diving into the grey waters of the North Sea shortly afterwards.

For this type of operation the striking power of the twin-engined Beaufighter was formidable and it possessed a capability equalled by very few combat aircraft of the time. Sid Watson flew with the Beaufighters on many anti-shipping strikes and recalls some of his impressions of these attacks:

These strikes would (usually) consist of thirty-six Beaufighters, twelve as anti-flak utilising their 4 × 20mm cannon and 6 × 0.303 machine-guns, twelve with their rockets and/or their normal armament, followed by twelve torpedo-carrying Beaus. From our side of the effort we would supply three squadrons of Spitfires as escort. The rendezvous would be Cromer on the Norfolk coast, so thirty-six Spitfires would make sure to be in position to wait for the arrival of the Beaufighters coming down from the north. We never had to wait very long, but in the meantime we had all those Spitfires in squadron formation orbiting under 500ft (we kept at low altitude to fox the enemy radar). Just to the west of Cromer there were several very tall radio towers and we always seemed to get very close to them while we were orbiting at this low level. I don't know why we didn't do all this just off the coast.

Once the whole formation headed out to sea at zero feet, it was a sight to behold. Seventy-two aircraft, the Beaus flanked on all sides by the Spitfires, all heading for a convoy we knew was there. Everyone knew what they had to do and as we approached the target the whole formation climbed to about 600ft. The Spitfires quickly dispatched any enemy fighters or they wisely fled the scene. The Wing Commander of the Beaufighters calmly, but quickly, instructed his pilots what ships they would go for and then repeated 'Attack', 'Attack', 'Attack'.

For us in the escort, we stayed at maybe 600ft above the convoy and it was almost like watching a movie. The Beaufighters wheeling and diving among the ships, great spouts of water rising high in the air, ships on fire, aircraft diving vertically into the sea. I wondered how the people on those ships felt when they saw that great armada of aircraft approaching. After the attack, heading for home, Spitfires would formate on shot-up Beaus and shepherd them back to the UK, some of them landing wheels up at our base of Coltishall.

The day after their successful escort operation, 118 Squadron was brought down to earth with a bump during an afternoon Roadstead which was carried out by eleven of its aircraft. Having made landfall at Ijmuiden, the Spitfires then split up with 'A' Flight turning north for Texel, while 'B' Flight headed south for the Hook. 'Dickie' Newbery, at the head of 'A' Flight, soon spotted two ships of approximately 800 and 1,000 tons steaming northwards and immediately ordered the attack. During the course of a brief but chaotic action, both steamers were badly damaged, the smaller vessel being set on fire, but defensive fire was extremely accurate and EN966, flown by Flying Officer Frank Brown, suffered a serious glycol leak on its run in to the target when still 1,000 yards away. In spite of the damage inflicted, Brown continued his attacking dive, his fire setting the vessel alight. Afterwards he managed to coax his aircraft up to 900ft but his engine soon spluttered to a halt and he was forced to bale out into the sea. Pilot Officer Flight, his No.2, gallantly dropped his own dinghy which fell within fifty yards of Brown's position, but he was unable to reach it and eventually disappeared from sight altogether. It was later assumed that Brown had become entangled in the rigging lines of his parachute harness and had drowned.

No.611 Squadron's first major engagement in 12 Group occurred on 25 July during Ramrod 154, an attack by twelve Mitchells of 180 Squadron on the Fokker works in Amsterdam. With 118 and 402 Squadrons protecting the bombers, 611 Squadron broke away to ward off a mixed gaggle of Me 109s and Fw 190s, and during the ensuing dogfights three Me 109s were shot down by Flying Officer Hickin, Flying Officer Hodgkinson and Pilot Officer Walmsley. Having already damaged an Me 109, Squadron Leader Charles (AR610) attacked an Fw 190, which blew up at close range directly in front of his Spitfire. His aircraft's engine was hit by debris from the blast and he was forced to bale out into the sea twenty-five miles off the Dutch coast. Charles's position was fixed by Flight Lieutenant Colloredo-Mansfield, and later, a daring ASR operation led to him being plucked from the sea by a Walrus virtually from under the Germans' noses.

Towards the end of July the escort of medium bombers was extended to include Mitchells of 2 Group and the newly operational Martin B-26 Marauders of the USAAF's Eighth Air Force. On the 27th twelve Mitchells of 180 Squadron carried out 12 Group Ramrod 20, an evening attack on the *Luftwaffe* fighter airfield at Schiphol, with protection provided by the Spitfires of the Coltishall and Digby Wings.

All squadrons became heavily engaged on the approach to the target as they attempted to stop a force estimated to be around thirty to forty-five Me 109s getting to the bombers. No.402 Squadron, acting as top cover, went into action first with Pilot Officer J.D. Mitchner claiming a 109 destroyed and Lloyd Chadburn another probably destroyed. No.416, in the meantime, was also busy, Squadron Leader Grant sending another 109 spinning to the ground, while Flight Lieutenant R.H. Walker and Sergeant G.F. Burden claimed one and two damaged respectively. Burden's Spitfire was badly damaged itself during the fight and was subsequently classified Cat. B on its return.

Due to the effective work of the top escort squadrons, very few Me 109s got anywhere near the Mitchells and those that did were quickly dealt with by 118 Squadron. Flying Officer Talalla (AR450) and Pilot Officer Flight (W3320) latched onto one, alternately attacking from the port and starboard beams. Flight's fire hit the 109 on its fuselage near the wing-root and Talalla, known to all as 'Jimmy', saw further strikes following two quarter rear attacks. The 109 fell away out of control and was last seen, still spinning, at around 3,000ft. In a separate action, Second Lieutenant Liby (Red 2) fastened onto another 109 and indulged in a dogfight which lasted around fifteen minutes and ended with the German aircraft crashing in flames near Gouda.

On 28 July 118 Squadron accompanied USAAF B-26 Marauders for the first time on a feint Ramrod which was intended as a diversion to draw fighters away from the real attack going in on the coke ovens at Zeebrugge. The B-26 had been introduced to service in northern Europe in May 1943 in the low-level role but prohibitive losses had brought about a change to medium-level attack. It was regarded as being something of a 'hot ship', indeed its speed posed problems for the close-escort Spitfires who were hard-pressed to fly a 'defensive weave' around the bombers, especially after they had dropped their bombs. As yet the American crews did not have full confidence in their aircraft and they also lacked operational experience. This became evident the following day during a raid on Amsterdam when they turned back ten miles short of the target, jettisoned their bombs in the sea and made for home. Sadly, two of 118 Squadron's Spitfires collided on their return to Coltishall killing Pilot Officer Buglass (EP191) and Flight Sergeant Hollingworth (AR447).

By now all pilots were fully conversant with the LFVb and were beginning to revel in its low-altitude performance. Although the use of clipped wings had brought about a marked improvement in the aircraft's rate of roll and increased its top speed, it was found that climb rate and stall speed had been adversely affected by the reduction in wing area. These factors were only affected marginally, but a situation was created in which some pilots chose to retain the wingtips, whereas others had them removed.

Pilot Officer (later Air Vice-Marshal) Bill 'Paddy' Harbison recalls that 118 Squadron possessed relatively few aircraft with clipped wings, and that these were often flown in mixed formations, occasionally with amusing results. During a formation landing one day, Harbison was flying a clipped example as No.2 to his CO, Squadron Leader Freeborn, whose aircraft retained its classic wing profile. With its slightly increased stall speed, Harbison's Spitfire touched down first, which brought an immediate response from Freeborn questioning just who was leading the flight!

August saw a return to escort work with Coastal Command's Beaufighters and another highly successful operation on the 2nd. A large convoy was sighted at 1127 hrs steaming at eight knots south of Den Helder comprising six merchant ships headed by M-Class minesweepers with flak ships on either flank. As the Beaufighters dived on the ships, 402 Squadron swept into the attack, Geoff Northcott firing at an Me 109 which crashed into the sea soon after. He then went for another 109 which was also confronted by 416 Squadron coming around the convoy the opposite way. The German pilot tried to escape by executing a violent half roll, but in doing so lost control and dived straight in.

At the rear of the convoy Lloyd Chadburn engaged one of four 109s, firing a long burst which used up all of his 20mm ammunition. The attack was then taken up by Pilot Officers Booth and Pow, both of whom damaged the 109 further, forcing its pilot to bale out. Flight Lieutenant Rae of 416 Squadron got behind another of the group and fired several short bursts which produced an explosion near the cockpit. It immediately half-rolled and crashed into the sea. Yellow section of 118 Squadron was also involved in the skirmishing, although it did not have as much success as the Digby squadrons, its only claim being a probable to Flight Lieutenant Shepherd.

Shortly after this operation, on 9 August, 402 and 416 Squadrons moved to Merston to prepare for their involvement in Operation Starkey, a large-scale deception that was intended to disrupt troop movements to the Italian front by giving the impression that landings were about to occur in northern France. They were joined later in the month by 118 Squadron, which had initially moved to nearby Westhampnett.

The climax to the hoax occurred on 9 September when large numbers of amphibious craft left south-coast ports in the early morning heading for Boulogne, but before this there was a period of intensive bombing which formed one of the busiest periods of the year for the close-escort squadrons. In addition to attacks on targets in north-east France, Pilot Officer Doug Love of 416 Squadron recalls that the Canadian Wing was

Two views of a 118 Squadron Spitfire LFVb which crashed as a result of engine failure on take-off. The pilot, 2nd Lt Liby, escaped unhurt. (*Watson*)

engaged in operations over a wide area with escort missions being carried out from Matlaske, Friston, Bradwell Bay, Martlesham Heath and Exeter. Generally, the *Luftwaffe* was not taken in by the attempted ruse and relatively few combats took place, although a notable exception occurred on 4 September during Ramrod S.31 Part III, an operation that Love described as 'a real show' in his logbook. Another of those taking part was Flying Officer Art Sager, who recorded his experiences in a wartime journal:

September is a busy month. Nearly all of the twenty-five shows are Ramrods, escorting 36 or 72 Marauders on bombing raids of aerodromes, marshalling yards, docks and bridges in France, Belgium and Holland. The Wing is fuelled and briefed for these missions at Coltishall, Bradwell, Wellingore, Merston, Manston and Lympne.

On 4 September, on a Ramrod to the marshalling yards at St Pol, 15–20 Me 109s climb to attack the first box of bombers on the return leg. Chad, leading 416 with you as his No.2, turns into them. They split up and there's a wild shamozzle. On a turn to starboard, Chad fires at one and continues breaking. You, close on Chad's tail, give a two-second burst at the same Hun, now less than a 100 yards away. You see flashes on the fuselage as he goes under you. Wheeling around to follow Chad, you fire at another Hun, also close, and black smoke pours from him. Suddenly the sky is clear. The Hun attack has been dispersed.

Chad reforms on the port side of the Marauders with about half of the squadron, 'B' Flight having been separated in the mêlée. Lagging behind, it is attacked from above by a dozen yellow-coloured Fw 190s which are reported first as friendly aircraft. They're firing explosive ammunition from long range which looks like flak. Chad, some distance away, is the first to call a break as he turns and dives into the gaggle. He fires at the leader head-on. The Hun bursts into flames and crashes on the cliffs above a beach. The rest of the 190s make a wide turn in close formation, apparently for another attack, but when the squadron dives down after them, they head east and disappear in the haze at deck level.

Dave [F/O D.F. Prentice – BL532] is hit in the first attack and he is forced to bale out about ten miles from the French coast. He is picked up later by the courageous crew of an air-sea rescue plane and returns to base with nothing more serious than a damp and creased uniform. Seldom have the Huns been so ferocious. In a separate engagement, 402 – giving rear cover on the starboard side of the last box – breaks up another attack on the bombers and in

The end result of a take-off swing – BM556, F/O W.G. Dodd of 402 Squadron, 4/9/43. (*Watson*)

doing so destroys four Me 109s and damages another. The total score for the Wing is six destroyed and two damaged with the loss of one Spitfire, but no bombers.

It is interesting that the Fw 190s, which were from II/JG26, were at first reported as 'friendly'. This was due to the fact that they were seen to be flying in fours, line astern, tactics that may have been used deliberately in an attempt to infiltrate the RAF formations. The successful pilots in 402 Squadron were Pilot Officer L.A. Moore, Sergeant J.N. Thorne and Flight Lieutenant J.D. Mitchner, the other claim being shared by several pilots.

After their involvement in Starkey, 402 Squadron returned to Digby on 19 September with 416 Squadron joining them the following month, after a short stay at nearby Wellingore. By now 416 were led by Squadron Leader R.H. 'Kelly' Walker, although his command was to be relatively brief as he would shortly be replaced by Squadron Leader F.E. 'Freddy' Green DFC. Over at Coltishall, 64 Squadron had taken over from 118 Squadron, which had been withdrawn to Peterhead.

Although nominally back in 12 Group, 402 and 416 Squadrons still carried out most of their operations from 11 Group bases in the south, as Art Sager's war journal reveals:

The Wing is now regularly commuting to Merston, Tangmere and Coltishall. On 22 September the usual force of 72 Marauders in boxes of 18 has a go at Evreux fighter base and again the Hun responds, 50 plus being reported in the target area. They are all Fw 190s and Chad, leading 416, bounces some of them as they climb to attack the bombers. They split up. Leading a section, you chase a couple down to 3,000ft, close to 250 yards on the trailing one and fire a short burst, seeing flashes on the fuselage as it goes into cloud. Climbing with your section to rejoin the bombers, you encounter another 190 coming down, its round nose getting bigger in seconds, and you get in a short head-on shot. It goes right through the section, miraculously missing everyone, trailing a stream of white smoke. You claim a damaged on these two exchanges.

The following day the Wing operates again from Tangmere, escorting Marauders to Beauvais. You lead Green section in an attack on several Fw 190s who've got into the bombers. The Huns get away but none of the bombers are lost, although you learn later that a rear gunner is wounded. Attacks on aerodromes in Normandy are provoking a lively enemy reaction and so Operations call for another attack on Beauvais on 24 September. Again there are lots of Huns about and 416 break into some of them who come roaring down out of the sun. After the break you return to the bombers but Chad, leading with 402 and flying above and to starboard, dives

64 Squadron Spitfire LFVb displays wing stripes used for Operation Starkey. (*Cooper*)

after them. He gets one and Mitchner, a Flight commander, gets a probable. A Wing of Spit IXs on high cover gets into another gaggle and destroys six for the loss of two. When you return to base you find there's a sizeable hole in the tail unit, a lucky miss by one of the Huns who'd come through.

There are two shows on 27 September. Operating from Wellingore for the first, the Wing flies across the North Sea to Den Helder to provide cover for Fortresses returning from a bombing raid on Emden. While most of the bombers are still in close formation coming out, four straggle behind, presumably damaged by flak. No Huns are seen. After re-fuelling the Wing is ordered to Tangmere where, in the afternoon, it covers Marauders on a Ramrod to the aerodrome at Conches. 416 Squadron, as close escort, can do no more than break into a gaggle of Fw 190s as they come through the outer screen, but 402, again led by Chad, get into a mass of them. One is destroyed, three probably destroyed and one is damaged. No bombers are lost.

W/C Lloyd Chadburn and S/L Freddie Green re-enact the Wild West in deepest Lincolnshire. (*Booth*)

In addition to these operations the wing flew two more Ramrods from Tangmere on the 24th and also participated in a shipping strike by Beaufighters off the Dutch coast on the 25th, its first for eight weeks.

For the Digby Wing the first major action of October occurred on the 3rd during a raid by B-26 Marauders on Schiphol. As the bombers and lead escorts crossed the Dutch coast on their way home, 402 Squadron were attacked by twelve Me 109s. Two sections of 416 Squadron, led by Lloyd Chadburn, went to 402's assistance, Chadburn himself selecting one of four 109s that were chasing after a single Spitfire to the west of Ijmuiden. Opening fire from 300 yards, one of the Messerschmitt's wheels soon dropped and a further burst from close range produced an explosion in one wing as though a cannon magazine had blown up. Both aircraft then entered cloud, but on emerging Chadburn witnessed a large splash as the enemy aircraft hit the sea, leaving a solitary tyre floating on the water. Several other pilots fired their guns during the dogfight, a probable being awarded to Flying Officer W.G. Dodd, with Geoff Northcott (EP120), John Mitchner (AR505) and Sergeant J.N. Thorne (W3445) all claiming Me 109s damaged. No Spitfires were lost, although Flight Lieutenant Dan Noonan inadvertently tried to even things up a little.

> On my 33rd op, 3 October, I was flying No.2 to the Wingco, Lloyd Chadburn, escorting 72 Marauders to Schiphol and we met bags of 109s. Chad chased one, turned around a low cloud and I lost sight of him briefly. As he opened his throttle I heard him say, 'Go get him, Danny!' Then I saw a plane emerge from the cloud and I hit the gun button – just for half a second – then I saw the round wingtips, it was Chad's Spit! My heart sank, I hoped I hadn't hit my leader. Soon we were on our way back across the Channel and I heard Chad say 'My engine's a bit rough, but I'm OK' Again, my heart sank, but we got back all right. When I landed, I went over to Chad to apologise and by then they had spotted one bullet hole in his radiator. Chad just laughed and said, 'Never mind Danny, you're not the first one of my gang to take a shot at me!'

Five days later an unusual and extremely one-sided combat took place during an ASR patrol by four Spitfires of 402 Squadron. Flight Lieutenant de Niverville, Flying Officer Dodd and Pilot Officers Moore and Woloschuk happened upon a three-engined Dornier Do 24, one of a number used by the *Luftwaffe* for its own ASR duties along the Dutch coast. Each pilot attacked in turn and all secured strikes on the flying-boat, but a second attack by Moore delivered the *coup de grâce* . His cannon shells ripped off sections of the aircraft's wing, after which it immediately plunged into the sea. There were no survivors.

162

Doug Booth, Freddie Green and Al McFadden of 416 Squadron. (*Sager*)

Bad weather for much of early October severely hampered operations and it was not until the middle of the month that an attempt could be made to re-launch the medium bomber offensive against airfield and communications targets in northern Europe. Even so, a Ramrod from Tangmere had to be cancelled on the 18th and four days later a similar operation was re-called due to 10/10 cloud over France. Although not strictly an operational sortie, the latter trip nearly proved to be the last for Flight Lieutenant Doug Booth of 416 Squadron.

We landed at Friston to refuel and my No.2 advised me I was puffing glycol in the circuit. My aircraft was DN-R and I dismissed the comment: no way, not with 'R for reliable'. We were supposed to rendezvous with some American bombers just off the French coast at 12,000ft and I guess Met had tried to squeeze a bombing run in between fronts because when we got to the enemy coast we were at 3,500ft under heavy cloud and rain, with static on the R/T. As we were loafing back across the Channel I could see Beachy Head off in the distance and, looking over the side, a stream of glycol. I called the CO and suggested a course for the nearest airfield and toughed it out a few moments more. Subsequently my temperatures went off the clock and I could see red under my engine cowling. I was close to shore and wondered if I could get over land, but I told the CO I was catching fire and his reply was, 'Bale out, bale out!'

Well we don't get to practise leaving single-engined aircraft so I remembered reading a recent account wherein S/L Jack Charles had had to vacate his aircraft at 20,000ft off the Dutch coast and had used the bunt procedure. Accordingly, I throttled back, slid my coupé top back and put the door on the half lock. I undid my oxygen, radio and straps, wound the trim forward and shoved the stick forward. As the aircraft nosed down, I popped up out of the cockpit – halfway: my chute had hung up on the finger pull on the front of the coupé top. The slipstream whipped my helmet off and I can remember tumbling over the starboard side and throwing up my arms for protection as the tail assembly whizzed by.

I pulled the ripcord and as I approached the surface I began to swing like a giant pendulum and hit the water backwards with a mighty splash. The next few minutes were a fight as I could not spill the chute because of the strong wind blowing. Eventually I got rid of it and then the CO_2 bottle on my Mae West did not inflate. When I reached around for my dinghy cord, that was gone. At this point I was under the water, up for a breath, then under again. The waves were in the order of four feet, and I remember thinking, this is a hell of a way to go.

Eventually an air-sea rescue launch (No.513) arrived, it had a large arm and net with two sailors hanging on. As they came along-side, one minute they were shaking hands with me, the next they were out of reach. I thought, if they don't pick me up pronto the ship will go aground (I had drunk that much water), but then they got a boat hook under my Mae West and dumped me on the deck like a wet rag. They pumped my ribs and took me below and for the first time in my life I passed the offer of a drink of rum! I was put ashore and spent one night shivering and shaking in a rest home on Beachy Head before being released and lorried to Brighton, the first stage of my journey back to Digby.

Following two Ramrods to Montdidier and Schiphol on the 24th, a blanket of fog descended over much of the south-east of the country. In fact, the weather was so bad that 416 Squadron had to remain at Hawkinge (where it had landed after the Schiphol trip) for eight days, before finally making it back to its home base. Having done so, the fog clamped in once again and did not lift until the 3rd, when another Marauder escort mission was laid on, the target, once again, being Schiphol. The disappointments of recent weeks would be quickly forgotten as the Digby Wing took off for what would be its most successful day of the war. Art Sager, by now a Flight Lieutenant, was one of those airborne.

On this show (Ramrod 290) the Digby Wing is assigned to close escort of 72 Marauders flying in boxes of 18 at 14,000ft. The Coltishall Wing is to fly above and ahead of the bombers. The day starts out badly with fog at Digby but it clears by eleven and after an early lunch, the Wing gets airborne and arrives at Coltishall in time for the briefing. It's cool, clear and cloudless, ideal weather for bombing and for air fighting.

We rendezvous with the Marauders as they climb over the North Sea. Chad, leading 402, takes position slightly above and to starboard of the two leading boxes while Freddy Green with 416 covers the last two, also on the right. When light flak appears at the Dutch coast the extra fuel tanks are released. On the way into the target the flak intensifies and the sky is full of black and dirty grey blotches, some showing red as they explode. They bracket the bombers and it seems impossible that any will get through without being hit, but they plough steadily on, the boxes remaining intact.

Over Schiphol – you can just make out the aerodrome ahead – the leading box of 18 drops its bombs and begins to turn port, still in close formation, back to the coast. The second box follows and now you can see the explosions below. They're right on target, on the aerodrome itself and on buildings around it. When the last box releases its bombs – a waterfall of silver in the middle of the flak – 416 wheels with it, north and then west, staying close.

As the first box of bombers reached the coast a gaggle of around fifteen Me 109s of II/JG3 made a somewhat half-hearted attempt to get behind the leaders but were prevented from doing so by 402 Squadron, engagements continuing for the next fifteen minutes from the coast to approximately eighteen miles offshore. Lloyd Chadburn (Red 1) dispatched two enemy aircraft in quick succession, each victory backed up by other members of his section. In the short gap between each combat, Chadburn saw three other aircraft going down in flames and two parachutes.

Geoff Northcott (Blue 1) led his section in to attack the second of a pair of 109s and fired a burst from thirty degrees off on the port side. He was then forced to break sharply when informed that his wingman was missing, at which point he saw an aircraft disintegrating in flames which he took to be that of his No.2 (Flying Officer Graham). Graham was still around, however, having lost his leader in haze, and later reported that the aircraft that had blown up was the 109 that Northcott had been firing at.

By now the Messerschmitts had been split up and were in complete disarray. Flight Lieutenant John Mitchner noticed a lone 109 coming in from behind the bombers, and although he managed to get onto its tail, he was not able to open fire as it carried out a series of steep turns to left and right. Suddenly it straightened out, but just as Mitchner was closing in for the kill, he saw the hood fly off and the pilot bale out. Looking back, he observed another mêlée about five miles away and quickly joined in. He had no difficulty closing onto another 109 and fired several bursts which struck its forward fuselage. Soon after, the aircraft flicked onto its back and burst into flames, its pilot also taking to his parachute.

At the head of 416 Squadron's Green section, Art Sager dived down onto four 109s, two of which broke away to head inland, Sager attacking the right-hand Messerschmitt while his wingman, Flying Officer W.H. Jacobs, went for the other. A short burst damaged the 109, but a cannon stoppage then made aiming impossible. He need not have worried unduly as his attack was taken up by Dan Noonan, who secured further hits, the 109 crashing in flames on the outskirts of Zandvoort. Sager then pulled up to witness the aircraft that had been attacked by Jacobs coming down a short distance away, but it was clear that his wingman had been hit as his Spitfire was pouring glycol. He did not return.

Following his initial victory, Noonan climbed steeply from ground level up to 2,000ft where he saw a solitary 109 approaching from the west. It flew towards him and at first attempted to get on his tail by turning steeply, its pilot then trying to make him overshoot by closing his throttle. Despite such action, Noonan was able to out-manoeuvre the 109 quite easily and fired several bursts from 100 yards, securing hits on the fuselage. The cockpit hood flew off, but before its pilot could bale out it flicked onto its back and dived vertically into the ground.

The final combat involved Flight Lieutenant Doug Booth.

> I was leading White section as we escorted the third box of bombers away from the target and headed for home. We had crossed out over the enemy coast and there was a lot of chatter on the R/T as the forward echelons were obviously in a scrap. I spotted three Me 109s approaching from the sea about 1,000ft below. I peeled off to port and dove to attack. As I closed, the 109 took evasive action while diving to the deck. I fired several short bursts and then it levelled out before suddenly half-rolling and diving into the sea. I wondered if they were heading back to base, out of ammo. In any event I think

they were caught by surprise, not expecting us coming from the land.

As most of the action had taken place towards the middle and rear of the bomber formation, the Coltishall Wing had little to do, although 64's CO, Squadron Leader M.G.L. 'Mike' Donnet DFC, was able to put in a claim for a probable. Of those shot down, Flying Officer Jacobs was killed when his aircraft crashed near Zandvoort, and on the German side, five pilots were killed including the *Kommandeur* of II/JG3, *Major* Kurt Brandle.

With large-scale bombing raids becoming less frequent due to the onset of winter weather, thoughts turned once again to Rhubarbs over Holland, although all too soon the folly of such operations became apparent. Reports had been received of German torpedo-bombers training over the Zuider Zee and on 13 November an attempt was made to attack them. Eight aircraft departed for Coltishall in the early morning to be refuelled and briefed, the intention being that four would carry out

Lloyd Chadburn and Geoff Northcott prepare to speak to the press after the successful operation on 3/11/43. (*Sager*)

Digby Wing pilots 3/11/43 (L to R) Noonan, Booth, Green, Sager, Mitchner, Northcott and Chadburn. (*Booth*)

the mission, while the remainder would take off twenty minutes later to provide withdrawal cover. The attack formation was to be led by Art Sager in EN950 with Flight Sergeant H. Dubnick (EP564) as his No.2, the second pair comprising Dan Noonan in EP452 and Flying Officer J.B. Gould in AB910.

The section crossed the North Sea at low level, in wide line abreast formation. As land came into view, overload fuel tanks were dropped and speed increased, but almost as soon as the coast was crossed, Sager's aircraft was hit by flak, a large hole being torn in the fuselage just aft of the cockpit. A quick inspection by Noonan revealed serious damage but this could not be communicated to Sager as his radio was dead. Using sign language, Noonan made it clear that the operation would have to be aborted, and after a forty-minute flight back across the North Sea, a very relieved section leader landed at Coltishall.

It soon became apparent just how lucky Sager had been. A shell had entered his aircraft on the port side just a few feet behind his head and had then exploded inside the fuselage exiting as shrapnel, evidenced by numerous small holes on the starboard side. Only the armour plating behind his seat had saved him. Rhubarbs were usually flown at the discretion of Squadron and Flight Commanders, some of whom thought that the risks were too great in view of the amount of damage that could actually be inflicted. Indeed, further mishaps in the weeks to come would lead to the Digby Wing phasing out this type of operation.

F/L Art Sager shows off flak damage to EN950 on 13/11/43. (*Sager*)

Over at Coltishall, 64 Squadron's introduction to life in 12 Group had been relatively troublefree, their first confirmed combat success occurring during a Beaufighter shipping strike in the afternoon of 23 November. Gold section, led by new CO Squadron Leader E. Cassidy DFC, remained on the western side of the ships to offer protection to the Beaufighters on their way out. One of the Beaus was hit by flak and before Cassidy could swing his section round to assist, an Me 109 appeared at low level and shot it down with a single burst. The Spitfires gave chase and caught up with it just as it was about to launch an attack on another Beaufighter. Cassidy fired several bursts which hit the 109 in its forward fuselage causing a glycol leak and setting its engine on fire. When all of his ammunition had been used up, Flying Officer Kelly (Gold 3), together with Sergeant Thorne, went into the attack and the Messerschmitt was eventually shot down into the sea to the west of Egmond.

Back over the convoy, Flight Lieutenant Johnny Plagis DFC (Charlie 1) was engaging one of a pair of Fw 190s which were attempting to regain land after delivering a brief attack on one of the Beaufighters. Plagis closed in and fired from 400 yards' range, noting a number of strikes on the Focke-Wulf's fuselage. Although there was no sign of smoke, his fire

X4257 of 64 Squadron first flew as a Mark I on 17/8/40 and was written off in a crash-landing on 3/7/44. (*Cooper*)

had crippled the 190 which shortly afterwards dived into the sea about five miles north-north-west of Den Helder.

One of the last big operations of the year for 12 Group's Spitfire squadrons took place on 26 November when USAAF Marauders raided the airfield at Cambrai-Epinoy (Ramrod 336 Part III). Once again 402 and 416 Squadrons provided close escort and, after taking off from their forward base at Manston, met up with the bombers off Dungeness at 13,000ft. For once the German reaction was too slow and a *Schwarm* of Fw 190s were seen making a hasty take-off just before the first bombs began to fall. While the rest of the squadron stayed with the Marauders, Art Sager took his section down in a steep dive after the 190s which were streaking away at low level in a desperate attempt to find safety.

Using his height advantage to good effect, and with his airspeed registering in excess of 460mph, Sager quickly caught up with the Focke-Wulfs, one of whom was lagging behind the other three. Making sure that his aircraft was correctly trimmed, he closed in behind the straggler and fired a burst of cannon and machine-gun into its fuselage. It immediately burst into flames, turned sharply to the right and hit the ground at a shallow angle, before exploding as it hit a railway embankment. As it did

Lt Chapin of 64 Squadron with BL 370. (*Cooper*)

so, Sager became aware of his No.2, Flight Sergeant Dubnick (EN908), flashing past on his left-hand side, so close that his aircraft was damaged by debris thrown up in the blast. Although he could have gained sufficient height to bale out, Dubnick elected to carry out a force-landing but misjudged his speed and was killed when his aircraft hit the ground and broke up. The pilot of the Fw 190, who was also killed, was *Leutnant* Hans Fischer of 5/JG26.

During the first half of December 402 and 416 Squadrons at Digby managing only 128 flying hours between them due to poor weather, and on the 19th both departed to Scotland for two-week gunnery courses, 402 going to 14 APC at Ayr, with 416 flying further north to Peterhead. At Coltishall, one of 64 Squadron's senior pilots, Flight Lieutenant Tony Cooper, flew only six ops in the month, four of which were hampered by thick cloud. Although 12 Group's Spitfire V pilots would continue to operate their aircraft on long sea crossings to the Dutch coast whenever they could, they were not the only ones faced with such demanding conditions.

ELEVEN

Perranporth Wing, September 1943– January 1944

W hile the Spitfire V was taking the war to the enemy over Holland and northern France, at the other end of the English Channel it was carrying out the vital task of protecting long-range Sunderland flying-boats from attack in the south-west approaches. By the autumn of 1943 the threat posed by U-boat strikes on Allied shipping in the North Atlantic had largely been overcome, but it was vitally important that maximum pressure be maintained, as any resurgence by Admiral Dönitz's forces would have seriously jeopardised the build-up to invasion. As Coastal Command's aircraft were coming under threat of attack as they flew to their patrol areas in the Bay of Biscay, Spitfire squadrons based in the far south-west of Cornwall flew frequent 'Instep' patrols in an attempt to stop the activities of the *Luftwaffe*'s long-range fighters which operated from airfields in the Brest peninsula. In the forefront of these actions were the units stationed at the airfield of Perranporth.

Opened in April 1941 as a satellite of Portreath, Perranporth was situated above the sheer cliffs on the Cornish coastline approximately ten miles north-west of Truro. Its exposed location gave little protection from bad weather and operations were frequently hampered by rain and strong winds. The airfield offered only the most basic of facilities consisting of three runways, with blast pens arranged around the surrounding perimeter track. Shelter for aircraft was provided by a single 'T2' hangar and a number of blister hangars.

By mid-September 1943 two Spitfire V squadrons were based at Perranporth: No.453 (RAAF) led by Squadron Leader K.M. Barclay and No.66 commanded by Squadron Leader Keith Lofts DFC, a pre-war Auxiliary pilot who had fought in the Battle of France. In addition to Instep duties, the units also took on the usual routine of bomber escorts, offensive sweeps and convoy patrols.

On 24 September the Perranporth squadrons were briefed in the morning by Wing Commander 'Jack' Charles, now Wing Leader at Portreath, for a Ramrod operation to the combined airfield and seaplane base at Lanveoc/Poulmic near Brest. Rendezvous was made with twelve Mitchells at the Lizard and a course set for the objective, initially at low level to avoid radar detection. After sixteen minutes the force began to climb and by the time they passed Ushant, 66 were at 16,000ft, with 453 at 18,000ft. Shortly after, twelve Me 110s were seen heading westwards to attack the bombers and 66 (led by Wing Commander Charles) broke immediately to commence a series of running engagements in the area around Pointe St Mathieu.

Flight Lieutenant George Elcombe (AA881 – Blue 1) selected one of two Me 110s away to his left and dived to attack. His initial burst from 350–400 yards was wide of the mark, but on closing to 150 yards he fired his remaining ammunition which hit the 110 in both engines and fuse-lage. It burst into flames and fell away to crash in the sea about ten miles west of Cap Chevres. Two parachutes were seen to open. In the mean-time, Elcombe's No.2, Flight Sergeant G. Thomas (AD260), was after another 110 which he attacked on the port quarter with a two-second burst, setting fire to its port engine. Very soon the whole left-hand side of the 110 was wreathed in flames and it was last seen in an uncontrolled dive towards the sea. Flight Sergeant R. Logan (BL426 – Blue 3) saw two 110s turning left in front of him and latched onto the right-hand one, following it through a number of extremely violent 'corkscrew' manoeuvres as the German aircraft attempted to get away. At first his fire did not have any effect, but on closing to 250 yards he saw strikes on the port engine, which began to smoke badly and eventually caught fire.

Having led 66 Squadron into attack, Wing Commander Charles (BL631) used his height advantage to close on the second in a section of four Me 110s, firing three separate bursts, the last at no more than 100 yards. Several pieces of debris came back from the 110's starboard engine, and as Charles broke away, he saw it flick into a spin and catch fire. One of its crew managed to bale out before it hit the sea, eleven miles west of Brest.

Yellow section also saw combat with Sergeant A. Hopkins (EP597 – Yellow 4) diving after two 110s which were already coming under attack from a pair of Spitfires. As these broke away, Hopkins moved in and followed one of the German aircraft down to sea level as it made a desperate attempt to escape. By now they were nearly at the entrance to Brest harbour, but at a range of 200 yards Hopkins fired all of his ammu-nition which put both the Messerschmitt's engines out of action. Shortly after it hit the sea and broke up. As the 110 had already been hit during

Pilots of 66 Squadron, Back row (L to R) Emery, Brunner, Hamer, Deytrekk, Logan. Front (L to R) Varey, Jackson. (*Varey*)

the previous attack, the victory was eventually shared with Flight Lieutenant V. Chocholin of 310 Squadron, who was himself shot down and killed a few minutes later. During the combat 453 Squadron stayed up as cover and were not engaged.

After a number of uneventful convoy patrols and ASR sorties, 66 and 453 Squadrons had a busy day on 3 October, one that provides a good example of the mobility that was now required of fighter squadrons. The day began with a dawn departure to Bradwell Bay in Essex, from where the wing took off in mid-morning to provide close escort for B-26 Marauders attacking Woensdrecht. After lunch they flew to West Malling to participate in 11 Group Ramrod 259, another Marauder escort, this time to the airfield at Beauvais. Following take-off at 1625 hrs, a successful rendezvous was made twenty miles north-west of Ault and the squadrons slotted into their positions on either side of the bombers, 1,000ft above. After the resting of Squadron Leader Barclay, 453 Squadron were being led by their new CO, Squadron Leader D.G. Andrews DFC.

Several reports of enemy fighter activity were received but nothing was seen until after the bombers turned away from the target. To the south-east of Oisemont, four Fw 190s dived down onto 66 Squadron to carry out a hit-and-run attack before continuing their dive to ground level. Although the action was over in a few seconds, their fire was deadly accurate and Flight Sergeant A.J. Edwards (BL762 – Red 3), who had been lagging behind, was shot down. Shortly afterwards Pilot Officer R.J. Darcey, at the head of 453 Squadron's Blue section, noticed two Fw 190s behind the bombers and turned to go after them, but immediately came under attack from another not more than 150 yards behind him. Breaking hard left, he spiralled down to 9,000ft giving the 190 a full deflection shot as it went past, but saw no strikes.

The two Fw 190s that Darcey had seen were then chased by Flying Officer L.J. Hansell, but they saw him in good time and performed a defensive split, each turning in opposite directions. Hansell went after the 190 which had broken to the right and achieved a number of hits on its starboard wing and wing-root, but by this time its partner was coming in from behind and he was forced to disengage by climbing into the glare of the sun. Forming up with Blue 1, he then made an uneventful return and landed with the rest of the squadron at Kenley. The only other member of 453 Squadron to fire his guns was Pilot Officer J.F. Olver (Blue 2), but he made no claim.

After staying overnight at Kenley, the wing flew back to base via Exeter on 4 October but a spell of poor weather hampered operations over the next few days and it was not until the 8th that offensive sorties could be resumed. Three separate formations of Spitfires departed Perranporth in the early morning to carry out patrols over the south-western approaches to provide protection to aircraft being delivered to the Mediterranean from No.1 Overseas Aircraft Despatch Unit (OADU) at Portreath. The first aircraft away were seven Spitfires of 66 Squadron at 0730 hrs, followed five minutes later by seven of 453 Squadron. The final section comprised four aircraft of 66 plus three of 453, together with Wing Commander P.J. Simpson DFC, who had recently taken over as Wing Leader at Portreath from Wing Commander Charles.

Instep patrols were carried out over triangular courses which extended up to 125 miles in a south-westerly direction from Perranporth. As the marauding *Luftwaffe* fighters invariably flew at low level, radar provided little help, and as a result contact with the enemy was a decidedly hit-and-miss affair. On this occasion the first and third patrols saw nothing, which was in marked contrast to the seven aircraft of 453 Squadron.

Having flown at 3,000ft for a short period to clear sea mist, the Spitfires dropped down to 300ft and flew on a course of 253 degrees for thirty minutes. At 0820 hrs they turned left onto 156 degrees for a further eleven minutes before making for home. Shortly after their final turn, Squadron

Leader Andrews saw eight aircraft heading north-west and identified them as Me 110s. They were flying at 200ft in two sections of four, 300 yards apart. As Andrews led the squadron in to the attack, the 110s began a slow turn to port and broke formation when the range was down to 500 yards. Within seconds all aircraft were involved in a hectic dogfight low over the sea.

Red section went into action first, followed by Yellow section, led by Pilot Officer C.R. 'Rusty' Leith, whose aircraft had suffered an electrical fault which had caused its R/T and reflector gunsight to pack up. Despite such a handicap he still managed to account for two of the 110s. Closing behind one at 150 yards, he fired a zero deflection shot with machine-guns only, which succeeded in setting fire to the enemy aircraft's port engine. The blaze rapidly spread to its mainplane and it gradually lost height and hit the sea at a shallow angle. Immediately afterwards Leith observed another Me 110 streaking for home and pursued it flat out. After a five-minute chase he was in position to launch a quarter attack which the German pilot countered by breaking sharply towards him. A turning match then ensued, but with his gunsight out of action, Leith stood little chance of obtaining any hits. Just as he was considering pulling up to dive on the 110 vertically, its pilot lost control when a wingtip brushed the water and it cartwheeled into the sea.

During the initial mêlée, Flying Officer P.V. McDade (Yellow 2) tried a couple of ineffectual 'squirts' head-on, but had better luck when he got on the tail of another of the Messerschmitts. The 110s appeared to be particularly vulnerable to fire damage and a short burst caused it to burst into flames, stall vertically and plunge into the water. Looking round for a second victim, he got behind another which had turned away from the main gaggle and struck the aircraft's port engine, mainplane and cockpit. Although McDade's Spitfire then suffered a cannon stoppage, the 110 was already on fire from its port engine and it was unable to maintain height and subsequently crashed.

The action was not entirely one-sided as Flying Officer H.M. 'Hal' Parker (EP252 – Yellow 3) was seen to dive into the sea at a steep angle, and Flight Lieutenant R.H.S. Ewins (EP364 – Red 3) was also in trouble. Having set the port engine of an Me 110 well alight, he was forced to break off his attack as he became aware of tracer rounds flashing past him. On attempting to rejoin the rest of the squadron, his engine began to run rough due to a serious glycol leak and he had no alternative but to bale out. While Flight Sergeant Ross Currie (Red 2) and Flying Officer Leo McAuliffe (Yellow 4) climbed to transmit for a position fix, Squadron Leader Andrews remained at low level to keep an eye on Ewins, who lost no time in getting into his dinghy and erecting its sail. He was eventually rescued in the early afternoon by a Royal Navy destroyer after five hours in the water. During this period he saw two further formations of Me 110s and witnessed one of their number being shot down by a Spitfire of 610 Squadron. Despite an extensive search, the body of Flying Officer Parker was not located.

The Me 110s that 453 Squadron had encountered all came from II/ZG1 who were to suffer further losses to the Perranporth squadrons later the same day during 10 Group Ramrod 91, yet another attack on Brest-Lanveoc/Poulmic. After briefing by Wing Commander Simpson, twenty-two Spitfires of 66 and 453 Squadrons took off at 1445 hrs to link up with eighteen Bostons (twelve from 88 Squadron and six from 342 Squadron) over Lizard Point at 14,000ft. With 66 Squadron to the right of the bombers and 453 to the left, the force proceeded to the target where around eight to ten Me 110s were seen climbing up to attack.

No.66 Squadron were in the best position to intercept and Squadron Leader Lofts (AR518 – Red 1) led his section down, positioning himself above and behind one of the aircraft in the rear of the enemy formation. During the dive he found that his overtaking speed was too great and he was forced to break away without achieving any hits. He then went for the last in a section of five 110s but came under attack himself and had to climb to stay out of trouble. Red 2 and 3 then took up the attack and succeeded in splitting up the enemy aircraft, which allowed the rest of the squadron to select individual targets.

Flight Lieutenant George Elcombe (BL583 – Blue 1) dived on a pair of Me 110s which broke in opposite directions as soon as they saw him coming. Selecting the left-hand aircraft, he opened fire at 600 yards but found he was closing so rapidly that he had to close his throttle completely to avoid overshooting. Positioning his Spitfire seventy-five yards behind and slightly above, Elcombe fired a one-second burst which produced an explosion in the 110's port motor and wing-root. As he was so close behind, he was forced to fly through the sheet of flame which spread back from the 110's port wing and experienced a terrific buffeting which buckled his elevators and put his fore and aft trim out of action. The Messerschmitt was last seen spinning down, out of control.

While Elcombe was dealing with this enemy aircraft, his No.2, Squadron Leader W. Foster (AA881), was chasing after another that had its sights set on a solitary Spitfire. Firing from 150 yards he witnessed several hits including a cannon strike on the starboard engine which gave off heavy smoke. Continuing his attack, Foster closed to thirty yards, narrowly avoiding a collision as he did so. The 110 eventually fell away in an uncontrolled spiral dive. The third member of Blue section, Flying Officer D. Baker (EP639), also met with success when he dived on a 110, hitting its starboard engine severely enough to set it alight. He then watched the aircraft as it descended and saw it explode as it hit the ground near a large wood.

Apart from an Me 110 damaged by Squadron Leader Lofts, the only other claim was a probable credited to Flying Officer C. Reeder (AD331 – Yellow 3), who attacked another 110, setting fire to its port engine. In marked contrast to 66 Squadron, 453 had an uneventful trip and all aircraft were safely down at Perranporth by 1630 hrs.

Another Ramrod operation (No.92) was flown the next day, but worsening weather led to the twenty-four Mitchells dropping their bombs on Morlaix instead of the primary target, the airfield at Brest-Guipavas. Low cloud and mist caused problems as the Spitfires returned, only two of 453 Squadron's aircraft making it back to base with two more landing at Exeter and the rest at Harrowbeer. The situation did not improve a great

F/O Arthur Varey of 66 Squadron. (*Varey*)

deal over the next few days and it was not until 13 October that unrestricted operations could be carried out once again.

At 1630 hrs eight aircraft of 66 Squadron took off to carry out an Instep patrol although two had to return early with technical trouble. The remaining six Spitfires flew the familiar course low over the sea, and just as they were turning onto their final leg, Squadron Leader Lofts (AR344 – Red 1) sighted a Ju 88 which was seen climbing steeply in an effort to reach the safety of clouds. The attack was commenced as soon as long-range tanks had been dropped with Lofts firing a long eight-second burst. His wingman, Flight Sergeant R. Casburn (W3168), then took over and maintained his fire as he followed the German aircraft into cloud.

The Ju 88 had already been hit several times and was unable to maintain its height, which allowed Flying Officer T. Hamer (EP639 – Red 3) to move in. He inflicted further damage, but was then forced to break to avoid getting in the way of Flying Officer A.W. Varey DFM (Yellow 1), who was already firing at the stricken Junkers. The other members of Yellow section, Lieutenant J. Thompson USAAC and Flight Sergeant J. Tidy, then attacked in turn by which time the Ju 88 was completely enveloped in flames and it eventually stalled and dived into the sea. The Spitfires orbited for a few minutes but there was no sign of survivors, and they returned to base after transmitting for a DF fix.

On 16 October 453 Squadron left Perranporth for Skaebrae in the Orkney Islands and were replaced by 341 (Alsace) Squadron, who carried out their first operational sorties the following day. No.341 Squadron had been formed at Turnhouse in January 1943 from Free French personnel who had previously formed *Groupe de Chasse* 1, which had been attached to various RAF fighter squadrons in the Middle East. Its CO was *Commandant* Bernard Duperior who had joined up with Free French forces in Canada in early 1941 having previously flown in the Vichy Air Force.

The next confrontation with the *Luftwaffe* took place on 23 October during an ASR operation looking for survivors of a naval action off the Ile de Batz. No.66 Squadron encountered four Fw 190s who showed little inclination to fight, two immediately climbing for the protection of the overcast above. Of the remaining pair, one was engaged by Yellow section while the other was seen in a tight left-hand turn low over the sea by Flight Lieutenant George Elcombe (BL583 – Blue 1). Tucking in behind the 190 at 160kt IAS, Elcombe saw white condensation trails streaming back from its wingtips as its pilot attempted to out-turn him. Within one and a half turns, however, he was in a firing position and achieved multiple strikes on the wing-roots of the 190, which then disappeared under the nose of his aircraft. On breaking to starboard he saw a patch of burning oil on the sea, his victory later being confirmed by Wing Commander Simpson. Its companion, which was attacked by Yellow section, was eventually shot down by Flight Lieutenant J. Jackson (AA839). Sadly, any feelings of elation at the successful outcome of this action were soon dispelled when EP639 and AD260 collided over Perranporth on their return, killing Flying Officer D. Baker and Warrant Officer D. Mace.

With daylight attacks on Germany by USAAF Eighth Air Force heavy bombers increasing in intensity, a number of *Luftwaffe* units were re-called in the latter half of 1943 to take part in the huge air battles now taking place over the Reich. This withdrawal of forces severely restricted defensive operations in other areas and had a profound effect on the air war over north-western France. Although the RAF's Ramrod operations continued whenever weather conditions allowed, for the close-escort squadrons at least, this reduction in opposition meant that combat with their opposite numbers became a very rare occurrence indeed. In its place were the hazards imposed by flak, which were particularly bad during an attack by Mitchells on Cherbourg docks on 24 October. As close escort, the Spitfires of 66 and 341 Squadrons flew 1–2,000ft above the bombers, a height which usually put them beyond the worst of the anti-aircraft fire. On this occasion, however, accurate heavy flak was experienced from 10–17,000ft which caused minor damage to two of 341 Squadron's aircraft.

The following day, 10 Group Ramrod 95 took twenty-four Mitchells of 2 Group to Lanveoc/Poulmic with the Perranporth Wing, as usual, in attendance. Once again flak was deadly accurate and scored a direct hit on one of the Mitchells, FR178 of 320 Squadron, which blew up with such force that FR162, its closest companion, was severely damaged and only just made it back to crash-land at Perranporth. Another Mitchell, FR166, was seen to dive into the Channel on the way back. The Spitfire of Flying Officer J. Stastny of 312 Squadron (AB372) was also hit by flak over the target and he was forced to bale out into the sea. Large numbers of ASR sorties were flown until last light and for the whole of the next day, but none of the missing aircrew was found.

Following this operation, convoy patrols and shipping recces took over for a while, with only occasional scrambles to liven things up. On 7 November 66 Squadron departed for Hornchurch where it began flying Spitfire IXs and was replaced by another French unit, 340 Squadron, whose aircraft proudly carried the Cross of Lorraine below the cockpit. From this point on, 340 and 341 Squadrons began a long and successful partnership that would ultimately see them form No.145 Wing as part of Second Tactical Air Force.

No.340 Squadron pilots sprint to their Spitfire Vbs. (*via Philip Jarrett*)

In the meantime they were set to continue with the Spitfire LFVbs that had been inherited from the outgoing squadrons, and their first operation as a wing took place on 16 November during 10 Group Circus 60, which consisted of a fighter sweep over the Brest peninsula in support of two squadrons of Bomphoons attacking Guipavas and Lanveoc/Poulmic airfields. The next day, 340 Squadron took off at 1625 hrs to commence a sea search for two enemy vessels reported to be in the Channel. Shortly after crossing the coast at low level near Lizard Point, BL583, flown by Sergeant P.N.A. Tummers, veered away and began a climbing turn to about 200ft before turning over and diving straight into the sea. Royal Navy minesweepers were operating close by and were quickly on the scene, but there was no sign of wreckage or of the pilot. The operation was continued, but the Axis ships were not seen.

In early November the medium bombers of 2 Group had commenced an offensive against V-1 launching sites that were now appearing in ever-increasing numbers, in the Pas de Calais. London was the primary target, but aerial reconnaissance had revealed more sites further to the west which threatened the vital south-coast ports that were needed for the forthcoming invasion. On 26 November a large-scale attack was carried out on the site at Martinvast to the south of Cherbourg by Bostons and

Mitchells drawn from seven squadrons, the bombers attacking in three waves at ten-minute intervals. Operating from Church Stanton, 340 and 341 Squadrons joined up with twenty-four Mitchells of 98 and 180 Squadrons near the Isle of Wight at 14,000ft, before proceeding to the target. A few Fw 190s were seen in the distance but these were adequately dealt with by Typhoons and Spitfire IXs flying top cover, the main danger, once again, coming from flak, which claimed one of the Mitchells and caused two others to collide.

After returning to Church Stanton, both squadrons were then obliged to stay there for the next three days as bad weather closed in, preventing all flying. Such were the conditions, they did not manage to get back to Perranporth until 1 December having spent a further two days at Portreath. This turned out to be a portent of things to come, and the offensive against the V-1 launching sites had to be put on hold until the 20th. In the intervening period a few convoy patrols were flown and the wing tried a Rodeo operation on 18 December which was again spoilt by the elements. No.341 Squadron became lost in cloud, while 340 Squadron climbed to 20,000ft in a vain attempt to find clear air before giving up and returning to base.

Further convoy patrols were carried out during the rest of the month, plus two fighter sweeps as withdrawal cover to Typhoons, but it was not until 30 December that contact was finally made with the enemy. On this occasion eight aircraft of 341 Squadron took off at 1410 hrs to complete an Instep patrol led by *Capitaine* Pierre Montet (AA846), who flew under the *nom de guerre* of Christian Martell. As they turned onto the final leg of

No.340 Squadron Spitfire Vbs prepare to take off. (*via Philip Jarrett*)

their patrol, they encountered four Fw 190s which immediately made off towards the nearest cloud cover. Firing a short burst at the last in the formation, Montet witnessed strikes on its fuselage before it disappeared from view. On coming down to sea level again, he fired at another which accelerated out of range, streaming smoke. *Sous Lieutenant* R. Borne (AB241) also attacked a lone Fw 190 with several bursts, during which debris was seen to fall from its tail. The 190 then sped away south-east with Borne in pursuit, but he was not able to close the gap and was eventually forced to break off due to fuel shortage.

In the morning of 5 January 1944 the wing was briefed for Rodeo 61, which was intended as support for attacks by USAAF B-17s on targets in western France. Before take-off an extremely unfortunate accident occurred, one that was repeated at many other wartime fighter stations and emphasised the Spitfire's lack of forward vision when on the ground. As Sergeant P. Fabesch of 341 Squadron was taxiing W3935 to the take-off point, he collided with *Sous Lieutenant* R. Chevalier, who was awaiting take-off clearance in BM317. Chevalier was killed in the pile-up and the impact was so severe that both aircraft immediately burst into flames. Fabesch managed to get out of his machine suffering from minor burns to his face. The operation itself was uneventful and nothing was seen of the Americans.

Over the next few weeks the Perranporth Wing provided close escort

View from Spitfire V emphasizing the pilot's many blind areas. (*Cooper*)

during a number of 11 Group Ramrods, accompanying 2 Group Mitchells and USAAF Ninth Air Force B-26 Marauders to various targets in north-east France. Forward bases for these missions were Ibsley and Tangmere, but once again there was no opposition and all of the operations passed off without incident.

In early February both 340 and 341 Squadrons were notified that they would shortly be re-equipped with Spitfire IXs, and the first of their new aircraft arrived soon after. By the middle of the month both squadrons were fully operational on the new variant and continued to fly from Perranporth until April, when they moved to Merston.

Although the Spitfire LFVb was still effective in its specialised low-altitude role, it was rapidly being superseded by more advanced versions of the Spitfire and it would only be a matter of time before the remaining examples were pensioned off, or relegated to be used by training units. Due to the demand for large numbers of fighter-bombers to cover the invasion, however, it would go on far longer than anyone at the time could have envisaged, and would write its name even more indelibly in the annals of Royal Air Force history.

TWELVE

THE DEANLAND WING

It had long been recognised that, for an invasion of northern France to be carried out successfully, large numbers of airfields would be needed along the south coast to house the massive numbers of fighters and fighter-bombers whose duty it would be to cover the ground forces. Proposals had been put forward as early as 1941 for advance landing grounds (ALGs) to back up existing stations, and eventually a total of twenty-three were constructed. All featured the most basic of facilities as they would only be required for a short period before and after the actual invasion.

The ALG at Deanland was situated five miles to the north-east of Lewes in Sussex and had first been put forward as a suitable location in 1942, the necessary land being requisitioned in early 1943. Preparatory work took the form of levelling, together with the removal of hedges, and this was followed in July by the arrival of No.16 Airfield Construction Group of the Royal Engineers who began work to upgrade the site to full ALG standard. Two runways were formed at ninety degrees to each other composed of Sommerfeld tracking, an all-weather surface constructed from heavy steel netting. Taxiways were similarly protected, and four blister hangars were erected so that maintenance could be carried out under cover. Unlike permanent stations, there was no accommodation for personnel as many of the squadrons amassed along the south coast would be required to relocate to France at short notice, and consequently everyone had quickly to get used to living under canvas.

Deanland became operational on 1 April 1944 with the arrival of three Polish Spitfire IX squadrons (302, 308 and 317) who stayed until the 26th, when they moved to another ALG at nearby Chailey. They were replaced three days later by the Spitfire LFVbs of 64 and 611 Squadrons from Coltishall, and the similar aircraft of 234 Squadron which flew in from Bolt Head. No.64 were commanded by New Zealander Squadron Leader John Mackenzie DFC, whose air combat record of six enemy aircraft destroyed was matched by Squadron Leader Bill Douglas DFC of 611, the Scot having secured all but one of his victories in Malta during 1942. No.234 Squadron was led by

Squadron Leader Phil Arnott, who had been awarded a DFC during his first tour with 130 Squadron.

In the run-up to the invasion the Deanland squadrons would be heavily involved in the 'softening up' process with attacks on gun batteries, communications and aerodrome targets, either directly in the form of armed reconnaissance sorties and sweeps, or indirectly in the escort of medium bombers. For personnel who had never experienced anything other than permanent stations, Deanland (or Tentland as it became known) took some getting used to, as Flight Lieutenant Tony Cooper of 64 Squadron recalls:

> Deanland was a bit of a come-down; luckily it was summer time when we suddenly found ourselves on this hump in the middle of the Downs. We were in tents and it took me back because my father in the First World War had had a truckle bed which was a wooden contraption over which canvas was stretched, with the same for a bath and wash stand, and it turned out that I had to use exactly the same thing. At night it was very cold, but when D-Day came up we didn't get much sleep as we were doing up to four shows a day and we were very busy.

In contrast to Tony Cooper's sleeping arrangements, certain enterprising ground crew discovered that sections of Sommerfeld wire-mesh

64 Squadron Spitfire LFVb undergoes maintenance in one of Deanland's blister hangars. (*Cooper*)

track, cut to the required size and laid over wooden uprights hammered into the ground, formed excellent mattresses.

Flying Officer George Sparrow of 234 Squadron remembers that the food consisted of little but rice and the air was full of Buzz bombs. In fact the V-1 flying bombs began to appear in increasing numbers shortly after D-Day and the barrage put up by the local gun defences led to many a sleepless night. Although all pilots were keen to have a go at shooting them down, they had been warned against attempting interceptions as the cruising speed of the V-1 usually varied between 350 and 400mph which was beyond the capability of the Spitfire V.

Another 234 Squadron pilot, Flight Sergeant Stan Farmiloe, was also unimpressed with the food at Deanland and recalls that the best meal of the day was usually to be had just before nightfall. Sitting around a blazing log fire, eggs were either boiled or poached and eaten with toast, all washed down with beer brought down from the local pub. Some of the Free French pilots proved to be particularly adept at catching and skinning rabbits, which were then roasted over an open fire, and there is also evidence that a surprising number of local chickens suffered a similar fate after being deemed 'lost'. In keeping with the rudimentary accommodation, toilet facilities were also rather basic, the latrines consisting of a deep trench over which one balanced on two parallel poles, the stench

S/L Phil Arnott of 234 Squadron. (*Halloran*)

187

being eased from time to time by the addition, and subsequent burning, of waste engine oil.

Over the next seven weeks all personnel would be pushed to the absolute limit and the stress of frequent operations would often be relieved by pranks and tomfoolery which would take place whenever the opportunity presented itself. One of the chief perpetrators of such activity on 234 Squadron was its CO, Phil Arnott, as Flying Officer David Ferguson witnessed on more than one occasion.

> Arnott had a remarkable party trick, usually produced when things were in full swing. He would suddenly feign illness, retire to a corner of the room, face the wall and we would be treated to what sounded like a ferocious expulsion of vomit! Only those in the know realised that he had, secreted inside his jacket, a full siphon of soda-water from which he released liquid in lengthy bursts. Disgusting, but very, very, realistic!

Following sector recces, operations got under way from Deanland on 2 May when its squadrons accompanied a force of seventy-two Marauders that attacked the railway marshalling yards at Valenciennes. On this occasion, at least, everything proceeded according to plan,

AR373 of 611 Squadron lands wheels-up. (*Cooper*)

bombing results were excellent, no flak was experienced and no enemy aircraft were seen.

By now the final preparations were being made for the D-Day landings and over the next three days the Deanland squadrons took part in Exercise Fabius, which was, in effect, a full dress rehearsal for the invasion. The exercise took place on the south coast between Littlehampton and Shoreham and involved the Spitfires in a pre-dawn take-off before flying low-level cover, the role they would undertake over the beaches of Normandy. As Deanland still had limited facilities for night flying, sorties in connection with Fabius were carried out from nearby Tangmere.

Despite the fact that three squadrons of Spitfires were set to operate from little more than an overgrown meadow, accidents would be relatively few, although there was hardly any room for error. Inevitably there were occasional mishaps, one of which caused a considerable fright for Flight Sergeant Charlie Potter of 234 Squadron.

> The Spit V was a wonderful aeroplane to fly with no vices in the air, but the narrowness of the undercart was a problem if a tyre burst on landing, which happened to me on the temporary narrow wire netting runway at Deanland. I found myself veering uncontrollably right towards a line of Spits parked alongside the runway. The only solution was to apply full right rudder, writing off the undercart and ending up a few feet from the line in a tangled heap! [this incident resulted in Cat. Ac damage to AD515 and occurred on 29 May after a Ramrod to Le Treport.]

Flight Sergeant Ian Walker of 611 Squadron had arrived at Deanland after everyone else following a period of leave. Having flown over from Coltishall in the unit's Tiger Moth, he carried out his first sector recce in Spitfire Vb AR373 (FY-J) on 7 May. Not having flown a Spitfire for some time he failed to ensure that his wheels were down and locked as a result of which his aircraft ploughed a neat furrow through the wire-mesh tracking on landing. Damage was minimal, but having carried out such a *faux pas* in full view of everyone, he thus said goodbye to any chance of a commission for the next six months! (Walker eventually left 611 Squadron with the rank of Flying Officer, having been mentioned in Despatches.)

Offensive operations were resumed on the 8th with a fighter sweep of the area around Rouen during which 64 Squadron's Gold section (comprising Flight Lieutenant Plagis and Flying Officers Law, Wellman and Thorpe) dropped down to strafe a 500-ton river boat that had been spotted on the Seine near Duclair. Any means of transport could now be considered a legitimate target and by the time the four had finished their attack, the boat was alight from end to end. Although a number of enemy aircraft were seen in the distance, they made no attempt to engage.

Another reconnaissance carried out the following morning produced no worthwhile targets, but Flying Officer D.N. 'Charlie' Greenhalgh of 234 Squadron, flying BL594, was soon in trouble as his engine lost power as the Spitfires swept along the route Berck sur Mer–Arras–Furnes. He turned back immediately, together with his No.2 Flight Sergeant Pete Bell, but shortly afterwards his aircraft was hit by flak. Although he announced that he was baling out, he did not have enough height to do so and was killed in the subsequent crash-landing.

More bomber escorts were flown over the next few days as protection for Mitchells and Bostons of 2 Group, but in the main *Luftwaffe* fighters were conspicuous by their absence and the only threat came from the German flak defences. Such operations could often be tedious, but on 12 May, during a Ramrod to the gun emplacement near Ault, 64 Squadron were allowed a more offensive role and were given clearance to strafe the guns after the bombing attack had been completed.

Bad weather over the next few days brought a temporary halt to the offensive, which gave pilots the opportunity to practise re-arming their aircraft, in addition to paying visits to Eastbourne baths to sharpen up their dinghy drills. On the few occasions when flying was possible, defensive patrols and practice interceptions were carried out, the rest of the time being spent huddled inside tents, trying to keep dry.

Operational flying recommenced in the evening of 19 May when the Spitfires of 234 and 611 Squadrons escorted Marauders to Dieppe. After the bombing had been successfully carried out the wing was vectored onto 'bandits', which turned out to be USAAF P-47 Thunderbolts. Both sides recognised each other before any harm was done, but this incident was the precursor of a serious problem that would be encountered around the time of D-Day, one that would lead to a number of Allied losses due to 'friendly fire'. In the meantime 64 Squadron was revelling in a low-level beat-up of the area around Le Havre, during which a barge was attacked and destroyed at Caudebec en Caux. From the pilots' point of view, this type of work could be exhilarating at times, and was especially so on this occasion as the Spitfires had to deliver their attack having flown under high-tension cables.

Two days later 64 and 234 Squadrons had an early start when they took part in a large-scale fighter operation from Manston which had the aim of causing maximum disruption to the rail system in northern France and Holland. From midnight on the 20th French civilians had been barred from using the rail network and the operation was timed so that

F/Sgt Reg Hooker of 234
Squadron demonstrates his
culinary expertise.
(*Fairweather*)

all aircraft were to be on patrol by 0730 hrs to achieve maximum surprise. The two squadrons had one of their most successful days in the run-up to D-Day and went on to account for twelve locomotives destroyed, seven by 64 and five by 234. All returned safely, although Lieutenant 'Mike' Bernard of 234 Squadron had a fright as his Spitfire snagged a cable which then coiled round the fuselage of his aircraft (BL646), restricting rudder movement. As the cable had also wrapped itself around the canopy, there was no possibility of him being able to bale out if control was lost, but after a very careful flight home, he succeeded in landing at Manston without mishap.

For the rest of the month bomber escorts were flown with monotonous regularity, although on occasion the Spitfires were able to go hunting for ground targets once their responsibilities to the bombers had been fulfilled. An evening operation to the coastal gun battery at Longues on 27 May provided the ideal opportunity, and afterwards the squadrons split up to look for targets of opportunity. As 234 Squadron contented themselves with strafing goods wagons near Beauchamp, 611 went for a tug and three barges on the Seine and later destroyed a locomotive south of Longues. No.64 Squadron did even better, finding a large number of targets and was somewhat spoilt for choice. These ranged from staff cars to military lorries and locomotives, although Pilot Officers Coupar and

De Verteuil did well to avoid a stationary train which opened up with light and medium flak as they circled it at 3,000ft. Two days later 64 and 611 Squadrons had further success during a sweep to the south-east of Dieppe, shooting up goods wagons and a signal box, in addition to destroying several military vehicles near Neufchatel.

After a hectic month, the pace of operations reduced considerably in early June and speculation began to mount that the Allied invasion of northern Europe might be imminent. The little flying that was carried out was mainly of a defensive nature, and on 3 June the 234 Squadron ORB noted 'a feeling of tension' as everyone wondered whether the big day was finally about to happen. On the 4th an order came through for all aircraft to be painted in special recognition markings, consisting of eighteen-inch wide black and white stripes to wings and fuselages, and in the afternoon pilots and ground crews set to with enthusiasm to apply these to their own machines. Unfortunately the good weather of recent days was not to continue and torrential rain in the evening washed off much of the paint that had been painstakingly applied during the day.

An improvement the following day allowed the work to be completed, and at 1830 hrs the Wing Leader, Wing Commander Peter Powell, called a meeting of all pilots in the officers' dining marquee to outline the plan of action. Everyone was reassured to know that they would be involved from the very beginning, carrying out low cover over the American landings on Omaha and Utah beaches. After the meeting broke up the camp was placed under armed guard, with all personnel confined within its boundaries until further notice.

The honour of being the first RAF fighter unit over Normandy fell to 611 Squadron. Having been awakened at 0300 hrs, they were airborne at 0348 hrs and arrived over their patrol line to witness the last stages of the night bombing to suppress local defences. There was plenty to report as they landed back at Deanland at 0610 hrs but, surprisingly, there had been no sign of the *Luftwaffe*. Everyone had anticipated a determined response and all pilots had been keyed up, fully expecting to have to fight their way in and out. The lack of opposition, although welcome, was almost an anti-climax.

The situation was exactly the same for 64 and 234 Squadrons, who carried out the first of their cover patrols between 0520 and 0610 hrs; indeed, the only problems they faced were caused by trigger-happy naval gunners and the pilots of some Allied aircraft whose recognition skills were not as good as they should have been. No.234 Squadron's first patrol was uneventful, but one of their pilots, Flight Sergeant Dennis Sims, did not return. He was last seen flying at 500ft ten miles south of St Catherine's Point and it was later assumed that his Spitfire (AA936) had

F/Sgt Dennis Sims of 234 Squadron. (*Fairweather*)

disintegrated after being hit by anti-aircraft fire, either from Allied ships or coastal defences.

At the time he went missing, Sims was flying as No.2 to Flying Officer David Ferguson, who remembers some of the tension that surrounded Operation Overlord:

> One had to be very chary of US fighters – they would fire first and do aircraft recognition later; in fact a US Thunderbolt was reputed to have shot down a Spitfire on D-Day. The US Navy were even worse. Shortly after D-Day I was leading 'A' Flight before dawn, climbing in close formation to our operating height. As we approached the coast, the Yanks threw up a horrible load of explosive and incendiary stuff, intermingled with tracer, slap in front of us. Everyone broke; my No.2 was hit and went down to ground level behind the beaches, No.3 called me from 10,000ft and No.4 prudently went home. Shortly afterwards, a Wing Commander further down the coast called the operational control ship insisting that if the firing did not cease immediately, he would withdraw his wing not only for the morning, but for the rest of the f—ing war!

Flight Lieutenant Tony Cooper of 64 Squadron was among the first over the Utah beachhead in BM327 (SH-F), his logbook comments confirming some of the hazards that had to be faced: 'Patrolling at 0520 hrs. Navy shelling coast defences – first landing made at 0620 hrs. Nearly shot down by Thunderbolt, Spitfire in front actually was. Another Spit hit by naval shell and blew up.' His overall comment was that the whole affair was like a 'General Brocks "benefit"!' Sadly, these were not isolated incidents, and more Allied aircraft would be shot down in error over the coming weeks. Poor weather conditions were undoubtedly a factor as low cloud often forced top cover P-47 Thunderbolts to fly at the same level as the Spitfire squadrons. This resulted in a large number of aircraft milling around in a narrow band of sky, a situation that was exacerbated due to the fact that many of the surface vessels making for the invasion beaches were flying anti-aircraft balloons.

Throughout D-Day the Deanland Wing maintained round-the-clock cover with each squadron carrying out four patrols. The final operation was performed by 611 Squadron which took off at 2250 hrs, remaining over the patrol line until 0005 hrs by which time it was too dark to see anything. Over the next few days this hectic schedule would be continued, with minor variations, placing enormous strain on ground crews to maintain serviceability, and on pilots, who had to endure the wearing effects of constant operations. Most pilots flew one or two trips each day with Squadron and Flight Commanders flying anything up to three. Tony Cooper's experiences were typical, and on 7 June he flew three sorties, amounting to seven hours and twenty-five minutes flying time, of which two hours and fifty-five minutes was classed as night flying.

The first and last operation of each day posed particular problems, especially if weather conditions were poor. Tony Cooper recalls a patrol carried out in the late evening of 7 June which ended well after dark:

> We were flying in three sections of four and coming back the weather was appalling with heavy rain and 10/10 cloud, very low. We had been on patrol for quite a long time and were all short on fuel. We came straight back to the English coast around Brighton but I was given a warning to stay clear of obstacles which meant balloons that were being flown over all south-coast towns. I was given a vector towards the east which we flew on for quite a long time, and when I queried this they told me to continue. My No.4 was already very low on fuel so I called up another station and it appeared that the first vector had been a reciprocal given in-correctly. I found out afterwards that I was heading well out towards the North Sea and we should have all gone down in the drink. We

eventually made it back and they got me into Deanland by firing rockets. My No.4 didn't actually make it to dispersal, he ran out of fuel as soon as he landed so we were very, very lucky.

As the first patrol was usually away before 0400 hrs, the 'early risers' were faced with a night take-off and at least an hour of night flying before the first streaks of light appeared. Flight Sergeant Stan Farmiloe of 234 Squadron recalls one occasion when he was lit up by flares dropped from above, all part of the job for Lancaster and Halifax crews, but a rare experience for a pilot in a day fighter squadron! David Ferguson remembers that his aircraft was modified for operations over the D-Day period by the fitting of baffle plates or 'blinkers' to the forward fuselage to reduce glare from the exhausts during night flying. Patrols during the few hours of complete darkness were carried out by night-fighter Mosquitos.

During Operation Overlord the *Luftwaffe* was hopelessly outnumbered by the Allied air forces and there was little that it could do to influence the land battle. On D-Day itself it managed to fly just over 300 sorties, which compares with a total of 14,674 flown by the Allies. It was rarely seen in anything more than *Staffel* strength, and with RAF and USAAF patrols flying over the beachheads within designated areas and to a rigid timetable, any unit that made contact was extremely fortunate to do so. Of the Deanland-based units, 611 Squadron had all the luck when it came to engaging enemy formations and they took part in three

BL734 of 64 Squadron. (*Cooper*)

successful actions, the first occurring during a late evening patrol on 10 June.

Having taken off from Deanland at 2250 hrs, the Spitfires were over the patrol line at 2310 hrs flying in individual sections as the light was already failing. Five minutes into the patrol a twin-engined aircraft was investigated by Squadron Leader Bill Douglas, but this turned out to be a Mosquito night-fighter. Shortly afterwards bomb bursts and anti-aircraft fire were seen coming from the Carentan area and Douglas saw four aircraft approaching from the south at 5,000ft in close formation, silhouetted against a stretch of low cloud. Diving down underneath them, he came up from below and astern, keeping himself against the dark background in the east. The four aircraft could be seen in what little light remained to the north-west.

Identifying them as Junkers Ju 88s, he manoeuvred behind the machine on the right-hand side of the formation and opened fire at 70–100 yards' range. Strikes were observed on the port mainplane and fuselage, and without warning the Ju 88 blew up directly in front of Douglas's Spitfire, debris hitting it and causing momentary loss of control. Not knowing how badly his aircraft had been hit, he made an immediate return to base. On inspecting the damage he found that the spinner had been dented and one of the aircraft's exhaust blinkers was missing, as was the rear-view mirror.

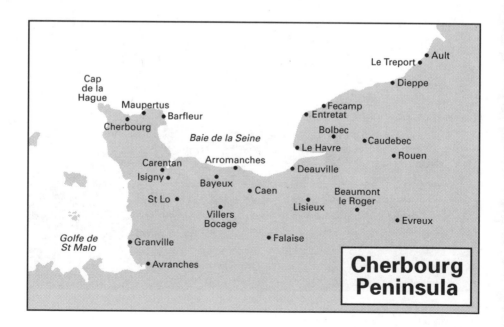

196

Shortly before Douglas's combat, Flight Sergeant J. Marquis (Green 4) trailed another Ju 88 as it flew west towards the Cherbourg peninsula. After flying abreast of it to starboard and below to obtain positive identification, he dropped back and fired with cannon and machine-guns, setting fire to its port engine. A second burst hit the Ju 88 in the fuselage and it turned sharply to port, diving almost vertically. For a moment Marquis was caught in its slipstream as it plunged down, and shortly after he saw an explosion as it hit the ground. As his starboard cannon had jammed during the attack and his hood was covered in oil, there was little point in remaining on patrol and he too returned to base.

Earlier in the day 64 Squadron had been greeted in traditional manner by the Navy as they took up station for an early-morning patrol over Omaha and Gold beaches. Flying Officer Wally Smart (BM129) escaped death by an extremely small margin when a 20mm shell punched a large hole, measuring a foot in diameter, in the fuselage of his Spitfire, aft of the cockpit. Fortunately nothing vital was hit and his aircraft continued to fly normally. The squadron ORB later noted, somewhat dryly, that the hole would have been where he was sitting if he had been flying 5mph slower!

On the next trip Flight Lieutenant Ted Andrews became the first 64 Squadron pilot to land in France.

> The needle in the temperature gauge started to go off the clock while over Omaha beach and I realised I would never make it back to Deanland. Only the night before we had been told that, in an emergency, we might land on a short strip which had been constructed in the beachhead. I found the strip, landed, and switched off the engine. I examined the radiator and found that a panel had come adrift and was blocking the airflow. I managed to get the panel off and got back into the aircraft as quickly as possible as the strip was unpleasantly close to the front line and battle noises and gunfire were close by. Fortunately the engine fired immediately and, despite an amphibious vehicle crossing in front of me, I was able to take off and rejoin the squadron.

The emergency strip that Andrews had landed on was to welcome another of the squadron's pilots later in the day when Warrant Officer Pugh was forced to put down in AA756 with engine problems. He did not get back quite so quickly and had to endure three days in France, where he got no sleep at all due to the incessant shelling. He eventually returned home in a tank landing craft, having received special permission to do so from an American General. On the fourth and final patrol, Pilot Officer De Verteuil was hit by flak in BM327 which punctured one of his tyres and caused him to nose over on landing.

Four days later, on 14 June, 234 Squadron carried out a patrol between Bayeux and Caen. Flight Lieutenant 'Johnnie' Johnston (BL415 AZ-B) was one of those taking part.

We took off at about 1400 hrs but, unbeknown to us, the Germans had put a counter attack in and they had pushed the front line back so we were patrolling not on our side of the line, but on the German side. At the halfway point we turned round to come back and the next thing that happened was that there was a hell of a bang and a great big flash as some 88mm anti-aircraft fire burst very close by. I was thrown completely upside down and two feet was taken off my starboard wingtip, opening up the end like blowing up a paper bag. The wingtip had gone up to the inboard hinge of the aileron, and the aileron itself was just dangling by a wire. As I was inverted there was another explosion underneath me which shattered the hood and broke open the first part of the side door, smashing the mechanism to pieces. I was then hit by a third round which took my radiator out.

I fought to get it reasonably level but the starboard wing was right down and it took all my strength to stop the aircraft turning completely over. At one point I even cocked my leg over the stick to try to relieve some of the control forces. Suddenly in front of me I saw a small landing strip. The last recorded speed that I remember seeing was 200mph, and as I thumped down, all I could say to myself was, 'Please don't let me burn.' The aircraft hit the ground with a hell of a smack and spun round and round. The impact broke my straps and I was flung forwards onto the gunsight, but fortunately I had my goggles down which prevented facial injuries.

The next thing I remember was being surrounded by men in khaki who, it turned out, were from the unit building the airfield. One of them stuffed a rifle in the hood and levered it open to get me out. On being led away I suddenly realised that I had lost my gold watch, so I staggered back to the aircraft to try to find it. The shock of hitting the ground must have been so great as to take it over my wrist and hand as I found it lying neatly over the throttle – not that I had had an engine to throttle! It turned out that the crew who were building the strip had brought over a crate of beer with them to share with the first aircraft to land at their brand new airfield. They reckoned that I had 'landed' so I enjoyed a nice bottle of cold English beer while I contemplated a very sad-looking Spitfire.

The airfield that Johnston had come down on was B.6 Coulombs and he was soon joined by Flying Officer Bill Painter and Flight Sergeant 'Joe'

Fargher, whose aircraft had also been hit by the anti-aircraft fire, although not as severely. Fargher had the misfortune to tip up on landing, which resulted in a badly gashed forehead, but apart from this, all three pilots were uninjured. As events were to prove, their adventures were far from over.

> We had to get back somehow. I didn't fancy staying where we were as the lads said they were under occasional fire from snipers. We asked for a vehicle to get us back through the lines and were given a staff car, with a Bren gun on the top, and a driver. We set off heading westwards along the main road from Caen to Bayeux and were stopped several times by our own Airborne people, eventually arriving outside an Army HQ. There was a battery of 4.5s firing away like hell nearby and we went in to see the officer in charge. We must have looked like a bunch of pirates with our gunbelts slung around us and knives in our boots and he said, 'Good God, what happened to you lot?' We explained things to him and he wrote us a note to flying control B.2 saying that we were returning to the UK to rejoin our unit, and to offer any assistance possible.
>
> We sent the Army lad away to get some dinner, and while he was away we pinched his vehicle. We took turns at the wheel and were driving merrily along the road when, suddenly, some Tiffies took off amid clouds of sandy dust and we knew we were near the airfield. A bit further along there was a Dakota standing and that meant England, it wasn't going anywhere else. By this time I was up at the front where the Bren gun was and Joe Fargher was driving. He stopped within a couple of feet of a group of people and my heart sank as the first person I saw was Air Chief Marshal Sir Trafford Leigh-Mallory (AOC-in-C AEAF), and beside him was Harry Broadhurst (AOC 83 Group, 2 TAF) and lots of frightened-looking hangers-on.
>
> Broadhurst came over and he was purple. He said, 'Do you know who I am?' I said, 'Yes Sir, you're Harry Broadhurst.' I forgot to say Air Vice-Marshal, which he didn't like, and then the AOC-in-C intervened and asked, 'What on earth are you people doing here in an Army car?' I explained and handed over our piece of paper. He had a good chuckle and said, 'Do you fancy a ride home?' After that the press lads got on the job and took a number of photographs, L-M milking the situation for the publicity it generated. Eventually we piled into the Dakota and were fed chocolate and drinks and flown back to Thorney Island where we stayed overnight. At nine o'clock in the evening the news came on and it said that three of our

aircraft had been shot down by anti-aircraft fire, but the pilots were believed to be safe!

Thanks to the prompt action taken by Air Chief Marshal Leigh-Mallory all three pilots were operational again the following day, having featured prominently in the morning edition of a national daily newspaper.

While 234 Squadron were patrolling to the west of Caen, 611 Squadron was flying further to the south near Falaise when they ran into a gaggle of approximately sixteen Me 109Gs. Both sides saw each other at the same time and joined combat after dropping their respective overload tanks. After a few minutes 'breaking and chasing', Squadron Leader Douglas (BL692) eventually got onto the tail of a 109 which attempted to escape in cloud. Its pilot was kicking on left and right rudder, to the extent that Douglas had great difficulty hitting it. With his cannon ammunition

F/Sgt T.P. Fargher, F/O W.H. Painter and F/L W.L.H. Johnston in front of AVM Leigh-Mallory's Dakota. (*Johnston*)

exhausted, he at last had some success, achieving De Wilde strikes on both mainplanes which produced twin streams of glycol from its radiators. He then had to break off on being attacked, but shortly afterwards saw a 109 hit the ground and burst into flames. Taking into account the statements that were later made by other pilots, it appears certain that this was the 109 Douglas had attacked.

White section was attacked by three 109s from behind, and as they broke Flight Lieutenant K.T. King lost contact with his No.2. With so many aircraft in the immediate area, he found that it was almost impossible to bring his guns to bear as he invariably came under attack himself first. During this time he saw a lone Spitfire go down on fire having been attacked from astern at close range. His chance finally came when he saw a 109 climbing steeply towards cloud at 3,000ft. Giving chase he fired at 200 yards' range, but just as he did so the enemy aircraft disappeared into the overcast. King continued to fire even though he could no longer see his opponent and was rewarded with the sight of it falling out of cloud with smoke and flames pouring from its engine and cockpit. It then dived vertically past him and exploded as it hit the ground.

Not far away another Me 109 was being harried by Sergeant G.S. Wilson (Green 2), who scored numerous strikes on its wing-roots before he was forced to break off as another Spitfire cut in front of him. This was the aircraft flown by Flight Lieutenant P.R. McGregor (White 1), who took up the attack and inflicted further damage which prompted the German pilot to bale out. Several other members of the squadron fired their guns; Lieutenant Carre claimed a probable with another damaged, and Flying Officer J.T. Clifford, Warrant Officer F. Delery and Flight Sergeant Marquis all put in claims for Me 109Gs damaged. The Spitfire seen on fire by Flight Lieutenant King was probably that flown by Flight Sergeant M.K. 'Kicker' Wilson, who failed to return.

As the Allied ground forces had consolidated their initial gains and were looking to break out to the south, Deanland's Spitfires were now venturing further inland, but were having to contend with some of the most intense flak yet experienced. No.64 Squadron had a particularly difficult day on 16 June and lost Flight Sergeant J.D.M. Duncan, who was shot down and killed during a patrol to the south-west of St Lô. Several other aircraft were hit and Flying Officers Law and de Jana were also badly knocked about. Later in the day the squadron flew a similar operation to the north-east of Caen and again ran into extremely accurate ground fire which boxed them up three times. Fortune favoured them this time however, and all aircraft returned safely.

Although the invasion appeared to be progressing as planned, prob-

F/L John Harder of 64 Squadron taxies out at Deanland. (*Cooper*)

lems were still being experienced with incidents of 'friendly fire'. The situation got so bad that Flight Lieutenant Ted Andrews of 64 Squadron was one of a number of pilots who were seconded to the Navy to advise on air operations and he spent an 'interesting' few weeks on a frigate attempting to educate the gunners in the art of aircraft recognition. Before this, 234 Squadron suffered further misfortune as it returned from France in the late evening of 17 June. It was already dark as the squadron approached Beachy Head at 3,000ft where it was fired upon by heavy and light anti-aircraft batteries situated along the coast. The fire was closest to Red section, and as they took evasive action Nos. 3 and 4 collided and Flying Officer Bill Painter, who had survived being shot down just three days before, was killed. The pilot of the other aircraft, Flying Officer George Sparrow, contemplated baling out but subsequently changed his mind and landed at Deanland safely.

Although he did not take part in this particular operation, David Ferguson can still bring to mind his CO's furious outburst after landing when he lambasted operations over what had happened. His anger was more than justified as great care had been taken to inform control of the exact position where the Spitfires would make their landfall and that they would be in close formation, with navigation lights on.

With so many aircraft and ships operating in a constricted area it was, perhaps, inevitable that mistakes would be made. Not long after this incident George Sparrow had another close shave. Having split from the squadron over the Channel with technical trouble, he was returning to the south coast in the dark when he heard the voice of a controller in the process of vectoring a Mosquito night-fighter onto an unidentified aircraft. Everything seemed to indicate that his was the aircraft being tracked, and just as things were becoming uncomfortably close, he saw a ball of flame not far behind him and the whoop of delight as the pilot of the Mosquito celebrated his victory.

A few hours before the tragic incident involving Bill Painter, 611 Squadron found itself in the right place at the right time again when it chanced upon a large formation of Focke-Wulf Fw 190s to the south of Bayeux. Lieutenant R.G. Gouby (BL472 – Black 1) led his section up to 16,000ft but they were not able to close until the German aircraft reversed their direction to the south of Carentan, which left the Spitfires up-sun and with height advantage. Diving to attack, Gouby singled out the leader of the first section, firing a burst which damaged its tailplane. The 190 then made a gentle turn to starboard so, with more deflection, he gave it a long burst achieving cannon strikes on its fuselage and engine, which immediately caught fire. It then rolled slowly onto its back and entered a spin which was not recovered before it hit the ground eight miles south-south-west of Peniers. The other 190s were not prepared to hang around and quickly dived away out of trouble, which was just as well as Gouby was short of fuel and had to land on one of the forward strips before returning to base.

In the meantime, Flight Sergeant 'Tam' Ward (Green 4) was also in action. After several inconclusive combats he used his Spitfire's superior turning performance to get on the tail of an Fw 190 and scored several hits on the aircraft's port wing-root and cockpit. He was then attacked from behind by another but lost it quite easily by kicking on coarse rudder and managed to regain his position on the original aircraft. Over 6,000ft was lost as the 190 made a desperate attempt to get away, but eventually a long burst at maximum deflection hit it near the cockpit. It then went down vertically, bursting into flames as it hit the ground. During a separate engagement Pilot Officer G.M. Shoebottom's Spitfire (BM641) was hit, which led to a crash-landing at an emergency landing strip with a severe glycol leak.

Weather conditions were still causing problems on occasion and in the early morning of 19 June, Flight Sergeant Ian Walker of 611 Squadron took off in AR608 as No.2 to Squadron Leader R.B. Cleaver, who had been attached to the unit as a supernumerary to gain operational experience following his return from India. Cloud was down to sea level over the Channel and the pair had no choice but to climb up through the overcast. It was still semi-dark and Walker soon began to have doubts as to his leader's ability to cope on instruments. Cleaver's Spitfire was seen to adopt increasingly unusual flight attitudes as its pilot gradually became disorientated, and shortly afterwards it rolled over, exposing its underside, before diving away out of control. Despite the conditions, Walker made a safe return to base but Cleaver was killed when his aircraft (BL520) crashed into the sea.

Although it was still less than two weeks since the invasion, the Airfield Construction Groups had been working hard in Normandy and several airstrips were already available so that aircraft could now be based on French soil. As this process continued, more and more wings were to transfer to the continent, and in the coming weeks the role of the ALGs along the south coast of England would diminish rapidly. It would be only a matter of days before the squadrons of the Deanland Wing moved on, the first departure being 234 Squadron, which left for Predannack on 19 June.

At this time the unit possessed twenty-four Spitfire LFVbs and the squadron Engineering Officer, Flying Officer Tony Creedon, recalls that all but one were made serviceable for the journey to Predannack, a fact that reflected well, not only on the ground crews, who had just had to contend with one of the most hectic periods of the entire war, but also on the Spitfire V itself. The aircraft departed in two separate formations, but the bad luck which had afflicted the squadron for several weeks was set to continue as Flight Sergeant Henderson was forced to bale out near the Eddistone lighthouse following a glycol leak. Despite the fact that he appeared to have baled out successfully, he was seen to be struggling in the water (Henderson was a non-swimmer) and his body was never found.

Nos. 64 and 611 Squadrons continued at Deanland for a few more days but they too moved further to the west on the 23rd, taking up residence at Harrowbeer and Predannack respectively. They were to have no immediate replacements and it was almost a month before the Spitfire XIVs of 91 and 322 Squadrons arrived, both units soon swapping their Griffon-powered machines for Mark IXs. Spitfire Vs did reappear briefly in the skies over Deanland when 345 (Free French) Squadron, led by *Commandant* Bernard, moved in from Shoreham on 16 August.

In the three-week period before they too converted to the Spitfire IX, 345 Squadron flew a number of close-escort missions, together with several armed recces on the lookout for surface transport. On 26 August two locomotives were destroyed during a sweep of the Calais–Ghent–Aulnoye area, and four days later a tug and six barges were shot up in the same region. On this occasion a Dornier Do 217 was also encountered to the north-east of Eindhoven and was duly shot down by four of

345's Spitfires flown by *Adjutant-Chef* Maurel, *Adjutant* Porchon, *Sergeant-Chef* Dromatakis and *Sergeant* Juventin. The latter's aircraft was hit by return fire from the Dornier, but Juventin managed to make a safe landing back at base.

No.345 Squadron received its Spitfire IXs on 6 September and continued to operate from Deanland until 19 October, when it moved to Biggin Hill. Although some permanent buildings had been erected in recent weeks for the accommodation of personnel, Deanland, like many other advanced landing grounds, closed shortly after, bringing to an end a brief but vital contribution to the invasion of northern Europe.

THIRTEEN

THE DRAGON STRIKES BACK

By mid-1944 the *Luftwaffe* was under the utmost pressure and was faced with the unenviable task of operating on three separate fronts. In addition to these duties, it was also being stretched to the limit in the face of strategic attacks by the USAAF's Eighth Air Force and RAF Bomber Command. As resources were concentrated for these vital battles, it was not unknown for RAF fighter pilots in other areas to complete a tour without coming into contact with their opposite numbers. This lack of opposition in the air, together with the Spitfire V's excellent low-level performance, meant that it was still a viable ground-attack machine, and in the coming weeks it would be busy seeking out transport and communications targets, albeit in greatly reduced numbers as squadrons converted to newer aircraft.

Of the squadrons that had comprised the Deanland Wing, 64 and 611 Squadrons began flying Spitfire IXs in early July, but 234 Squadron was to soldier on with its LFVbs until the end of September. Flying Officer Tony Creedon, whose job it was to maintain the old aircraft, found no major problems despite the fact that most of them were by now two to three years old and relatively high-time machines. He also recalls that most pilots were keen to remove the invasion stripes from their aircraft as soon as possible as the paint had been applied in a very rough and ready manner which resulted in a marked deterioration in the aircraft's top speed.

No.234 Squadron, whose badge consisted of a fire-breathing dragon together with the motto 'We Spit Fire and Revenge', was now based at Predannack, which had opened in May 1941 as a satellite for Portreath and was located on the exposed heathland of the Lizard peninsula in Cornwall. Although the camp was a big improvement on Deanland, many pilots were not altogether happy at their isolated position. One pilot wrote that he expected it to be – 'a stooge job – all readiness, stand-by and patrols'. Although early operations did consist mainly of defensive patrols and shipping reconnaissance sorties, within a matter of days it became apparent that their elderly Spitfire Vs were to become active in a new role: dive-bombing!

One of the squadron's main operational tasks was to reconnoitre the western approaches to the English Channel and prevent enemy ships interfering with the transport of supplies to the Allied forces in Normandy. In the event no seaborne threat emerged, and most of the bombing attacks that were eventually carried out were against coastal radar stations and communications targets a short distance inland.

Flight Lieutenant Ray Stebbings recalls that the usual procedure when bombing ground targets was to half-circle the objective at 6–8,000ft before commencing an attacking dive at around forty-five degrees, into wind. The target was viewed through the reflector gunsight until, at a height of 3,000ft, the nose of the Spitfire was gradually pulled up and the bomb released on the count of eight. Despite the rudimentary nature of this technique, results were remarkably good, and 234 Squadron carried out practice bombing on a regular basis, often using as convenient targets large patches of seaweed that were to be found at various places along the Cornish coast. Stebbings also remembers that take-off could be a nail-biting experience with a 500lb bomb suspended between the Spitfire's narrow track undercarriage. Ground clearance was reduced appreciably, and with all-up weight increased to 7,150lb, take-off performance could sometimes cause concern, especially on those aircraft which had seen better days.

'A' Flight of 234 Squadron. (*Johnston*)

The new method of attack was not favoured by Flight Lieutenant 'Johnnie' Johnston:

> For me dive-bombing in a Spitfire was a most unlikeable job. The bomb was slung underneath and the bomb cradle used the same supports as the overload tank with one or two alterations. The method of fusing was by double wire held together by a loop at each end and it wasn't until the bomb had dropped a certain distance that the pin was pulled out. It was supposed to be a fail-safe device in case you had a hang-up and had to land with it, although I can't recall this ever happening. In the dive the aircraft used to tuck its nose underneath itself and the faster you went, the more it tucked under, which made it difficult to pull out. It became the habit for some pilots to trim their aircraft nose-up and that was very dangerous because when the bomb was released and they started pulling back on the stick, it was easy to over-stress the airframe. One or two aircraft did lose their wings in the pull-out.

Occasionally low-level skip-bombing was tried, usually in an attempt to seal up the ends of railway tunnels. This brought fresh problems relating to the setting of the delayed-action bombs: too short a period of time and the attacking aircraft itself could be damaged, too long and the pilot of the following Spitfire could be affected by the blast.

As the squadron worked up towards their first bombing attack, they also flew a number of armed reconnaissance operations during which two pilots were shot down. Eight aircraft took part in Rhubarb 303 on 4 July when storage tanks and railway wagons were strafed at Quimper, but defensive fire hit BL233 flown by Flight Lieutenant F.D. Rumble and he was forced to bale out. A similar operation was carried out the next day, during which the Spitfire flown by Flying Officer 'Red' Bage (EP756) was hit by flak as it crossed the French coast. Bage immediately turned back, together with his No.2, Flight Sergeant Len Stockwell, but only got a short distance over the Channel before his engine caught fire. Stockwell saw his leader attempt to bale out but his parachute failed to open and his body was later seen floating in the water. An ASR operation that was launched later in the day had to be abandoned due to worsening weather, before Bage could be found.

No.234 Squadron's first attempt at dive-bombing took place on 8 July during an afternoon raid on a radar station near Ushant. Two direct hits were noted and four more bombs fell within the designated target area. After the bombing was complete the Spitfires dropped down to shoot up aerial arrays and buildings with cannon and machine-guns.

The following day seven aircraft joined forces with 611 Squadron (flying one of their last operations with the Spitfire V) in bombing the radar station at Pointe du Raz. The target was found to be obscured to the north by 7/10 cloud cover which meant that the attack had to be delivered from a direction that was far from ideal. It was not very successful; most bombs undershot and much of the damage that was caused can be attributed to the subsequent strafing attack which hit one of the Freya installations and several camouflaged buildings. Squadron Leader Arnott also attacked and silenced a light flak post.

Having been shot down shortly after D-Day, Flight Sergeant 'Joe' Fargher had the experience repeated on 11 July in AA973 during a low-level armed recce of the Brest peninsula. He later wrote:

> We hugged the contours of the ground, barely clearing treetops and telegraph wires, the pilots concentrating on scanning the sky for enemy aircraft and the ground ahead for targets of opportunity. Maintaining open battle formation at 100ft and 260mph was not easy, particularly when the leader changed course suddenly. As I breasted a low ridge I spotted anti-aircraft guns squarely in my path. With no chance to turn away, I tore across the gun site as low as I possibly dare. There was a loud bang (they said that if you heard an anti-aircraft shell explode, you had usually been hit) but my controls responded normally and the engine note hadn't changed, so I kept my place in the formation. Nothing was said on the R/T, radio silence was the rule until the first engagement.
>
> The terrain was undulating and most of the fields were very small and surrounded by trees, so it was certainly no place for a forced landing. Then I noticed the temperature rising and the oil pressure dropping, perhaps I would have to make a forced landing after all! I pulled back on the stick automatically to gain as much height as I could and weighed up the prospects of a landing I could walk away from. Frantically searching for a suitable field, I mentally checked the drill for baling out. I was up to 2,400ft now and still had some speed left when the Spitfire caught fire. That settled it, I would have to jump! A short R/T transmission: 'Hatstand Blue 3, on fire – baling out.' I jettisoned the canopy and out I went.

Other members of the squadron saw Fargher land safely and bundle his parachute under a hedge. Fortunately for him, the only people in the immediate vicinity were French farm workers who quickly spirited him away from the nearest German forces and into the care of the local *Maquis*, who organised his escape.

We were having a meal in the sitting room of a farmhouse one day when two German soldiers came to the kitchen door to buy eggs. There was no time to move and from the adjoining room I heard the farmer's wife meet their request courteously and the Germans say that they would return in two days for further supply. Like many other French people at that time this lady was leading a double life; politely correct to any Germans they encountered, but also deeply involved, at considerable risk to themselves and their families, in hiding Allied airmen on the run.

While keeping out of sight as much as possible I gave a hand with the hay-making where I could, and when news of a supply drop came I assisted in laying out the flarepath lights. Amidst great excitement, several hundred men, women and children turned up to watch 16 Halifax bombers parachute a great many supply containers holding small arms, ammunition and explosives. It was while waiting for the supply drop that I met a French parachutist officer who introduced me to the escape route. I was taken to meet two other pilots who had been shot down and a British intelligence agent who was taking vital information back to England concerning German strengths and dispositions in the area. We were to return by boat direct across the English Channel and that day set out for the coast just north of St Brieuc. There were only two stopping points at safe houses on the way but at the second, disaster almost overtook us.

Whether we had been followed or not I never found out, but in the small hours of the morning, shots were fired through the window of the cottage and in the ensuing confusion one of the German visitors wounded his NCO, which enabled us to make our getaway. We hid for the whole of the next day in a large gorse bush for we were now in the coastal zone where special restrictions were in force. After dark we were escorted down to the beach by a party of men and women of the Resistance, along paths through sandhills which had been heavily mined. This hazard was overcome by shuffling along in single file behind a 20 year-old girl who placed a white handkerchief on each mine embedded either in the path or close to it. After a short wait on the beach a rowing boat appeared and I was soon on board a Royal Navy gunboat. Next morning I was back in England and after a spell of leave, rejoined my squadron.

Following an uneventful sweep on 19 July, four aircraft carried out a patrol near Lorient on the 22nd during which three locomotives were attacked and damaged at Hennebont. One aircraft was lost, that flown by Flying Officer J.L. Coward. Later the same day, at 1913 hrs, eight aircraft took off to escort three Mosquitos of 151 Squadron who were to attack a château near Lorient which was being used as accommodation for German naval personnel. Apart from the bombing attack itself, the whole mission was flown at zero feet. Everything went well until half way across the Channel when Pilot Officer Johnny Metcalfe had to return with R/T problems. Much to his disgust, Flight Sergeant Stan Farmiloe had to go with him. The château was badly damaged during the attack, the remaining Spitfires following in behind the Mosquitos to strafe the building with cannon and machine-guns. Light flak was experienced in

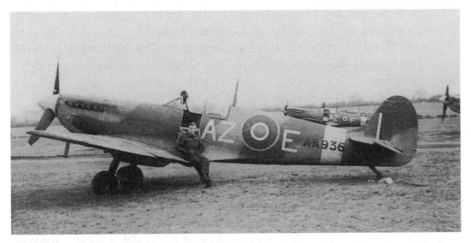

Two views of AA936 of 234 Squadron. (*Fairweather*)

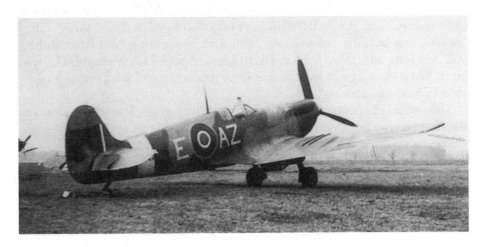

the target area, Lieutenant 'Mike' Bernard's aircraft receiving minor damage to its starboard mainplane.

On 24 July half the squadron took off to attack a target near Landivisiau and were equipped for the task with 500lb bombs. Flight Sergeant Stan Farmiloe's experiences were recorded in his wartime diary:

> The target was a petrol dump supposedly containing one million litres in the railway siding just south of Landivisiau. Eight aircraft of 611 went in first, we followed about fifteen minutes later. The C.O. was leading (I was his No.2) and after a little 'wandering' we located the target, half circled same at 8,000ft and then went down. Secured seven hits in the target area, the other being a mere fifty yards out. Didn't get a good run in myself owing to slight cloud but nevertheless my bomb dropped slap in the middle of a largish warehouse in the middle of the yard. Pulled up after bombing to 4,000ft and then dived down again and strafed the yard in general. Unwittingly I wasted most of my shots on the building I'd hit previously!

Later in the day a second bombing attack was carried out in the same area, this time on a viaduct carrying a railway line. Once again eight aircraft took part and the viaduct received one direct hit and several near misses which caused damage to its superstructure. Trucks and buildings were also strafed at the railway station nearby.

Three days later the squadron flew Rhubarb 323 which involved a sweep along the south-western coastline of the Brest peninsula. Having crossed into France at Plouescat at 6,000ft and above cloud, the Spitfires descended to carry out a strafing attack on the airfield at Kerlin Bastard before proceeding along the coast towards Lorient. It was here that they were bracketed by highly accurate flak which hit AR343 flown by Flying Officer E.R. 'Ben' Lyon (Red 3). Severely damaged, it dived away out of control, trapping its unfortunate pilot and preventing him from baling out. Not long after, Red leader, Flight Lieutenant W.C. Walton DFC, was hit in BM200, but he at least was able to retain control long enough to be able to bale out successfully.

The rest of the Spitfires made it back safely, but the loss of Walton was a serious blow. Fortunately, the squadron was able to replace him from within its ranks and 'A' Flight was taken over by the highly experienced 'Johnnie' Johnston, who had been a member of the unit since October 1943 as supernumerary to Squadron Leader Arnott. By coincidence, 234 had also recently lost its 'B' Flight commander with the posting of Flight Lieutenant C.H. Lattimer DFC to HQ ADGB, his replacement being Flight Lieutenant Tim Berry from 611 Squadron.

On 29 July 234 Squadron took part in the bombing of the village of Serignac, an attack that had been specifically requested by local resistance forces. Flight Sergeant Stan Farmiloe's war diary gives his view of the mission:

Something else new, this time a low level bombing attack – one certainly gets variety down here. The target was a village – Serignac, south of Morlaix which had been taken over by a battalion of Germans. We were requested to do the bombing before 0800 hrs by the Maquis. Four squadrons were detailed, the Harrowbeer Wing (64 and 126 Squadrons), 611 Squadron from Bolt Head and the great 234 – forty-eight Spits in all carrying roughly twelve tons of bombs.

Briefed at 0630 hrs and set off at 0655 hrs. The squadrons were to bomb at five minute intervals starting at 0730 hrs, we were to be third in, and all to be carried out at tree top height. Crossed in at Plouescat, reached the village at 0738 hrs and found we were almost the first there. Passed over the target and split into sections of four to bomb. We had to make two runs in (Blue section) as at the first attempt Yellow section cut us out and their bombs were exploding just as we were about to go in.

No flak seen at all – bags of Spits all over the place. Second run was O.K., aimed at the church, being the most solid looking

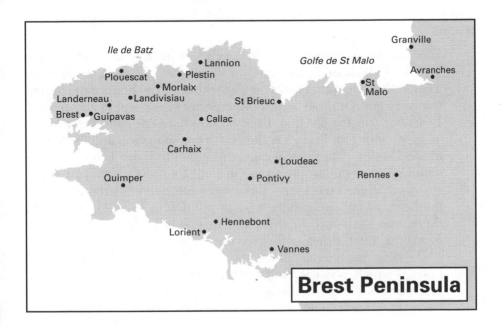

building – bombs have a habit of bouncing. Two of our section's did in fact, and burst in a field far past the village. Only saw a little damage as I went over but when 611 came in (third) they said the place was pretty well devastated. Intelligence has reported since that 80% was destroyed. Damn good prang all around!

It is interesting that Farmiloe claimed to have aimed his bomb at the village church. 'Johnnie' Johnston, who also flew on this operation, recalls that the pilots were warned against attacking the church as the arms of the Resistance had been hidden in the crypt!

The next day eight aircraft attacked a locomotive and its trucks on the Landerneau to Loudeac line, and on the 31st another bombing attack was carried out, this time on the radar station at Ushant. Two bombs overshot and one failed to drop, but the rest were on target and one Freya installation was believed to have been destroyed.

There was little excitement over the next few days, apart from a two-aircraft scramble on 1 August; shipping reconnaissance sorties were the order of the day and it was not until the evening of the 5th that 234 flew once again in squadron strength. After flying over to Bolt Head to be refuelled, they took part in one of their more unusual escort operations, which involved providing cover for Halifaxes towing Hadrian gliders on a special operations mission (Dingson 35A). Each glider contained a jeep together with three men and their equipment and the intention of the force was to create as much disruption as possible to German communications in the area to the north of Lorient. Stan Farmiloe takes up the story:

> Our job was to rendezvous with ten gliders and tugs and escort them to a point about mid way between Vannes and Lorient. It was quite a late show – we didn't meet the gliders until 2130 hrs, but the timing was very good and all were at the rendezvous point dead on time. I was No.2 to the C.O. and our section took over the front of the 'gaggle', with Tim Berry's at the rear. The navigation and the timing of the Halifax chaps was wizard throughout. There was also some damn good organisation on the ground by the French. Just as we approached the target area, three huge fires were started alongside the fields where the gliders were to put down. In one of the fields there was even a T to show the direction of landing. Saw the first three touch down before we turned away.
>
> The only flak we saw throughout was a little from the direction of Lorient which was catching a pounding from the air. I could see great clouds of smoke rising up. We escorted the Halifaxes out as far as the French coast. It was then too dark to be of any further use

so we reformed and set course for Predannack, landing back there a little after 2300 hrs in pitch darkness.

By now the Allied armies were making rapid progress in clearing the Germans out of north-western France and it would only be a matter of days before their forces were driven out of 234 Squadron's area of operations. As a result there was little chance of seeing any action unless they were called to operate from bases further to the east. This occurred on 11 August when a request was made for them to escort four Mosquitos of 151 Squadron, who were to raid a tank repair factory near Rheims. The operation was carried out from Manston and involved a one-hour-and-forty-five-minute positioning flight, which was only ten minutes shorter than the operation itself. No enemy aircraft were seen, but heavy flak was experienced when crossing the coast and there was intense and accurate light flak in the target area. As there was insufficient daylight to return to Predannack, the squadron flew back the following day.

Three days later the long trek along the south coast was being made once again, this time to Tangmere, from where an armed reconnaissance was flown to the north-west of Paris. Targets proved to be largely elusive although one section shot up a number of railway trucks near Beauvais. On the 19th four aircraft of 'A' Flight had the honour of escorting the Duke of Gloucester, who was flying in a Sunderland to Mount Batten where he was to carry out an official visit. Having completed their duties, the section then went to Harrowbeer where they met up with him again and escorted him for a second time (this time in a Dakota) to Polebrook. Bad weather en route, however, led to them having to divert to Charmy Down.

On 23 August 234 Squadron made one of its deepest penetrations into occupied territory during a Rodeo flown from Manston. They flew as far south-east as Verdun, the intention being to seek out *Luftwaffe* fighters returning from intercepting an Eighth Air Force bombing raid. The skies turned out to be clear of enemy aircraft however, Blue section having to be content with shooting up between fifteen and twenty barges to the south of Douai and an Me 109 that was spotted on the ground west of Mezières. Red and Yellow sections also found suitable targets, attacking barges at Valenciennes and Ypres.

Low cloud and rain prevented the squadron's Spitfires returning to Predannack until the 25th but when they did get back there was little for them to do apart from providing cover for HMS *Warspite* and her attendant destroyers as they bombarded the port of Brest. With the prospect of little action, morale began to slip, but there was heartening news on the 27th when a signal was received that the squadron would

EN858 of 234 Squadron at North Weald, September 1944. (*RAFM*)

shortly be moving to North Weald in Essex. In fact the move took place the following day, and from its new base 234 was ideally placed to continue offensive sorties over northern France and Holland.

Sector recces were flown to get accustomed to their new surroundings, and the squadron's Spitfires flew their first operation from North Weald on 30 August with an armed reconnaissance of the area around Lille and Douai. A large convoy of army trucks was attacked near Douai, while two barges, a dredger and a locomotive received the full treatment at Bethune. Although the month of August had proved to be largely disappointing, 234 had still managed to fly nearly 600 hours, of which 236 hours were operational.

With Allied fighter-bombers ranging far and wide over northern France and the Low countries, the German re-supply network had been virtually paralysed during daylight hours. The highly successful attacks carried out by rocket-firing Typhoons may have taken the headlines, but the contribution of the Spitfire squadrons to the ground war was equally, if not more, important. Like any modern army, the *Wehrmacht* had an insatiable demand for fuel, so by targeting its supply network, comprising soft-skinned vehicles, locomotives and barges, the transport of this precious commodity was restricted to an amount that represented a small fraction of the total required. Of all the German tanks and armoured vehicles that were eventually taken during the Allied advance, it was found that the majority had not been destroyed by air attack, but abandoned out of fuel.

No.234 Squadron maintained the pressure with two armed recces on the morning of 1 September, three barges being attacked on a canal to the north of Ypres on the first, with two locomotives and ten loaded barges coming in for similar treatment during the second, which took place near Courtrai. On the 5th the squadron turned its attentions to Holland, and during a sweep to the north-east of Rotterdam, a locomotive was left on fire and another damaged. A small steamer was also attacked and set on fire at Schoonhoven.

Not long after, on 8 September, the first V-2 rocket landed in Chiswick, soon to be followed by several others, one of which put a sudden halt to an inter-squadron football match being played at North Weald. The V-2 launch sites were in the vicinity of The Hague, and over the next few days many sorties would be flown in an attempt to find and destroy them. The prospect of having large quantities of explosive or liquid oxygen blow up at close range was not particularly comforting, but the nearest 234's pilots came to locating anything connected with the V-2s occurred on the second of two recces carried out on the 9th when a large articulated lorry was shot up near Rotterdam.

At first it was thought the V-2s were controlled by some form of radio guidance system, and 192 Squadron, which normally monitored the German night-fighter control frequencies, was brought in to see if there was any possibility of using radio counter-measures. On 14 September the squadron's Halifax and Wellington aircraft flew so-called 'Anti Big Ben' patrols off the Dutch coast, 234 Squadron putting up pairs of aircraft throughout the day as cover.

Concern over V-2 rockets had to be put to one side as the Allies launched Operation Market Garden on 17 September, the attempt by the airborne forces to seize and hold a number of vital bridges around Arnhem and Nijmegen. No.234 Squadron provided cover to some of the vast number of transports and glider tugs that were being used, but with the virtual eclipse of the *Luftwaffe* day fighter force, there was little for them to do, as Stan Farmiloe recalled in his wartime diary:

> Rather a big day. The 1st Allied Airborne Army staged the largest airborne invasion by far, it left the one on D-Day in the shade. The targets were all in Holland, chiefly around Arnhem and Nijmegen. Our job was to act as anti-flak over the first part of their journey, from the Scheldt estuary and for about sixty miles inland. I have never seen so many aircraft in all my life, there must have been

thousands. Dakotas carrying paratroops, Halifaxes and Stirlings towing gliders, bombers, and every type of fighter including Tempests, Mustangs and Spits acting as cover. In fact we spent most of our time over there dodging other aircraft, usually batches of 100+ Dakotas who were flying at our level of 600ft.

When we arrived we found very little to do except to look on. There was no sign of flak anywhere, it had apparently all been silenced by the first wave of fighters (we were in second). I saw a Stirling spin in on fire from 1,000ft, it was alight from stem to stern and looked just like a fiery cross. A Dakota also made a forced landing whilst on fire. Saw a few paratroops dropped and a small number of gliders released and that's about all. It seemed as if all Holland was out watching us go over, all in their Sunday best too!

If they had been mere spectators on the opening day of Market Garden, a more active role was undertaken on the 18th. The airborne forces were taking two distinct routes towards Arnhem and were encountering problems along their northernmost track, which took them close to Schouwen Island. A number of flak barges had been positioned just off the coast and the route was patrolled for an hour in mid-afternoon, several attacks being made on these and flak positions on Schouwen itself.

Already the position of the ground forces around Arnhem was

After operational use many Spitfire Vbs served as trainers including this example with 61 OTU (note bomb racks under wings). (*Cooper*)

Another 61 OTU Spitfire Vb (revised codes). (*Varey*)

becoming desperate and their situation was not helped by a sudden deterioration in the weather, which prevented many of the Allied fighter-bombers from coming to their assistance. No.234 Squadron also had their problems. Stan Farmiloe later wrote:

> It was supposed to be another escort job, more tugs and gliders out to Holland. We had to do quite a little cloud flying in order to gain some height and the squadron became split into fours. We also failed to find the bomber stream so it couldn't be called a success exactly. I was in Blue section with Tim [Berry] leading and after getting well and truly lost somewhere over northern France we obtained a homing which led us slap bang over Calais which was still in Jerry's hands. We were in a tight vee at around 1,500ft and boy the flak!, it was easily the worst I'd seen, Lord knows how we all escaped.

Weather conditions were no better the following day and another escort and anti-flak patrol had to be abandoned due to low cloud and bad visibility. No.234 Squadron's last involvement with the ill-fated Arnhem operation took place on the 23rd when it carried out an uneventful patrol from Bourg Leopold to Eindhoven.

Word had been going around for some time at North Weald that new equipment was on the way, but it was not until 29 September that the rumours turned to reality when the first of the squadron's Mustang IIIs arrived. Despite the fact that nearly all of the replacement aircraft had previously been flown by a Polish squadron, most pilots were more than happy that they now had a machine which possessed the performance and range to take the war to the enemy for the remainder of the European conflict. More examples of the North American fighter arrived over the next few days and the squadron was taken off operations for a short period to work up on the new type.

In early October most of 234 Squadron's old Spitfire LFVbs were dispersed to various OTUs where the dangers of operational flying were replaced by hazards of a rather different nature. Three of its aircraft were to be more fortunate, however, and were eventually refurbished by Reid and Sigrist for export to Portugal in 1947. These aircraft were BL646, BL981 and BM131.

By now the war was rapidly moving beyond the Spitfire V's radius of action, but it still clung precariously to operational status, a situation that would continue until the end of the war in Europe.

FOURTEEN

FINAL OPERATIONS

One of the last fighter units to fly the Spitfire V in northern Europe was 63 Squadron, which had begun flying the type just before D-Day, having previously carried out tactical reconnaissance duties with Mustang Is. During the invasion period they had taken on the vital task of gunfire spotting for the Navy's heavy guns, which were bombarding fortifications along the French coast between the River Orne and the River Vire. The unit carried out this role from Lee-on-Solent as part of the Air Spotting Pool (also known as No.34 Recce Wing, 2nd TAF).

During a maximum effort on D-Day 63 Squadron flew a total of seventy-six sorties amounting to 108 hours and 25 minutes flying time. Patrols were normally carried out in pairs with the Section Leader calling the fall of shot, while his wingman flew about 2,000ft above as cover. Many successful 'shoots' were carried out against heavy and medium gun batteries, troop concentrations and enemy armour, although Flying Officer G.R. Duff was shot down by flak during the first wave. As the bombardment continued throughout the day there was a noticeable drop in the amount of flak encountered, and by the end of the day it was noted as being largely light and ineffective.

Despite observations on the first day of the invasion, flak, some of it from the Allied side, was to remain a problem. On 7 June, Flight Sergeant Jim Harris was hit but made it back to crash-land at Hamble, and the day after Flying Officer C.N. Gall was forced to bale out of P8747 near Bayeux. At first it was thought that he had been shot down by Me 109s, but on his return two days later he was able to report that the trouble had in fact come from defensive fire put up by Navy vessels in the Channel.

As the Allied forces made progress inland, requests were made for assistance with shoots away from the immediate coastal area, and on 14 June thirty-two sorties were made in connection with attacks on field guns, mobile batteries and HQ buildings around Caen. In some cases the proximity of Allied troops made it impossible to engage individual targets. On the 16th a number of enemy aircraft attempted to 'bounce' spotting aircraft, but they made no effort to hang around when engaged

F/Sgt Jim Harris later flew with 234 Squadron and was killed on 7/2/45 in Mustang III FB115. (*Halloran*)

and were quickly driven off. The main danger, as ever, came from the ground and Flight Lieutenant N.A. Doniger's aircraft was hit by 'rocket flak', resulting in a crash-landing at an advanced landing ground near Bayeux.

Over the next few days many sorties had to be aborted due to bad weather, but this did not stop an increased effort by the *Luftwaffe,* six Fw 190s attacking Flight Lieutenant E.R. Lowry and Flying Officer F.H. O'Neill. Although the combat proved to be ineffectual, the decision was made to provide a section of four aircraft for each spotting pair in future.

Having survived several scares, the squadron's luck took a turn for the worse on 24 June when Flying Officer A.T. Witney's aircraft developed engine trouble on the way back from a sortie. Fumes leaked into the cockpit and during an attempted crash-landing in a field near Gosport, the aircraft burst into flames, killing its pilot. The following day thirty-six sorties were flown as the Navy attacked heavy coastal batteries and forts near Cherbourg. Flying Officer B.F. Cleeton (BL753) was last seen diving steeply towards the ground, and although not seen to crash, he did not return and was posted missing. Flying Officer Duff was hit once again by flak and force-landed in France, returning to the squadron five days later.

With the advances made by the Allied ground forces, suitable targets became increasingly difficult to find, and on 3 July 63 Squadron transferred to Woodvale with a detachment operating from Ballyhalbert in Northern Ireland. The unit remained in the north-west until 21 September, when it flew to North Weald to take part in bomber escort operations along the Dutch coast. Although Antwerp had been taken by the Allies in early September, its port facilities could still not be used as the Germans held the banks of the Scheldt estuary, and the heavy guns situated on the island of Walcheren dominated the approaches. As the island was largely below sea level, the aim was to utilise heavy bombers to breach the sea walls which, it was hoped, would flood a number of gun batteries and disrupt defences.

Having flown practice battle formations, 63 Squadron's first mission occurred on 26 September when it formed part of the escort for Mitchells attacking a ferry at Breskens which was being used to transport German troops retreating from the Allied advance. The first attack on Walcheren took place on 3 October when 240 Lancasters succeeded in destroying the sea wall for a length of 100 yards at Westkapelle. Four days later 121 Lancasters of 5 Group breached the walls near Flushing. Although all of the bombers returned safely, one of 63 Squadron's aircraft suffered engine failure in the target area as a result of flak damage. Flying Officer Bridgford (EN837 – Black 2) carried out a crash-landing at Blankenberge, escaping with superficial injuries, although his aircraft was a Cat. E write-off.

Due to adverse weather conditions only two further attacks were possible during October, raids being carried out on heavy gun positions on the 12th and 28th. Thereafter 63 Squadron reverted to its old duties of spotting for the Navy before Walcheren finally fell to the Allies in early November after a week of ground fighting. With the front line rapidly moving to the east there was now little for the unit's Spitfires to do apart from occasional VIP escorts and sorties carried out by single aircraft acting as airborne relays. The squadron was finally disbanded at North Weald on the last day in January 1945.

Although the Spitfire V was never to be operated from bases on the continent as a first-line fighter, some did operate from airfields in France and Belgium in the wake of the Allied advance. In late 1941 the air-sea rescue organisation had been re-organised, one of the pioneer units being 276 Squadron which formed at Harrowbeer on 21 October. The unit then led a somewhat fragmented existence with flights based at various airfields throughout the south-west operating Lysanders, Ansons, Walruses and Warwicks. The Spitfire IIC (later re-designated ASR.II) was also used from 1942 to provide a rapid response capability to locate downed airmen, a secondary role being the provision of cover for slow-flying Walrus amphibians. The aircraft were modified so that a dinghy and survival gear could be stowed in the flare chutes, and they were used until late April 1944 when they were replaced by Mark Vbs.

Several of the Spitfire Vbs that 276 Squadron received were fitted with engines that featured the so-called 'Basta' modifications, which allowed operation up to 25lb/sq.in boost pressure for a period not exceeding five minutes. These included AD111, BL379 and EP171. Performance was improved at low level, but overhaul life was reduced and 150 octane fuel had to be used in place of the regular 100 octane. Fuel consumption also went up by approximately 25% when the higher boost setting was used in conjunction with max. revs.

On 18 September the squadron HQ and 'B' Flight, comprising five Spitfires and two Walruses, transferred to Querqueville before moving to Amiens-Glisy (B.48) at the end of the month. A further move was made to St Croix near Bruges on 26 October, from where the unit's Spitfires carried out regular patrols over the North Sea that were timed to coincide with bomber streams returning from raids on Germany.

On 14 December 'B' Flight moved again to Knocke (B.83) on the North Sea coast where it would stay for the remainder of the war. Despite numerous scrambles in search of aircraft and crews, it was not until 17 February 1945 that the first successful pick-up was made from the continent when a B-17 navigator was pulled from the sea by one of the Walruses. This marked the unit's 300th rescue since being formed. Sadly, successes like this were few and far between; on most occasions there was either no sign of wreckage, or there was nothing that could be done to help. On 22 February a section of Spitfires searching for a Dakota located only a waterlogged dinghy with a body face down in the water, and three days later all that could be found of a Wellington crew was a dinghy with a motionless body inside it.

What was probably the final time a Spitfire V fired its guns in anger occurred on 12 March. The port of Antwerp was being used as an offloading point for supplies destined for the advancing Allied armies, but ships involved in this operation were coming under threat of attack from German 'Biber'-Class midget submarines. To deter such activity 276 Squadron's Spitfire Vbs flew a number of patrols over the Scheldt estuary, and Flight Lieutenant K.S. Butterfield attacked and sank one of these 'mini U-boats' off Domburg in BL379.

On 20 March reports were received that a fighter had ditched in the sea twelve miles north-west of The Hague and a section of Spitfires immediately took to the air to search the area. The pilot was soon located and a Walrus directed to effect a rescue. Due to the rough state of the sea, however, the Walrus (L2220) was unable to take the pilot aboard and then came under attack itself by shore-based guns. The waves were such that the Walrus was unable to take off again and its pilot, Warrant Officer Bowe, was forced to taxi his aircraft out to sea where he and his crew were picked up by a USAAF Catalina, which then sank the Walrus with gunfire. This unfortunate episode was covered by the Spitfires until their fuel ran low, but the drama was not quite over as the Catalina could not take off either and had to remain on the water until the following morning, when it was finally able to get airborne. (An international distress call was put out for the pilot in the dinghy and he was eventually picked up by a German rescue launch.)

Two more rescues were carried out before the end of the war, although tragedy struck during the first. On 5 April a B-17 came down in the sea ten miles off Dunkirk, five of the crew being located by a section of Spitfires which orbited overhead as a rescue launch made its way to pick them up. As they did so Pilot Officer N. MacDonald reported engine problems in BM414 and almost immediately dived straight into the sea with black smoke pouring from his aircraft. Although help was quickly at the scene, no trace of aircraft or pilot was found. On 13 April another sea search found a dinghy occupied by a survivor from a German midget submarine who was handed over to the Royal Navy at Ostend.

No.276 Squadron's final sorties of the war occurred on 29 April during an unsuccessful search for the crew of a B-17 reported in the sea off Overflakkee, an operation which was severely hampered by fire from coastal gun batteries and bad weather.

Although the duties of the ASR Walruses were set to continue, the conclusion of the war in Europe on 8 May meant that the squadron's Spitfires were not required any more, and they were given up shortly after the unit returned to Andrews Field on 8 June. Most did not see any further service and were struck off charge later in the year.

Over the years the Spitfire V has been subjected to a fair amount of adverse comment, particularly regarding its performance deficiency when compared with the Focke-Wulf Fw 190. Fighter Command's losses, especially in 1942, were extremely serious, but it would be wrong to assume that this situation was brought about entirely by the weaknesses of the Mark V; indeed, large-scale offensive operations over northern France had been called into question as early as November 1941 when the main opposition was still the Messerschmitt Me 109F.

By operating over enemy territory the initiative was often handed to the *Luftwaffe*, whose pilots had plenty of time to get airborne and climb above the incoming RAF fighters. With height advantage they were able to dictate terms and only attacked if the odds were heavily stacked in their favour. As a result the RAF invariably fought at a tactical disadvantage, and most of the aircraft that were lost were shot down within the first few seconds of an attack. Occasionally engagements would take place between individual aircraft where there was no advantage either way. Under such circumstances a well-flown Spitfire V was still a worthy opponent, and many Fw 190 pilots paid the ultimate price when they attempted to mix it in one-to-one combat.

With the advent of the 'cropped blower' LF, the Spitfire V's performance was augmented at low levels so that it was able to fulfil a useful role until the end of the war. Pilot reaction to flying the LF varied considerably – almost without exception it is referred to as the 'clipped, cropped and clapped' Spitfire, although there would appear to be two schools of thought regarding the term 'clapped'. For many it relates to the aircraft's age, but there are still those who maintain that the appellation refers to the fact that it virtually fell out of the sky above 12,000ft. Perhaps the final word on the Spitfire V should be left to some of those who flew the aircraft in combat.

Flight Lieutenant Dave Glaser – 234 Squadron:

> The one I liked the best of the lot was the 'clipped and cropped' Spit. I really loved it because it had a super rate of roll and you could really pull it in. We did mainly escort work with it and it was ideal for that height (10-12,000ft). I found it was very good against the Fw 190 and I never had any trouble dealing with them.

Flight Lieutenant Art Sager – 416 Squadron:

> While later I came to appreciate the greater speed and power of the Spit IX and XVI, the Spitfire V was my first love. In spite of being outmatched at times by the Me 109 and Fw 190 at some altitudes and in steep dives, it gave you complete confidence because of its ability to out-turn the Hun. You knew that with it, if you were alert, he'd never get on your tail. Because of its feminine lines and deadly sting, I called my Spit 'Ladykiller', not appreciating at first that pretentious and macho connotations might be attributed to the pilot!

Pilot Officer Bill Harbison – 118 Squadron:

> The Mark V Spitfire was, in my view, the most pleasant Spitfire to fly and handle. It was relatively light on the controls and had good performance at low and medium altitude. However, with a single-

stage blower, it ran out of steam as the boost dropped off at altitude where it was out-performed by the Fw 190. The clipped version had an excellent rate of roll and was a good performer at low level. The contrast between the Mark V and the Mark VII was marked, particularly as far as agility was concerned.

Warrant Officer Roy Fairweather – 234 Squadron:

The Spitfire LFVb was a delightful aeroplane to fly for the purpose for which it had been modified – low-level combat with the Focke-Wulf Fw 190. It did not deserve the tag 'clapped' (a humorous afterthought) because our maintenance crews kept it in top condition. It had simply been superseded and out-classed by later marks of Spitfire and other higher-performance aircraft.

Flight Lieutenant Clive Gosling – Supermarine test pilot:

The Mark V to me seemed underpowered; indeed, it was not until the airframe was fitted with the Merlin 61 that the full potential of the aircraft appeared to be realised. The LFV was a little 'hot rod', it was very nimble and light, and with an exhilarating low-level performance.

Squadron Leader Johnny Freeborn – 118 Squadron:

The Spitfire V played a great part in the war and was, indeed, the fighter workhorse, but I hated the b—y thing! It wasn't a patch on the Spitfire II which was replaced by them. The airframe was standard but the engine was, in my opinion, makeshift, underpowered and rated at the wrong altitude. It could not cope with the Fw 190 and the modifications to the engine did not help. On 118 Squadron we got re-equipped with the cropped blower engines – the effect was a great rate of climb to 12,000ft and thereafter not much more. How I wished for Mark IXs or XIVs, but at least the V was reliable and got us there and back.

FIFTEEN

SPITFIRE V SURVIVORS

Relatively few examples of the Spitfire V still exist, although the
burgeoning interest in classic warbirds has resulted in three examples returning to the skies, and another being restored for static
display. This chapter details the histories of those aircraft that are
currently preserved in the UK, or have been resident in recent years. (For
a full list of all operations flown by these aircraft, see Appendix B.)

AB910

Perhaps the best known of all the airworthy Spitfire Vs, AB910 was built
at Castle Bromwich and was initially allocated to 222 Squadron at North
Weald on 22 August 1941. Its stay was relatively short and only lasted to
the end of the month when it was damaged in a forced landing at
Lympne. After repair by Air Service Training at Hamble, it was passed
to 37 MU at Burtonwood, before being issued to 130 Squadron at
Perranporth. AB910 completed a total of twelve operations with its new
squadron and flew as escort on both daylight raids against the *Scharnhorst*
and *Gneisenau* in December 1941 (Veracity I and II). On the latter
mission it was flown by Pilot Officer Jones, who was attacked by two
Me 109s. Although squadron records state that no damage was inflicted,
AB910 did not fly any further ops with 130 Squadron and by 15 January
1942 was with Westland Aircraft for repair.

After a spell with 6 MU at Brize Norton, AB910 was next delivered to
133 (Eagle) Squadron at Biggin Hill on 13 June. During the next two
months it flew twenty-nine operational sorties and was flown twice by
Pilot Officer Don Gentile, who later achieved fame as one of the Eighth
Air Force's leading aces. On 19 August AB910 flew on four occasions
during the Dieppe Raid, Flying Officer E. Doorly using it to damage a
Dornier Do 217 during the second patrol of the day, with Flight Sergeant
R.L. 'Dixie' Alexander destroying another on the third.

Towards the end of August 1942, 133 Squadron undertook air-firing
practice prior to converting to the Spitfire IX, and by early September
AB910 was with 242 Squadron at Digby. The unit was about to be

transferred to the Middle East and 910 only flew non-operational sorties before being transferred to 12 MU at Kirkbride on 12 November.

Following a lengthy period of storage, its next operational duties were with 416 Squadron at Digby, its first sortie occurring on 6 July 1943 when it was flown by Sergeant J.L.A. Chalot on an ASR patrol. Two days later it was delivered to 3501 SU to be fitted with a new M-Series Merlin, but from this point the aircraft's history, as recorded in Form AM78, differs markedly from Squadron ORBs. The movement card would have us believe that it was passed to 402 Squadron after its return from Cranfield and remained with the unit until transfer to 53 OTU on 20 April 1944. The ORBs, however, show that it continued to fly with 416 Squadron until they converted to Spitfire IXs at the end of January 1944 and was then taken over by 402, with whom it served until mid-July 1944. During the invasion it flew numerous cover patrols over the Normandy beach-heads from its base at Westhampnett.

AB910 did eventually make it to 53 OTU, and on 4 April 1945 Flight Lieutenant Cox was carrying out power checks prior to take-off from Hibaldstow, with the help of WAAF Margaret Horton who was leaning over the tail to hold it down. Assuming she had jumped clear, Cox opened the throttle and took off, unaware that she was still desperately clinging onto the tailplane. Flight Lieutenant Tony Cooper, OC 'A' Flight, recalls what happened next:

> I was leading a section of three pupils and we were at the end of the perimeter track waiting to take off, looking to the right for aircraft coming in. I noticed this peculiar silhouette but couldn't think what sort of aircraft it was – it looked like a Spitfire but it had this hump on it which, as it got closer, I realised was someone draped over the fin. It went past us, landed on the runway, stopped, and this figure got off and walked to the edge of the runway and, it would appear, lit a cigarette. As events appeared afterwards, it was Margaret Horton and all the press came down the next day to interview her. I understood at the time that she said it was a protest because she wanted to join the Air Transport Auxiliary, and they wouldn't allow her to go onto flying duties!

On 17 May AB910 was allocated to 527 Squadron at Digby, a unit that flew Oxfords, Wellingtons, Dominies, as well as Spitfires on a variety of duties, including calibration work, communications and practice interceptions. By early 1946 the unit was at Watton and had evolved into the Radio Warfare Establishment, but AB910 departed on 30 May for storage at 29 MU, High Ercall. It was then acquired by Group Captain (later Air Commodore) Allen Wheeler on 14 July 1947 and given the civil registration G-AISU. Re-painted in a blue colour scheme with white cheat line, it was used for air racing, wearing the number 82 during the National Air Races in 1949.

Thereafter it was sold to Vickers-Armstrong Ltd and was flown regularly by Jeffrey Quill until its donation to the Battle of Britain Memorial Flight on 15 September 1965. It has remained with the BBMF ever since and has suffered two accidents: an undercarriage leg collapse at Duxford in June 1976 and a collision involving a Harvard which swung on landing at Bex in Switzerland in August 1978. The second incident caused Cat. 3S damage, repairs being carried out at Abingdon, during which some components of Spitfire IX MK732 were used.

AR501

Spitfire Vc AR501 was built by Westland Aircraft Ltd at Yeovil and was delivered to 8 MU, Little Rissington, on 22 June 1942. Following a short spell with 6 MU at Brize Norton, it was passed to 310 Squadron at Exeter on 19 July. Its first operational sortie took place in the evening of 3 August when it was flown by Sergeant A. Skach on a convoy patrol. Over the next eight months AR501 flew a total of seventy-four operations ranging from anti-Rhubarb patrols, ASR sorties and scrambles to bomber escorts and sweeps over north-western France. It was flown on a number of occasions by Squadron Leader Frantisek Dolezal DFC, who had achieved air combat victories while serving in both the French Air Force and the Royal Air Force in 1940.

On 18 September Dolezal was flying AR501 during a squadron formation practice when a number of Fw 190s carried out a low-level attack on Dartmouth. The squadron were given vectors to carry out an interception and, having dived through cloud, they saw two 190s flying south-east at 3,000ft with four more a short distance away. Dolezal led the chase, but the enemy aircraft used their superior performance to pull away. Although he opened fire at extreme range, the raiders got away without damage.

AR501 was involved in action over the Brest peninsula on 29 January 1943 during close escort of twelve Bostons of 226 Squadron bombing a railway viaduct near Morlaix. It was flown on this operation by Flying Officer K. Drbohlav, a sharp engagement taking place when the squadron was attacked by nine Fw 190s of JG2. Squadron Leader E. Foit (AR498) and Flight Sergeant V. Popelka (AR521) both put in claims for Fw 190s destroyed, but Warrant Officers J. Sala (AB519) and M. Petr (EP464) were shot down and killed.

On 15 March AR501 was parked in a dispersal pen at Exeter when it was hit by a Mosquito of 307 Squadron which swung during an overshoot. It suffered Cat. B damage and was taken to 67 MU at Taunton for repair. Following short spells at 33 MU, 3501 SU and 504 Squadron, AR501 next served with another Czech squadron, 312, at Ibsley. Its first sortie occurred on 22 October 1943 when it was flown by Flying Officer V. Smolik on 11 Group Ramrod 280, a close-escort mission to Evreux that was carried out from Tangmere. Smolik also flew AR501 on 11 November, during which it carried out anti-flak support for Whirlwind fighter-bombers attacking shipping off Guernsey.

Over the next few weeks a number of close-escort sorties were flown to 'Noball' (V-1) sites in the Pas de Calais before 312 Squadron converted onto Spitfire IXs at the end of January 1944. On 27 February AR501 began a short spell with 442 (RCAF) Squadron at Digby, before transferring to 58 OTU at Grangemouth on 30 March. Within a month it had moved yet again and was with 1 Tactical Exercise Unit at Tealing.

On 4 July AR501 was allocated to 61 OTU at Rednal but suffered an accident on 9 September which necessitated its removal to Air Service Training at Exeter for repair. During this period it was also converted to LF standard. On emerging in its new guise, it spent time in store at 33 MU, before joining the Central Gunnery School at Catfoss on 24 April 1945. AR501 was flown on only a very few occasions at CGS, and on 22 August it was passed to 29 MU at High Ercall for further storage before being struck off charge.

Unlike many of its contemporaries, it escaped the scrapman and was delivered to the Department of Aeronautical Engineering at Loughborough Technical College on 21 March 1946. Total airframe hours on arrival were 511 hours and thirty-five minutes. It then served as a training airframe for the college's students before being taken on by the Shuttleworth Trust at Old Warden in 1961.

AR501 took to the air again as a result of its involvement in the film *Battle of Britain* for which it was restored to airworthy condition by Simpsons Aeroservices and Spitfire Productions Ltd at Henlow. During filming it flew approximately fifty hours and was placed on the civil register as G-AWII. After its starring role, AR501 spent time at Bedford and Duxford where it underwent a major rebuild which culminated in its first post-restoration flight on 27 June 1975, when it was flown by Neil Williams. It continues to be one of the highlights at Old Warden's summer airshows, where its classic lines can be admired in an authentic setting.

AR614

Spitfire Vc AR614 was built by Westland Aircraft Ltd and was delivered to 39 MU at Colerne on 24 August 1942 before being issued to 312 Squadron at Harrowbeer on 11 September. An air test was carried out by Squadron Leader Cermak the following day and its first operation took place on 18 September when Flight Sergeant J. Kohout used it on a convoy patrol. Over the next seven weeks it took part in twenty-two operations before Flight Sergeant S. Tocauer suffered a blown tyre as he attempted to take off on a cross-country exercise. Although damage was only classified as Cat. Ac, which was repaired on site, it does not reappear in squadron records until 10 April 1943 when new CO Squadron Leader Tomas Vybiral flew it on a Rodeo over north-western France.

Vybiral was also at the controls on 14 May as 312 and 313 Squadrons joined forces for 10 Group Fighter Roadstead No.2, which consisted of a strafing attack on Axis shipping in St Peter Port, Guernsey. A number of E-boats and other small warships were damaged, but Vybiral's wingman, Flying Officer Jaroslav Novak, was shot down and killed in EP539. AR614 was also damaged when a cannon shell hit the rear fuselage, wrecking the R/T and IFF, but after several anxious moments Vybiral was able to make a safe return to base.

Repairs were carried out by Air Service Training, after which AR614 was issued to 610 Squadron at Bolt Head, although it only flew two operational sorties before the unit began flying Spitfire XIVs in January 1944. It was then taken on by 130 Squadron at Scorton, but its flying was all of a non-operational nature before the unit disbanded on 13 February, its aircraft being ferried to nearby Catterick. Following a short spell with 222 Squadron at Acklington, AR614 underwent an overhaul at 3501 SU prior to being issued to 53 OTU on 16 September, where it remained until June 1945.

It then passed through 33 MU, Lyneham, before being allocated to 4 School of Technical Training (SoTT) at St Athan as an instructional airframe with the identity 5378M. In the 1950s it became a static display machine, eventually appearing in a distinctive all-silver colour scheme, but by 1963 was to be found on the dump at 60 MU, Dishforth. The following year it was bought by the Air Museum of Calgary where it remained until its sale in 1970 to Donald Campbell of Kapuskasing, Ontario, in whose ownership it took on the identity C-FDUY.

AR614 was eventually brought back to the UK by Ray Hanna and was placed on the civil register as G-BUWA on 19 March 1993. It was then acquired by Sir Tim Wallis's New Zealand-based Alpine Fighter Collection and was rebuilt to airworthy condition by Historic Flying Ltd at Audley End, Essex. Its first post-restoration flight took place on 5 October 1996 in the colours of 312 Squadron. In 1999 AR614 was sold to the Flying Heritage Collection of Seattle and was handed over to its new owners at Duxford on 14 May, prior to being transported to the USA.

BL614

Built at Castle Bromwich, BL614 was delivered to 8 MU, Little Rissington, on 4 January 1942 to be fitted out with its operational equipment, prior to joining 611 Squadron at Drem on 7 February. Its first sortie took place on 18 February when it was flown by Flight Sergeant W.L. Miller on a patrol over the Firth of Forth.

BL614's history then becomes unclear as there is a discrepancy between its Form AM78 and squadron records. The movement card shows Cat. B damage occurring on 8 March with no further use until June, whereas 611 Squadron's ORB notes six operational sorties, mainly convoy patrols and scrambles, carried out between 16 March and 23 May. There is no doubt that BL614 joined 242 Squadron at Drem on 2 June, with which it flew ten operational sorties commencing with a scramble by Flight Sergeant Mather on 7 June.

BL614 was then taken on by 222 Squadron, again at Drem, on 10 August, although it departed for Biggin Hill four days later to participate in the Dieppe Raid. On 18 August 614 was flown by Sergeant J.W. MacDonald on a Rodeo in the Calais/Cap Gris Nez area, an operation that saw one Fw 190 destroyed by Don Blakeslee of 133 Squadron. For Operation Jubilee on the 19th it was flown by MacDonald during an early-morning patrol off Dieppe, and again in the evening. Both sorties were uneventful.

Having returned to Drem, BL614 went through a quiet period before it flew with the squadron to Ayr, where it was eventually taken on by 64 Squadron which arrived on 28 March 1943 from Hornchurch. During this time it was engaged mainly on convoy patrols, the first of which occurred on 11 April when it was flown by Sergeant D. Ledington. It then moved to Friston on 7 August and to Gravesend on the 19th where it suffered minor damage which was repaired on site. Following another move to West Malling on 6 September, BL614 took part in five sorties as close escort for medium bombers attacking airfields and marshalling yards in northern France during Operation Starkey.

On 19 September 64 Squadron's Spitfire Vbs were passed to 118 Squadron which then moved to Peterhead on the north-east coast of Scotland where BL614 flew five defensive patrols before being transferred to 3501 SU. After the war it was allocated to No.2 SoTT at Cosford as 4354M, but shortly afterwards moved to No.6 SoTT at Hednesford. Around this time its identity became confused with AB871 (4353M), the most likely explanation being that the M-Series numbers were inadvertently transposed. This resulted in BL614 eventually being placed on the gate at RAF Credenhill painted as 'AB871'.

After use in the film *Battle of Britain*, it went to Wattisham and then to the aircraft collection at Colerne, where its true identity was revealed during re-painting. Following a period in store at St Athan, BL614 was put on show at the Manchester Air and Space Museum in 1982 where it remained until 1995, when it was delivered to Rochester for full restoration by the Medway Aircraft Preservation Society, a process that took over two years to complete. It is now on display at the RAF Museum at Hendon in the markings of 222 Squadron.

BM597

Having spent many years as gate-guardian at Church Fenton, BM597 is the most recent example of the Spitfire V to return to the air. Another product of the Castle Bromwich shadow factory, it was delivered to 37 MU at Burtonwood on 26 April 1942 before being passed to 315 Squadron at Woodvale on 7 May. Operational sorties consisted mainly of scrambles and defensive patrols, the first of which occurred on 23 May when it was flown by Sergeant Slonski. No.315 Squadron moved to Northolt on 6 September but BM597 was left behind for the incoming 317 Squadron, joining 'A' Flight as JH-C. Most of its flying over the next five months was non-operational and it suffered Cat. B damage during a move to Kirton-in-Lindsay on 13 February 1943.

After repair, BM597 went to 39 MU, Colerne, before being ferried to 222 MU, High Ercall, on 4 January 1944. Here it underwent a period of lengthy storage until it was delivered to 58 OTU, finally retiring from active service in October 1945. It then became a ground instructional airframe at No.4 SoTT at St Athan with the identity 5713M.

For many years BM597 took on gate-guardian duties at Hednesford and Bridgenorth until playing an important role in the *Battle of Britain* film when it formed the master from which glassfibre replicas were made by Spitfire Productions. In 1975 BM597 was put on the gate at Linton-on-Ouse before being moved to Church Fenton four years later where it was displayed in 609 Squadron's markings as PR-O. In the late 1980s it was acquired by Historic Flying and was stored at HFL's base at Audley End, awaiting its turn in the restoration schedule.

In 1994 it was bought by the Historic Aircraft Collection, who commissioned Historic Flying to restore it to airworthy condition, a complex task that came to a successful conclusion on 19 July 1997 when it made its first flight in over fifty years. Registered G-MKVB, it carries markings as worn during service with 317 Squadron.

EP120

Built at Castle Bromwich in early 1942, EP120 was delivered to 45 MU, Kinloss, on 23 May before being issued to 501 Squadron at Ibsley. Wearing the code letters SD-L, it was flown by Sergeant E.H. Moore on two cannon tests in the morning of 6 June before Pilot Officer R.C. Lynch took it on its operational debut the same day during an escort of twelve Hurri-bombers attacking Maupertus airfield. Over the next few weeks it flew a number of offensive sweeps together with defensive patrols and scrambles but, for the time being at least, it was not to come into contact with its counterparts on the other side of the Channel.

On 16 July EP120 was involved in a collision at Ibsley which resulted in Cat. Ac damage. Flying Officer F.T. Brown of 118 Squadron suffered a burst tyre on landing in AB403 and had just pulled up by the side of the runway as Pilot Officer Lynch in EP120 was hurrying to the take-off point to take part in a shipping recce. Lynch hit the stationary aircraft amidships, Brown just having sufficient time to scramble clear. Repairs were carried out at Ibsley and EP120 eventually re-emerged with new code letters as SD-Y. Operations resumed on 14 August, when it was flown by Sergeant H.R. Kelly on an early-morning scramble to 20,000ft over St Albans Head. Five days later it flew three sorties in connection with the Dieppe Raid, two by Flight Sergeant R.J. Long and one by Wing Commander Pat Gibbs. During the latter sortie Gibbs destroyed a Dornier Do 217, his aircraft suffering combat damage when attacked by an Fw 190 (see page 114).

Following repair, EP120 was delivered to 19 Squadron at Perranporth on 6 September, its first operational sortie occurring on the 24th during an anti-Rhubarb patrol off Lizard Point with Sergeant W.H. Mills at the controls. For the remainder of the year it was used mainly on defensive patrols and did not venture over to France until 3 January 1943, when it was flown by Flying Officer S.N. Chilton on a sweep to Landivisiau and Guipavas at 18,000ft. Operational flying then ceased on 9 February as preparations were made for Exercise Spartan, which took place between 1 and 12 March, 19 Squadron flying from Middle Wallop and Membury.

On 22 April EP120 was issued to 402 Squadron at Digby, its first operation taking place on 14 May, when it was flown by Flight Lieutenant M. Johnston as rear support to bombers operating off the Dutch coast. In early June EP120 was flown on several occasions by 402 Squadron's CO, Squadron Leader Lloyd Chadburn, but after his promotion to Wing Leader on the 13th, it became the regular machine of his successor, Squadron Leader Geoff Northcott. Over the next ten months Northcott flew sixty operational sorties in EP120, shooting down four Me 109s and two Fw 190s between 27 June and 3 November.

EP120 remained with 402 Squadron until 12 February 1944, when it was damaged in a crash-landing, the repair process lasting until 8 June. Following short stays at 33 MU and 3501 SU, it went to 53 OTU at Kirton-in-Lindsay on 12 October for its final period of service flying, which lasted until 19 April 1945. Minor damage was repaired by Vickers prior to it returning to 33 MU, from where it was passed to No.4 SoTT at St Athan as 5377M.

After use as an instructional airframe, it was put on the gate at various RAF establishments including Wilmslow, Bircham Newton and Boulmer, where it was restored in 1964 using components from Spitfire XVI TD135. After playing a static role in the film *Battle of Britain*, it was put back on gate-guardian duties, this time at Wattisham. Although renumbered 8070M, it did not carry this identity and continued to wear its correct serial number, together with the code letters QV-H.

EP120 was brought indoors in 1989, and after a short period in storage was sold to the Fighter Collection, for whom it was rebuilt to airworthy condition by Historic Flying. Its first flight after restoration took place on 12 September 1995 and the aircraft is currently based at Duxford. In recognition of its historic past it wears the 'City of Winnipeg' titles and AE-A codes, as carried during wartime service with 402 Squadron, in place of its civil identity G-LFVB.

APPENDIX A

DETAILS OF SELECTED OPERATIONS

Pilots and aircraft on selected operations (details as recorded in Squadron ORBs).

Biggin Hill Wing – Circus 103B – 27 September 1941

72 Squadron		92 Squadron		609 Squadron	
S/L D.F.B. Sheen	W3380	S/L R.M. Milne	W3817	S/L G.K. Gilroy	P8699
Sgt Pocock	W3440	P/O P.H. Beake	W3444	F/O J.A. Atkinson	W3850
Sgt Dykes	AB822	F/L J.W. Lund	W3459	F/O V. Ortmans	W3625
F/L Kosinski	W3511	P/O P. Humphreys	W3375	F/O G.E.F. Dieu	AB975
P/O N.E. Bishop	W3441	Sgt Atkins	W3599	P/O D.A. Barnham	W3621
Sgt J. Rutherford	AB818	P/O Cocker	W3762	F/O R.E.J. Wilmet	X4666
F/L Hall	W3704	Sgt Carpenter	R8640	F/L J. Offenberg	W3574
Sgt A.F. Binns	AB843	P/O E.A.G.C. Bruce	AB779	Lt M. Choron	AB901
Sgt Falkiner	AB922	Sgt Woods-Scawen	W3710	P/O I.G. Du Monceau	P8585
Sgt J.G. Merrett	P8560	Sgt W.L.H. Johnston	AB395	Sgt T.C. Rigler	AB802
P/O E.P.W. Bocock	W3429	P/O P.L.I. Archer	AB847	Sgt J.E. Van Schaick	R6882
Sgt B. Ingham	AB893				

Ibsley Wing – Veracity II – 30 December 1941

118 Squadron		234 Squadron		501 Squadron	
S/L H.B. Russell	W3943	S/L H.M. Stephen	W3835	S/L C.F. Currant	W3846
Sgt E.J. Ames	AD210	F/L J.B. Shepherd	AD725	F/L R.D. Yule	BL240
Sgt H.C. Kerr	AD581	Sgt Goldsmith	AA722	Sgt A. Vendl	AD200
P/O Fulford	AD239	P/O G.R. Bland	W3967	F/Sgt A. Dvorak	W3768
P/O I.S. Stone	AD309	Sgt D.N. McLeod	AA944	P/O J.J. Guerin	W3840
Sgt D. Claxton	AA741	Sgt R.W. Joyce	AB854	Sgt A.A. Toller	P8741
Sgt Freeman	AD187	P/O Le Bas	W3631	P/O A.E. Drossaert	W3939
F/L Robson	AA740	P/O R.S. Woolass	AA727	F/Sgt D.S. Thomas	W3703
P/O R.W.P. MacKenzie	AA729	Sgt Drinkwater	W3935	Sgt K. Vrtis	W3841
P/O Booth	W3832	F/L E.D. Glaser	W3936	P/O Palmer-Tomkinson	W3894
P/O P.B. Jones	AD209	P/O Denville	AA728	Sgt R.C. Lynch	AD538
Cdr A. Jubelin	-	P/O Cameron	W3937	P/O J.O. Harrison	AB965
Sgt Buettel	AA724				
W/C I.R. Gleed	IR-G				

Debden Wing – Circus 178 – 1 June 1942

65 Squadron

W/C J.A.G. Gordon	BL936
Sgt R.E. Parrack	BL647
P/O J.R. Richards	AR391
F/L C.R. Hewlett	BL899
Sgt V. Kopacek	AB133
Sgt Stevenson	AD268
Sgt P.J. Hearne	AB982
P/O V. Lowson	W3604
F/L G. Wellum	BL586
Sgt R. Brown	AR388
Sgt Smith	AD469
F/Sgt Bentley	AR362

71 Squadron

S/L C.G. Peterson	BL449
Sgt W.B. Morgan	W3957
F/L O.H. Coen	BM293
P/O Helgason	BM249
P/O Andrews	AB941
P/O O'Regan	AD564
F/L G.A. Daymond	BL583
P/O E.G. Teicheira	BM386
P/O Potter	W3761
P/O Gray	AD111
P/O R.S. Sprague	W3368
P/O McMinn	AD127

111 Squadron

S/L P.R.W. Wickham	BM185
Sgt R.C. Bryson	AB938
Sgt G.C. Heighington	BM629
F/L F.H.R. Baraldi	BL423
Sgt Y. Henriksen	W3814
Sgt H.D. Christian	AR281
Sgt A. Williams	W3716
F/L R.C. Brown	AB905
Sgt D.J. Telfer	W3122
F/O J. Hartman	AD325
Sgt W.H. Cumming	BL728

350 Squadron

S/L D.A. Guillaume	BL381
P/O A.M. Plisnier	BM564
P/O X.L. Menu	AA933
P/O F.A. Venesoen	EN769
Sgt F.E. Boute	BL621
F/L I.G. Du Monceau	BL540
F/O R.J.L. Laumans	AB173
Sgt J. Ester	AB980
P/O H.A. Picard	W3446
P/O R. Schrobiltgen	W3646
Sgt J.L. Hansez	W3626
F/Sgt G.J. Livyns	BL822

Czech Wing – 10 Group Ramrod 23 – 23 June 1942

310 Squadron

S/L F. Dolezal	AD338
Sgt A. Skach	AR343
F/L B. Kimlicka	AD374
Sgt M. Petr	AD582
W/O J. Skirka	AD328
Sgt A. Stanek	AD365
F/L E. Foit	AD542
Sgt L. Valousek	BL579
F/L F. Burda	AD366
F/O J. Hartman	BL923
F/L V. Chocholin	BL591
F/L H. Hrbacek	BM400

312 Squadron

W/C A. Vasatko	BM592
S/L J. Cermak	EN841
Sgt J. Mayer	R7158
F/O Perina	AD572
P/O J. Novak	BL260
F/L Kaslik	AA970
F/L A. Vybiral	BL289
Sgt J. Novotny	BL487
F/L K. Kasal	BL343
Sgt V. Ruprecht	-
F/Sgt Sticka	BL340
Sgt R. Ossendorf	BL254

313 Squadron

S/L K. Mrazek	BM419
F/L Raba	BM424
Sgt J. Hlouzek	P8709
P/O Prihoda	BM295
Sgt Horak	BL819
F/Sgt Cap	P8324
Sgt Vendl	W3965
F/Sgt Vavrinek	BM273
F/O Hochnal	EP109
Sgt Prerest	AR428
P/O Kucera	AR432
Sgt Dohnal	AA751

12 Group Ramrod 16 – 3 May 1943

118 Squadron		167 Squadron		504 Squadron	
S/L E.W. Wootten	AR447	S/L A.C. Stewart	VL-X	S/L J.R.C. Kilian	EE624
F/L R.A. Newbery	AB403	F/O F.J. Reahill	VL-F	Sgt P.D. Bailey	EP555
F/O F.T. Brown	EN966	P/O J. Jonker	VL-D	F/L G.C.T. Richards	BM471
Sgt J. Hollingworth	EN959	F/L A.R. Hall	VL-B	F/O R.A. Milne	EE620
Sgt R.J. Flight	EP413	P/O J.D. Ramsey	VL-A	Sgt J.D. Gerrard-Gough	AA968
F/O C.L.F. Talalla	AR453	F/O C.T.K. Cody	VL-E	F/O D.G. Biasissi	EE619
F/L J.B. Shepherd	EP515	P/O J.W. van Hamel	VL-H	F/L C.C. McCarthy-Jones	AR503
W/C H.P. Blatchford	EN971	F/L V.C. Simmonds	VL-W	Sgt J.L. Seelenmeyer	EE621
P/O S.A. Watson	P8753	Sgt A. Stening	VL-P	F/Sgt P.J. Doyle	EN773
Sgt C. Anderton	EP124	Sgt J.M. Ketcham	VL-Z	Sgt R.O. Dyer	EE603
F/Sgt T.J. de Courcy	BL303	Sgt F.A. Lewis	VL-T	F/Sgt K.F. Roberts	AB254
F/Sgt A. Buglass	EP126	F/O J. van Arkel	VL-K	F/O R.H. Orlebar	EN953

Digby Wing – 3 November 1943

402 Squadron		416 Squadron	
W/C L.V. Chadburn	LV-C	S/L F.E. Green	EP452
S/L G.W. Northcott	EP120	F/L R.D. Booth	AR383
F/O A.J. Morris	AA880	Sgt G.F. Burden	EE637
F/O C.A. Graham	BM535	F/O J.C. McLeod	P8751
F/O W.G. Dodd	EP445	P/O E.E. Gall	EE685
F/O W.G. O'Hagan	EE661	P/O G.H. Farquharson	P8640
F/L J.B. Lawrence	AA753	F/L A.H. Sager	BM471
F/O W.S Harvey	AD489	F/L D.J. England	W3128
F/O D.R. Drummond	W3454	F/L D.E. Noonan	AB284
F/L J.D. Mitchner	BM211	F/O J.T. Wilson	AR383
F/O K.S. Sleep	AR493	F/O W.H. Jacobs	BL430
F/O J.F. Richardson	AR503		
P/O J.A. MacLeod	W3630		

Perranporth Wing – 10 Group Ramrod 91 – 8 October 1943

66 Squadron		453 Squadron	
S/L K. Lofts	AR518	W/C P.J. Simpson	-
F/L A. van den Houte	AB140	S/L D.G. Andrews	AA966
F/O W. Varey	AD508	P/O J.F. Olver	EP644
Lt Thompson	BM512	F/O L.J. Hansell	EP560
F/O C. Reeder	AD331	P/O G.J. Stansfield	EP361
F/L G. Elcombe	BL583	P/O R.G. Clemesha	AB199
S/L W. Foster	AA881	P/O C.R. Leith	AR607
F/O D. Baker	EP639	F/O R.R. O'Dea	EE618
F/Sgt J. Woodward	W3168	F/Sgt R. Logan	BL426

Deanland Wing – 21 May 1944

64 Squadron		234 Squadron	
S/L J.N. MacKenzie	AB143	S/L P.L. Arnott	EN903
F/O A.T. Thorpe	W3320	Lt M. Bernard	BL646
F/L J.A. Plagis	BL734	F/O J. Metcalfe	EN861
F/O D.A.B. Smiley	AB403	F/L F.E. Dymond	BL235
F/O W.A. Smart	BM129	F/Sgt T.P. Fargher	W3426
Cpt Sassard	AR292	F/L W.C. Walton	BL233
F.L J.W. Harder	AA972	F/O D.P. Ferguson	BL563
F/O D.F. O'Neil	BM414	F/O E.R. Lyon	AD515
F/O Wellman	AD132	F/Sgt P.J. Bell	BM992
F/O Law	BL374	F/L W.L.H. Johnston	BL594
F/O W.B. Brooks	W3656	Sgt O.C. Potter	AB279
F/Sgt W.A. Livesley	P8585		

APPENDIX B

OPERATIONS LOGS OF SPITFIRE V SURVIVORS

Operational histories of Spitfire Vs that are currently preserved in the UK, or have been resident in recent years. Information is from Squadron ORBs.

AB910

222 Squadron

Date	Pilot	Times	Operation
26/08/41	P/O Ramsey	1800-1935	Patrol off E.Goodwin
27/08/41	P/O Ramsey	0705-0900	Top cover – Blenheims – Arras
28/08/41	P/O Ramsey	1345-1530	Convoy patrol off Harwich
29/08/41	P/O Ramsey	0650-0850	ASR off Dunkirk for W/C Gillan
29/08/41	P/O Ramsey	1015-1120	ASR off Goodwin sands
31/08/41	P/O Ramsey	0625-0830	Cover for naval craft

130 Squadron

Date	Pilot	Times	Operation
13/12/41	P/O MacDonald	0845-1045	Convoy Patrol
15/12/41	Sgt Young	1030-1200	Convoy Patrol
15/12/41	Sgt Young	1245-1440	Convoy Patrol
18/12/41	F/L New	1205-1330	Bomber escort – Brest – Veracity I
20/12/41	P/O Jones	1225-1240	Scramble
20/12/41	F/L New	1630-1740	ASR – found Beaufort crew
23/12/41	Sgt Cox	1125-1200	Scramble
24/12/41	P/O Jones	0920-1045	Convoy Patrol
25/12/41	Sgt Cox	1400-1530	Convoy Patrol
28/12/41	Sgt Ogilvie	1645-1750	Convoy Patrol
30/12/41	P/O Jones	1330-1450	Bomber escort – Brest – Veracity II

133 Squadron

Date	Pilot	Times	Operation
23/06/42	P/O W.C. Slade	1110-1230	Sweep off Dunkirk
24/06/42	P/O J.C. Nelson	0710-0830	Convoy Patrol
26/06/42	P/O E. Doorly	1105-1235	Channel Patrol
29/06/42	Sgt G.E. Eichar	1540-1710	Cover – Bostons – Hazebrouck
12/07/42	P/O G.I. Omens	0615-0800	Convoy Patrol

12/07/42	F/O E. Doorly	1845-2100	Cover – Bostons – Abbeville
15/07/42	P/O D.D. Gudmundsen	1155-1315	Diversionary sweep – Abbeville
21/07/42	P/O D.S. Gentile	1835-1915	Cover for massed Rhubarb
22/07/42	P/O D.S. Gentile	0920-1045	Convoy Patrol
26/07/42	F/O E. Doorly	0720-0910	Convoy Patrol
26/07/42	F/O E. Doorly	1250-1425	Sweep – St Omer
28/07/42	F/O E. Doorly	1230-1355	Rodeo Etretat – Fecamp
01/08/42	F/O E. Doorly	1615-1750	Sweep Brugge – Knocke
02/08/42	F/O E. Doorly	1810-1945	Convoy Patrol
02/08/42	Sgt C.H. Robertson	2055-2205	Convoy Patrol
03/08/42	Sgt C.H. Robertson	1010-1135	Convoy Patrol
04/08/42	F/O E. Doorly	0715-0840	Convoy Patrol
05/08/42	P/O D.D. Smith	0655-0830	Roadstead Boulogne – Le Havre
09/08/42	F/O E. Doorly	0520-0640	Patrol
09/08/42	F/O E. Doorly	1725-1835	Rodeo – St Omer
17/08/42	F/O E. Doorly	1710-1830	B-17 escort Fecamp – St Valery
18/08/42	F/O J.C. Nelson	1310-1420	Rodeo Dunkirk – Sangatte
19/08/42	F/O E. Doorly	0720-0840	Patrol Dieppe
19/08/42	F/O E. Doorly	1015-1130	Top cover 12,000ft – Do 217 damaged
19/08/42	F/Sgt R.L. Alexander	1225-1345	Patrol Dieppe – Do 217 destroyed
19/08/42	F/O E. Doorly	1955-2055	Patrol 10m SE of Eastbourne
20/08/42	P/O D.D. Smith	0855-1015	Patrol
20/08/42	F/O E. Doorly	1625-1735	Rodeo – St Omer

416 Squadron

06/07/43	Sgt J.L.A. Chalot	1615-1830	ASR for W/C Rabagliati
06/07/43	Sgt J.L.A. Chalot	1935-2135	ASR for W/C Rabagliati
07/07/43	Sgt J.L.A. Chalot	0635-0830	ASR for W/C Rabagliati
17/07/43	P/O J.C. McLeod	1045-1100	Ramrod (from Matlaske) – aborted
18/07/43	Sgt H.V. West	1955-2140	Beaufighter escort
25/07/43	P/O J.C. McLeod	1915-2120	ASR for S/L Charles
02/08/43	F/L R.D. Forbes-Roberts	1040-1105	Beaufighter escort – early return
12/08/43	P/O J.C. McLeod	1000-1150	R-196 B-26 – Ault
12/08/43	P/O J.C. McLeod	1835-1925	R-198 B-26 – Poix
15/08/43	P/O J.C. McLeod	0955-1155	R-199 B-26 – Woensdrecht
16/08/43	P/O J.C. McLeod	1035-1205	R-203 B-26 – Bernay
16/08/43	Sgt E.E. Gall	1615-1745	R-205 B-26 – Bernay
17/08/43	P/O J.C. McLeod	0955-1135	R-206 B-26
17/08/43	P/O J.C. McLeod	1510-1645	R-207 B-26 – Poix
18/08/43	P/O J.C. McLeod	0945-1145	R-208 B-26 – Woensdrecht
19/08/43	F/O H.R. Finlay	1130-1300	R-209 B-26
25/08/43	Sgt R.W. Beall	1830-2000	R-S.2 Mitchells – Bernay
26/08/43	P/O J.C. McLeod	1520-1725	10Gp R-78 Bostons (from Exeter)
27/08/43	F/L R.D. Forbes-Roberts	0830-0935	R-S.6 Mitchells Bernay (recalled)
30/08/43	F/O J.L. Campbell	1810-1940	R-S.14 Venturas – target nr St Omer
31/08/43	P/O J.C. McLeod	0735-0905	R-S.16 Mitchells – Monchy Breton
02/09/43	F/O A.J. Fraser	1805-1940	R-S.24 Pt II B-26

03/09/43	P/O J.C. McLeod	0910-0955	R-S.26 Pt II B-26 – Beaumont le Roger
04/09/43	S/L R.H. Walker	1750-1805	R-S.32 Pt III – R/T failure
05/09/43	F/O F.R. Bartlett	0825-1040	R-S.33 Pt III – Woensdrecht
06/09/43	P/O J.C. McLeod	0645-0830	R-S.35 B-26 – Rouen m.yards
06/09/43	F/L R.D. Forbes-Roberts	1705-1845	R-S.36 Pt I B-26 – Serquex m.yards
07/09/43	P/O J.C. McLeod	0800-0940	R-S.38 Pt V B-26 – St Pol m.yards
08/09/43	F/O F.R. Bartlett	0925-1110	R-S.41 Pt III Mitchells – Vitry-en-Artois
03/10/43	P/O J.C McLeod	1025-1210	R-257 B-26 – Schiphol
24/10/43	P/O L.G.D. Pow	1130-1330	R-283 B-26 – Montdidier a/d
24/10/43	P/O L.G.D. Pow	1530-1720	R-284 Mitchells – Schiphol
13/11/43	P/O J.B. Gould	0925-1120	Rhubarb
07/01/44	P/O J.C. McLeod	1120-1235	R-431 target nr Cherbourg
14/01/44	F/L W.F. Mason	1045-1250	R-452 Pt II Mitchells 'Noball' – N of Abbeville

402 Squadron

01/03/44	S/L G.W. Northcott	1650-1850	Roadstead – Beaufighters
26/03/44	S/L G.W. Northcott	1240-1410	Ramrod – Bostons – Ijmuiden
31/03/44	S/L G.W. Northcott	1625-1835	Roadstead
02/05/44	S/L G.W. Northcott	1500-1725	R-822 Bostons – Tournai
03/05/44	S/L G.W. Northcott	1340-1505	R-826 Mitchells
04/05/44	S/L G.W. Northcott	0615-0845	Fabius I
04/05/44	S/L G.W. Northcott	2045-2305	Fabius I
05/05/44	S/L G.W. Northcott	0700-0845	Fabius I
07/05/44	S/L G.W. Northcott	1445-1625	R-841 Mitchells – Serquex m.yards
08/05/44	S/L G.W. Northcott	0900-1050	R-845 Sweep
08/05/44	S/L G.W. Northcott	1815-1955	Sweep – Mons area
09/05/44	S/L G.W. Northcott	0955-1145	R-855
10/05/44	S/L G.W. Northcott	1700-1840	R-864 aborted due to haze
11/05/44	S/L G.W. Northcott	1010-1050	R-866 early return – mech. trouble
11/05/44	S/L G.W. Northcott	1615-1755	Sweep – Douai area
12/05/44	S/L G.W. Northcott	1815-2005	R-879 – Sweep
13/05/44	F/O G.B. Lawson	1010-1155	R-880 – Sweep
13/05/44	W/O H.C. Nicholson	1515-1700	R-884
15/05/44	S/L G.W. Northcott	0850-1050	R-889 target nr Etretat
18/05/44	S/L G.W. Northcott	2055-2205	Cantab patrol – Selsey Bill
19/05/44	S/L G.W. Northcott	1910-2000	R-897 early return – mech. trouble
02/06/44	F/O G.B. Lawson	2130-2330	Patrol – Solent area
05/06/44	F/O D.R. Drummond	0400-0600	Patrol – Foreness area
05/06/44	F/O K.M. Collins	1250-1400	Patrol – Beachy Head area
05/06/44	F/O G.B. Lawson	1620-1800	Patrol – Beachy Head area
05/06/44	F/O G.B. Lawson	2020-2155	Patrol – Beachy Head area
06/06/44	F/O G.B. Lawson	0945-1215	Beachhead cover (eastern area)
06/06/44	P/O H.C. Nicholson	2200-2359	Beachhead cover
07/06/44	F/O G.B. Lawson	0430-0710	Beachhead cover
07/06/44	P/O K.A. Heggie	0940-1045	Beachhead cover (spare)
08/06/44	F/O G.B. Lawson	0435-0705	Beachhead cover

08/06/44	F/O E.L. Mouland	0940-1205	Beachhead cover
10/06/44	F/O G.B. Lawson	0440-1700	Beachhead cover
10/06/44	P/O H.C. Nicholson	0940-1200	Beachhead cover
10/06/44	F/O G.B. Lawson	1700-1830	Convoy Patrol
10/06/44	P/O K.A. Heggie	2130-2359	Patrol
12/06/44	P/O C.H. Bavis	0930-1200	Beachhead cover
12/06/44	P/O K.A. Heggie	2205-2315	Beachhead cover
13/06/44	P/O K.A. Heggie	0445-0615	Beachhead cover
13/06/44	F/O G.B. Lawson	2205-2355	Beachhead cover
14/06/44	F/O E.L. Mouland	0400-0600	Beachhead cover
16/06/44	F/O G.B. Lawson	1130-1400	Beachhead cover (western area)
16/06/44	F/O G.B. Lawson	1455-1715	Beachhead cover
16/06/44	F/O E.L. Mouland	2200-2359	Beachhead cover
17/06/44	F/O G.B. Lawson	1135-1405	Beachhead cover
17/06/44	F/O E.L. Mouland	1635-1905	Beachhead cover
21/06/44	F/O G.B. Lawson	2115-2245	Beachhead cover
22/06/44	F/O G.B. Lawson	1435-1610	Convoy Patrol
22/06/44	F/O G.B. Lawson	2220-2350	Beachhead cover
25/06/44	F/O J.A. MacLeod	0415-0640	Beachhead cover
27/06/44	F/O G.B. Lawson	0725-0935	Beachhead cover
27/06/44	F/O G.B. Lawson	1930-2130	Beachhead cover
28/06/44	P/O K.A. Heggie	0430-0630	Beachhead cover
29/06/44	P/O K.A. Heggie	1130-1320	Beachhead cover
29/06/44	F/O G.B. Lawson	1725-1935	Beachhead cover
30/06/44	F/O E.L. Mouland	1430-1630	Beachhead cover
05/07/44	P/O K.A. Heggie	0705-0715	Early return – mech. trouble
06/07/44	W/O R.L. Pascoe	1225-1410	R-1063 Mitchells – Cerences
10/07/44	W/O R.L. Pascoe	1140-1320	Shipping Patrol
10/07/44	P/O K.A. Heggie	1530-1650	Shipping Patrol
10/07/44	F/L K.S. Sleep	1930-2100	Shipping Patrol
12/07/44	P/O K.A. Heggie	1905-2120	R-1081 Lancasters – Vaires m.yards
13/07/44	P/O K.A. Heggie	1050-1230	Convoy Patrol

AR501

310 Squadron

03/08/42	Sgt A. Skach	1840-2005	Convoy patrol
04/09/42	P/O J. Doucha	1255-1435	Patrol
08/09/42	Sgt A. Skach	1050-1140	Rear support to shipping recce
10/09/42	S/L F. Dolezal	1840-1940	Rear cover for Whirlwinds
11/09/42	Sgt A. Stanek	1525-1645	Convoy patrol
12/09/42	F/Sgt F. Mleinecky	1210-1240	Scramble
13/09/42	Sgt A. Skach	1340-1505	Anti-Rhubarb patrol
14/09/42	Sgt A. Skach	1005-1130	Convoy patrol
15/09/42	S/L F. Dolezal	1700-1810	Rear support Bostons – Cherbourg
17/09/42	F/L V. Bergman	1530-1645	Rear support to shipping recce

18/09/42	S/L F. Dolezal	1115-1205	Fired on 190s bombing Dartmouth
19/09/42	Sgt A. Skach	1350-1525	Convoy patrol
22/09/42	F/O R. Borovec	1125-1235	Anti-Rhubarb patrol
23/09/42	F/O R. Borovec	1025-1135	Rear support to shipping recce
23/09/42	F/Sgt M. Petr	1820-2010	Convoy patrol
01/10/42	P/O J. Doucha	1615-1750	Convoy patrol
01/10/42	P/O J. Doucha	1830-1925	Convoy patrol
09/10/42	S/L F. Dolezal	0900-1035	Diversionary sweep – Dutch coast
09/10/42	F/Sgt M. Petr	1830-1910	Convoy patrol
10/10/42	P/O J. Doucha	1405-1530	Convoy patrol
12/10/42	W/O A. Skach	0905-1035	Convoy patrol
12/10/42	F/L J. Hartman	1255-1440	Convoy patrol
15/10/42	S/L F. Dolezal	1350-1500	Rear support – Hurri-bombers
27/10/42	S/L F. Dolezal	1515-1650	10Gp R-17 supporting B-17s
28/10/42	S/L F. Dolezal	1440-1550	Rear support – Hurri-bombers
03/11/42	F/L J. Hartman	1330-1510	Anti-Rhubarb patrol
08/11/42	F/Sgt V.Popelka	0835-1010	ASR for P/O Doucha (shot down
08/11/42	F/Sgt V. Popelka	1255-1400	7/11 in AR502 – body found later)
09/11/42	W/O J. Skirka	1145-1305	Convoy patrol
09/11/42	W/O J. Skirka	1530-1725	Anti-Rhubarb patrol
11/11/42	S/L F. Dolezal	1420-1620	Sweep Cap de la Hague – Guernsey
14/11/42	S/L F. Dolezal	1115-1240	Rear support for B-17s – Lannion
14/11/42	S/L F. Dolezal	1355-1535	Sweep – Lannion
17/11/42	S/L F. Dolezal	1115-1305	10Gp R-37 – Lannion
10/01/43	P/O K. Zouhar	0910-1050	Convoy patrol
15/01/43	W/O A. Skach	1510-1530	Convoy patrol
21/01/43	S/L E. Foit	1245-1415	10Gp R-47 Bostons – Cherbourg
22/01/43	F/L R. Borovec	1010-1150	Anti-Rhubarb patrol
23/01/43	S/L E. Foit	1235-1415	10Gp R-48 Cover 23,000ft
26/01/43	W/O F.Trejtnar	1450-1615	10Gp R-49 Venturas – Morlaix
27/01/43	W/O F. Trejtnar	1600-1730	Convoy patrol
29/01/43	F/O K. Drbohlav	1325-1515	10Gp R-50 – Morlaix viaduct
03/02/43	Sgt A. Sveceny	1100-1250	Convoy patrol
11/02/43	W/O A. Skach	1540-1710	Anti-Rhubarb patrol
12/02/43	W/O A. Skach	1010-1130	Convoy patrol
13/02/43	W/O A. Skach	0810-0945	Patrol
13/02/43	F/L H. Hrbacek	1340-1540	10Gp R-52 Bostons – St Malo
14/02/43	F/O J. Hartman	0935-1100	Anti-Rhubarb patrol
14/02/43	F/O J. Strihavka	1405-1520	Anti-Rhubarb patrol
15/02/43	F/O J. Strihavka	0930-1110	Convoy patrol
15/02/43	F/O J. Strihavka	1140-1345	Convoy patrol
16/02/43	P/O O. Pavlu	1140-1330	10Gp R-53
17/02/43	P/O O. Pavlu	1055-1150	Convoy patrol
17/02/43	F/Sgt V. Lysicky	1405-1525	Patrol
18/02/43	F/L H. Hrbacek	1650-1825	Convoy patrol
20/02/43	F/O J. Strihavka	1400-1545	Convoy patrol
24/02/43	F/Sgt J. Stefan	1355-1520	Anti-Rhubarb patrol

24/02/43	F/O K. Drbohlav	1805-1910	Convoy patrol
25/02/43	Sgt A. Sveceny	1115-1300	Convoy patrol
27/02/43	F/L H. Hrbacek	1345-1530	10Gp R-54
27/02/43	W/O A. Skach	1745-1910	Anti-Rhubarb patrol
28/02/43	P/O O. Pavlu	1445-1615	10Gp C-17 Whirlwinds – Maupertus
28/02/43	P/O O. Pavlu	1820-1915	Anti-Rhubarb patrol
01/03/43	P/O O. Pavlu	1300-1310	Scramble – recalled
06/03/43	F/L H. Hrbacek	1330-1510	10Gp R-56 – Brest
08/03/43	F/L H. Hrbacek	1305-1450	10Gp R-57
10/03/43	F/L H. Hrbacek	0750-0920	Anti-Rhubarb patrol
10/03/43	F/O J. Strihavka	1600-1725	Anti-Rhubarb patrol
10/03/43	W/O F. Trejtnar	1820-1920	Convoy patrol
11/03/43	W/O F. Trejtnar	1000-1125	Convoy patrol
11/03/43	W/O F. Trejtnar	1845-2005	Gunboat patrol
13/03/43	F/L H. Hrbacek	0930-1115	Convoy patrol
14/03/43	Sgt A. Sveceny	0815-0950	Anti-Rhubarb patrol
14/03/43	Sgt A. Sveceny	1545-1710	10Gp C-18 Whirlwinds – Maupertus

312 Squadron

22/10/43	F/O V. Smolik	0930-1135	11Gp R-280 B-26 – Evreux
24/10/43	F/O F. Chabera	1440-1555	10Gp R-94 Mitchells – Cherbourg
25/10/43	F/O F. Chabera	1325-1525	10Gp R-95 Mitchells – Lanveoc
26/10/43	F/O V. Smolik	1200-1335	Convoy patrol
28/10/43	F/Sgt J. Zakravsky	1405-1545	10Gp R-96 Mitchells – Cherbourg
30/10/43	F/O V. Smolik	1455-1600	10Gp R-99 Bostons – Maupertus
01/11/43	F/O V. Smolik	1745-1805	Scramble
03/11/43	F/O V. Smolik	1010-1220	R-289 B-26 – St Andre
05/11/43	F/Sgt J. Zakravsky	1505-1555	10Gp R-100 – Cherbourg (abort)
07/11/43	P/O Motycka	0835-1025	R-297 Bostons – Bernay
08/11/43	F/O V. Smolik	0945-1105	ASR
10/11/43	F/O V. Smolik	1030-1150	Roadstead 78 – off Guernsey
26/11/43	F/O V. Smolik	1005-1115	10Gp R-107 Mitchells – Martinvast
20/12/43	F/O V. Smolik	1620-1740	Convoy patrol
22/12/43	P/O Motycka	1055-1245	R-383 'Noball' – south of Abbeville
23/12/43	F/O V. Smolik	0900-1040	R-389 'Noball' – 10m ESE Dieppe
24/12/43	F/O V. Smolik	1335-1455	R-393 'Noball' – 6m SE Cherbourg
30/12/43	Sgt Cermak	1355-1630	R-397 'Noball' – 10m NE Abbeville
04/01/44	P/O Kruta	1520-1710	R-422 'Noball' – 5m NE Abbeville
05/01/44	P/O Kruta	1105-1310	R-423 'Noball' – Mesnil Allard
06/01/44	P/O Kopecek	1105-1315	R-428 'Noball' – 9m SW Dieppe
23/01/44	F/O V. Smolik	1505-1650	R-472 'Noball' – Calais area
28/01/44	F/L Kasal	1540-1725	ASR
29/01/44	F/L Kasal	1330-1540	R-493 'Noball' – SE Dieppe

AR614

312 Squadron

18/09/42	F/Sgt J. Kohout	1020-1210	Convoy patrol
18/09/42	F/Sgt V. Ruprecht	1730-1905	Walrus escort
19/09/42	F/Sgt J. Novotny	1220-1405	Convoy patrol
19/09/42	F/Sgt J. Novotny	1535-1725	Anti-Rhubarb patrol
21/09/42	P/O S. Peroutka	1135-1300	Anti-Rhubarb patrol
21/09/42	F/Sgt J. Novotny	1600-1725	Convoy patrol
01/10/42	F/Sgt M.A. Liskutin	1205-1325	Walrus escort
01/10/42	F/Sgt M.A. Liskutin	1650-1805	Escort Whirlwinds – shipping attack
11/10/42	F/O J. Keprt	1520-1710	Convoy patrol
14/10/42	P/O V. Slouf	1225-1350	Convoy patrol
14/10/42	P/O V. Slouf	1650-1810	Convoy patrol
15/10/42	P/O V. Slouf	1330-1505	Escort Hurri-bombers
21/10/42	P/O J. Dvorak	1305-1435	Sweep – rear support B-17s – Brest
22/10/42	F/Sgt J. Novotny	1325-1455	Convoy patrol
25/10/42	F/L K. Kasal	1750-1840	Escort captured German aircraft
26/10/42	F/Sgt J. Kohout	0955-1035	Scramble
27/10/42	F/Sgt S. Tocauer	1515-1645	Sweep – Alderney area
28/10/42	F/Sgt S. Tocauer	1410-1545	Escort Hurri-bombers
03/11/42	F/Sgt J. Novotny	1110-1255	Convoy patrol
03/11/42	F/Sgt J. Novotny	1515-1645	Sweep – Jersey/Guernsey area
04/11/42	F/Sgt J. Novotny	1255-1315	Anti-Rhubarb patrol (abort)
06/11/42	F/Sgt R. Ossendorf	1020-1145	Shipping recce
08/04/43	S/L A. Vybiral	0955-1200	Rodeo 33 with Czech Wing
09/04/43	S/L A. Vybiral	1250-1440	Roadstead 55 – chased Ju 88
10/04/43	S/L A. Vybiral	0910-1050	Convoy patrol
13/04/43	F/L B. Budil	1405-1545	Scramble – patrol base 15,000ft
14/04/43	S/L A. Vybiral	1515-1735	Roadstead 57 – Whirlwinds
15/04/43	F/Sgt J. Kohout	1315-1510	Shipping recce
16/04/43	S/L A. Vybiral	1245-1440	10Gp R-64
18/04/43	F/L A. Vrana	0645-0820	Shipping recce
18/04/43	S/L A. Vybiral	1205-1345	Patrol
19/04/43	S/L A. Vybiral	0925-1100	Anti-Rhubarb patrol
19/04/43	F/L A. Vrana	1645-1845	Convoy patrol
20/04/43	S/L A. Vybiral	1615-1735	10Gp C-25 Venturas – Cherbourg
21/04/43	F/Sgt M.A. Liskutin	0940-1125	Shipping recce
23/04/43	F/Sgt M.A. Liskutin	1540-1640	Convoy patrol
26/04/43	F/Sgt F. Kotiba	1630-1750	Anti-Rhubarb patrol
27/04/43	S/L A. Vybiral	1130-1320	10Gp C-27 Venturas – St Brieuc
01/05/43	S/L A. Vybiral	0935-1135	10Gp C-28
04/05/43	S/L A. Vybiral	1850-2050	C-294 Venturas – Abbeville m.yards
05/05/43	F/L B. Budil	1555-1640	Scramble – Exeter 15,000ft
13/05/43	S/L A. Vybiral	1500-1650	Convoy patrol
14/05/43	S/L A. Vybiral	2000-2130	Shipping attack – Guernsey Cat. Ac

614 Squadron

22/11/43	F/L H.H. Percy	1530-1650	Shipping recce
09/12/43	Sgt C. Oddy	1325-1500	Convoy patrol

BL614

611 Squadron

18/02/42	F/Sgt W.L. Miller	1115-1245	Patrol
27/02/42	Sgt C.E. Graysmark	1730-1830	Scramble
16/03/42	F/Sgt Boyle	1640-1655	Scramble
26/03/42	Sgt Rogers	1615-1645	Scramble
26/03/42	Sgt Rogers	1920-2040	Dusk patrol
29/03/42	F/Sgt D.A. Bye	0805-0925	Convoy patrol
09/04/42	F/L Edwards	2055-2140	Convoy patrol
23/05/42	F/L W.M. Gilmour	0630-0650	Scramble

242 Squadron

07/06/42	F/Sgt Mather	1320-1350	Scramble
07/06/42	Sgt Hampshire	2110-2240	Scramble
16/06/42	F/Sgt Buist	0655-0710	Scramble
16 /06/42	F/L Benham	2345-0145	Night flying practice/Patrol
18/06/42	F/L Benham	2330-0020	Convoy Patrol
07/07/42	Sgt Sullivan	0850-0935	Scramble
07/07/42	F/L Benham	1325-1435	Scramble
15/07/42	Sgt Hamblin	1255-1320	Scramble
22/07/42	Sgt Hamblin	2030-2040	Scramble
23/07/42	Sgt Hamblin	0620-0755	Convoy Patrol

222 Squadron

17/08/42	Sgt J.W. McDonald	1520-1600	Feint Ramrod – Beachy Head area
18/08/42	Sgt J.W. McDonald	1305-1435	Rodeo over Dunkirk 19,000ft
18/08/42	Sgt J. Ekbery	1910-2030	Patrol
19/08/42	Sgt J.W. McDonald	0553-0735	Patrol off Dieppe
19/08/42	Sgt J.W. McDonald	1700-1820	Withdrawal cover for Dieppe
29/11/42	Sgt C.A. Joseph	1530-1700	Patrol

64 Squadron

11/04/43	Sgt D. Ledington	1200-1245	Convoy patrol
16/04/43	P/O B.C. Kelly	0720-0910	Convoy patrol
19/05/43	P/O F.R. Burnard	2105-2235	Convoy patrol
28/05/43	P/O B.C. Kelly	1230-1400	Convoy patrol
06/06/43	Sgt C.A. Rice	1955-2135	Convoy patrol
27/07/43	Sgt A. Pugh	1725-1855	Convoy patrol
15/08/43	F/O B.C. Kelly	1315-1400	Patrol Beachy Head – Shoreham

17/08/43	F/O B.C. Kelly	0500-0620	Patrol
06/09/43	F/O K.V. Calder	1710-1845	R-S.36 B-26 – Amiens m.yards
07/09/43	Sgt J.D.M. Duncan	0740-0855	R-S.38 Pt III Mitchells – St Omer
08/09/43	F/L G.B. Silvester	0930-1100	R-S.41 Pt III Mitchells – Vitry en Artois
08/09/43	F/O K.V. Calder	1705-1825	R-S.42 Mitchells – Boulogne
09/09/43	F/O K.V. Calder	1415-1545	R-S.43 Pt III Venturas – Merville
13/09/43	F/O K.V. Calder	1745-1910	Rodeo 253 Le Touquet – Abbeville
14/09/43	F/L G.B. Silvester	1655-1810	R-218 B-26 Lille-Nord

118 Squadron

22/09/43	Sgt S.V. Piper	0810-0835	Patrol
25/09/43	P/O J.M. Hemstock	1745-1930	Dusk patrol
28/09/43	F/Sgt F.L. Spencer	-	Dusk patrol
10/10/43	F/Sgt F.L. Spencer	1800-1845	Scramble
13/10/43	Sgt D.G. Ballard	0715-0830	Patrol
14/10/43	Sgt R.A. Hamilton	0710-0810	Patrol

BM597

315 Squadron

23/05/42	Sgt Slonski	1300-1440	Patrol over base 20–27,000ft
24/06/42	P/O Widziszowski	0855-0940	Scramble
03/07/42	P/O B. Semmerling	2005-2025	Defensive patrol
16/07/42	F/O H. Wyrozemski	1240-1315	Defensive patrol
04/08/42	F/Sgt J. Adamiak	1705-1725	Defensive patrol
04/08/42	F/Sgt J. Adamiak	1945-2030	Defensive patrol
12/08/42	P/O S. Blok	1630-1710	Convoy patrol
20/08/42	F/Sgt J. Adamiak	1825-1855	Scramble

317 Squadron

| 18/11/43 | P/O J. Zerozek | 1350-1440 | Scramble |
| 21/01/43 | F/Sgt J. Malinowski | 1220-1235 | Scramble |

EP120

501 Squadron

06/06/42	P/O R.C. Lynch	1630-1750	Escort Hurri-bombers – Maupertus
08/06/42	P/O R.C. Lynch	1045-1220	Sweep mid-Channel
08/06/42	P/O W.R. Lightbourne	1505-1545	Convoy patrol
08/06/42	P/O R.C. Lynch	2130-2215	Scramble
09/06/42	P/O R.C. Lynch	0515-0645	Convoy patrol
09/06/42	Sgt A. Vendl	1640-1730	Scramble
11/06/42	P/O R.C. Lynch	1420-1510	Patrol 25,000ft – St Catherines Pt
20/06/42	Sgt A.R. McDonald	1500-1620	Sweep with Biggin Hill Wing – St Omer

23/06/42	Sgt A. Lee	1935-2020	Scramble
26/06/42	Sgt A.R. McDonald	1640-1810	11Gp sweep from Redhill
27/06/42	Sgt A.R. McDonald	0530-0730	Convoy patrol
27/06/42	Sgt A.R. McDonald	2245-2345	Scramble to mid-Channel
29/06/42	P/O R.C. Lynch	1340-1445	Scramble
29/06/42	P/O R.C. Lynch	2140-2245	Convoy patrol
02/07/42	P/O R.C. Lynch	1510-1645	Convoy patrol
11/07/42	P/O R.C. Lynch	1620-1720	Scramble south of Portland
11/07/42	P/O R.C. Lynch	2125-2215	Scramble south of Portland
12/07/42	P/O R.C. Lynch	0640-0745	Patrol IOW-Portland
13/07/42	P/O R.C. Lynch	1055-1220	Patrol IOW-Portland
14/07/42	P/O R.C. Lynch	1125-1220	Cover for shipping recce
15/07/42	P/O R.C. Lynch	0835-1000	Sweep – Cherbourg peninsula
14/08/42	Sgt H.R. Kelly	0455-0550	Scramble – St Albans Head
17/08/42	F/Sgt R.J. Long	1640-1740	Diversionary sweep – Cherbourg
19/08/42	F/Sgt R.J. Long	0745-0815	Escort Blenheims – Dieppe – recalled
19/08/42	F/Sgt R.J. Long	1025-1150	Escort Hurricanes – Dieppe
19/08/42	W/C P. Gibbs	1455-1615	Patrol – Do 217 destroyed – damaged Cat. Ac

19 Squadron

24/09/42	Sgt W.H. Mills	1730-1910	Anti-Rhubarb patrol – Lizard
06/10/42	Sgt W.H. Mills	1605-1705	Convoy patrol
08/10/42	P/O H.A.L. Simpson	1420-1525	Convoy patrol
09/10/42	P/O H.A.L. Simpson	1655-1745	Convoy patrol
10/10/42	Sgt W.H. Sloan	1345-1505	Convoy patrol
11/10/42	P/O S.N. Chilton	0725-0900	Convoy patrol
11/10/42	P/O S.N. Chilton	1020-1145	Convoy patrol
13/10/42	P/O S.N. Chilton	0900-0915	Scramble
15/10/42	Sgt R.A. Hutchinson	1650-1815	Convoy patrol
24/10/42	P/O S.N. Chilton	1500-1620	Convoy patrol
26/10/42	P/O S.N. Chilton	1520-1705	Convoy patrol
27/10/42	P/O S.N. Chilton	1050-1145	Escort Tiger Moth to Scillies
28/10/42	Sgt R.A. Hutchinson	1320-1350	Patrol
31/10/42	Sgt R.E. Wass	1050-1115	Shipping recce (abort)
02/11/42	Sgt T.E. Winter	1035-1135	Patrol Lands End – Dodman Pt
06/11/42	P/O S.N. Chilton	1410-1535	Patrol Lands End – Dodman Pt
07/11/42	Sgt E.S. Opie	1135-1310	Patrol Lands End – Dodman Pt
08/11/42	P/O S.N. Chilton	0900-1030	Patrol Lands End – Dodman Pt
08/11/42	Sgt A. Glover	1130-1315	Patrol Lands End – Dodman Pt
10/11/42	P/O S.N. Chilton	1130-1315	Patrol Lands End – Dodman Pt
11/11/42	Sgt E.S. Opie	0935-1040	Convoy patrol
11/11/42	Sgt A. Glover	1135-1300	Convoy patrol
27/11/42	P/O S.N. Chilton	0930-1100	Convoy patrol
29/11/42	P/O D.W. Connor	1300-1420	Convoy patrol
01/12/42	P/O S.N. Chilton	1640-1800	Convoy patrol
02/12/42	P/O S.N. Chilton	1405-1535	Convoy patrol
05/12/42	P/O S.N. Chilton	1405-1520	Rear cover for Rhubarb
17/12/42	P/O I.M. Mundy	1100-1255	Instep patrol

20/12/42	P/O G.A. King	1400-1550	Instep patrol
24/12/42	P/O S.N. Chilton	0850-1025	Convoy patrol
26/12/42	P/O S.N. Chilton	1510-1610	Convoy patrol
27/12/42	P/O S.N. Chilton	0915-1120	Instep patrol
03/01/43	F/O S.N. Chilton	1315-1500	Sweep Landivisiau – Guipavas
10/01/43	P/O W.H. Mills	0930-1055	Roadstead – Whirlwinds
10/01/43	Sgt A. Glover	1410-1515	Convoy patrol
13/01/43	Sgt R.A. Hutchinson	1000-1125	Shipping recce – Ile de Batz
14/01/43	Sgt A. Glover	1230-1340	Convoy patrol
14/01/43	Sgt A. Glover	1630-1815	Convoy patrol
29/01/43	F/O G.A. King	1330-1535	Support for bombers – Morlaix
02/02/43	Sgt J.D. Baragwanath	1320-1445	Convoy patrol
02/02/43	P/O G.N. Bell	1535-1645	Convoy patrol
07/02/43	F/L P. Wigley	0920-1030	Liberator escort – not sighted

402 Squadron

14/05/43	F/L M. Johnston	0525-0735	Support for bombers off Holland
17/05/43	F/L M. Johnston	1540-1750	Beaufighter escort
18/05/43	W/O R.H. Prebble	1820-1855	Scramble
24/05/43	F/L M. Johnston	1115-1305	Roadstead – off Texel
27/05/43	F/L M. Johnston	0650-0800	Lagoon – off French coast
31/05/43	F/L M. Johnston	1645-1900	C-309 Pt I Mitchells – Flushing
05/06/43	S/L L.V. Chadburn	1230-1400	Roadstead – attacked armed trawler
11/06/43	S/L L.V. Chadburn	1145-1315	Sweep – Zeebrugge
11/06/43	S/L L.V. Chadburn	1815-1945	Lagoon
12/06/43	S/L L.V. Chadburn	1905-2040	R-91 Bostons – Rouen
22/06/43	P/O D.R. Drummond	1625-1800	Beaufighter escort
23/06/43	S/L G.W. Northcott	1650-1830	R-100 Bostons – Meaulte
24/06/43	S/L G.W. Northcott	0745-0915	Ramrod
24/06/43	S/L G.W. Northcott	1645-1810	Ramrod
25/06/43	S/L G.W. Northcott	0745-0905	12Gp R-19 Amsterdam (abort)
26/06/43	S/L G.W. Northcott	1825-2015	Rear support B-17s to Le Mans
27/06/43	S/L G.W. Northcott	1420-1600	Beaufighter escort – Me 109 destroyed
29/06/43	S/L G.W. Northcott	1945-2135	Ramrod
18/07/43	S/L G.W. Northcott	1420-1615	Beaufighter escort
18/07/43	S/L G.W. Northcott	1955-2140	Beaufighter escort
25/07/43	S/L G.W. Northcott	1410-1555	R-158 Bostons – Schiphol
27/07/43	W/O J.R. Richardson	1920-2120	12Gp R-20 Mitchells – Schiphol
29/07/43	S/L G.W. Northcott	0945-1115	B-26 escort – from Ludham
29/07/43	S/L G.W. Northcott	1745-1855	B-26 escort – from Bradwell Bay
30/07/43	S/L G.W. Northcott	1000-1130	12Gp R-23 Bostons – Schiphol
02/08/43	S/L G.W. Northcott	1040-1220	Beaufighter escort – 2 Me 109 destroyed
12/08/43	S/L G.W. Northcott	1000-1135	R-196 B-26 escort
15/08/43	F/O D.R. Drummond	0945-1200	R-199 B-26 – Rotterdam – from Martlesham
16/08/43	S/L G.W. Northcott	1030-1210	R-203 B-26 – Bernay
16/08/43	S/L G.W. Northcott	1615-1750	R-205 B-26 – Bernay
17/08/43	P/O J.D. Mitchner	0955-1135	R-206 B-26 escort
22/08/43	S/L G.W. Northcott	1805-1945	R-212 B-26 Beaumont le Roger – Fw 190 dest.

23/08/43	S/L G.W. Northcott	0740-0850	Ramrod – recalled
25/08/43	S/L G.W. Northcott	1830-2005	B-26 escort
26/08/43	S/L G.W. Northcott	1515-1715	10Gp R-78 Bostons – St Brieuc (from Exeter)
30/08/43	S/L G.W. Northcott	1810-1950	R-S.14 Venturas – St Omer area
31/08/43	S/L G.W. Northcott	0720-0900	R-S.16 Pt III – Mitchells – Monchy Breton a/f
31/08/43	S/L G.W. Northcott	1705-1825	R-S.18 – Venturas – Forêt de Hesdin
02/09/43	S/L G.W. Northcott	1800-1945	R-S.24 Pt II B-26 escort
04/09/43	S/L G.W. Northcott	1750-1930	R-S.31 Pt III B-26 – St Pol – Fw 190 dest.
05/09/43	S/L G.W. Northcott	0830-1040	R-S.33 Pt III Bostons – Woensdrecht
06/09/43	S/L G.W. Northcott	0645-0825	R-S.35 B-26 – Rouen m.yards
06/09/43	S/L G.W. Northcott	1705-1845	R-S.36 Pt I B-26 – Serquex m.yards
07/09/43	S/L G.W. Northcott	0755-0945	R-S.38 Pt V B-26 – St Pol m.yards
09/09/43	S/L G.W Northcott	0755-0955	Patrol over Channel
09/09/43	S/L G.W. Northcott	1355-1530	R-S.43 Pt I Bostons – Monchy Breton a/f
11/09/43	S/L G.W. Northcott	1655-1845	R-216 Pt II B-26 – Beaumont le Roger
13/09/43	S/L G.W. Northcott	1800-1945	Sweep Beaumont le Roger – Evreux
14/09/43	S/L G.W. Northcott	1640-1810	Ramrod – abort
18/09/43	S/L G.W. Northcott	0945-1135	R-228 Pt II B-26 – Beauvais
18/09/43	S/L G.W. Northcott	1625-1735	R-230 Pt II B-26 – Beaumont le Roger
21/09/43	S/L G.W. Northcott	0850-1030	B-26 escort to Beauvais – from Manston
22/09/43	S/L G.W. Northcott	1525-1715	R-237 Pt II B-26 – Evreux
23/09/43	S/L G.W. Northcott	0810-1000	B-26 escort to Conches a/f – from Tangmere
23/09/43	S/L G.W. Northcott	1450-1635	R-240 B-26 – Beauvais
24/09/43	S/L G.W. Northcott	1100-1250	R-242 Pt III B-26
24/09/43	S/L G.W. Northcott	1500-1650	R-243 Pt II B-26
25/09/43	S/L G.W. Northcott	1125-1245	Beaufighter escort
03/10/43	S/L G.W. Northcott	1035-1225	R-257 B-26 – Schiphol – Me 109 damaged
18/10/43	P/O G.B. Lawson	1600-1730	Ramrod from Tangmere
03/11/43	S/L G.W. Northcott	1550-1740	R-290 B-26 – Schiphol – Me 109 destroyed
05/11/43	S/L G.W. Northcott	1245-1415	Ramrod – 'Noball' nr Boulogne
05/11/43	S/L G.W. Northcott	1545-1645	Ramrod – Mitchells – missed r/v
07/11/43	S/L G.W. Northcott	1025-1140	Ramrod from Hawkinge
11/11/43	S/L G.W. Northcott	1510-1610	R-312 Mitchells – 'Noball' site
16/11/43	S/L G.W. Northcott	1335-1540	Beaufighter escort
23/11/43	S/L G.W. Northcott	1410-1525	Beaufighter escort
26/11/43	S/L G.W. Northcott	1140-1310	R-336 Pt III B-26 Cambrai
29/11/43	S/L G.W. Northcott	0945-1045	Ramrod from W.Malling – abort
01/12/43	S/L G.W. Northcott	0945-1145	R-343 Pt IV B-26 – Cambrai
04/12/43	S/L G.W. Northcott	1430-1550	R-349 Pt I B-26 escort from Manston
14/01/44	S/L G.W. Northcott	1045-1145	R-452 Pt II Mitchells – 'Noball' N of Abbeville
21/01/44	S/L G.W. Northcott	1155-1325	R-468 Pt II – 'Noball' nr St Omer
25/01/44	S/L G.W. Northcott	1540-1640	Ramrod from Bradwell Bay
29/01/44	S/L G.W. Northcott	1355-1540	Ramrod – 'Noball' S of Rouen
06/02/44	F/L R.A. Morrison	1000-1100	Lagoon
08/02/44	F/L E.P. Wood	0900-1030	Lagoon
09/02/44	F/L E.P. Wood	1320-1450	Lagoon

SPITFIRE V SQUADRONS IN FIGHTER COMMAND – JANUARY 1942

9 Group

Squadron	Code	Airfield	CO
457	BP	Jurby/Andreas	S/L P.M. Brothers
308	ZF	Woodvale	S/L Nowierski
131	NX	Atcham	S/L M.G.F. Pedley DFC

10 Group

Squadron	Code	Airfield	CO
312	DU	Angle	S/L A. Vasatko DFC
130	PJ	Perranporth	S/L E.P.P. Gibbs DFC
317	JH	Exeter	S/L H. Szczesny VM
306	UZ	Church Stanton	S/L A. Wczelik
302	WX	Harrowbeer	S/L Kowalski
118	NK	Ibsley	S/L J.C. Carver
234	AZ	Ibsley	S/L F.E.W Birchfield
501	SD	Ibsley	S/L C.F. Currant DFC

11 Group

Squadron	Code	Airfield	CO
41	EB	Westhampnett	S/L P.H. Hugo
129	DV	Westhampnett	S/L R.H. Thomas
602	LO	Redhill	S/L B.E. Finucane DSO DFC
452	UD	Kenley	S/L K.W. Truscott
485	OU	Kenley	S/L E.P. Wells DFC
72	RN	Gravesend	S/L C.A. Masterman OBE
124	ON	Biggin Hill	S/L R.M.B. Duke-Woolley DFC
91	DL	Hawkinge	S/L R.W. Oxspring
401	YO	Biggin Hill	S/L A.G. Douglas
64	SH	Hornchurch	S/L B.J. Wicks DFC
411	DB	Hornchurch	S/L P.S. Turner DFC
313	RY	Hornchurch	S/L K. Mrazek DFC
222	ZD	North Weald	S/L R.M. Milne DFC
403	KH	North Weald	S/L C.N.S. Campbell
121	AV	North Weald	S/L H.C. Kennard DFC

315	PK	Northolt	S/L S. Janus VM DFC
316	SZ	Northolt	S/L A. Gabszewicz
303	RF	Northolt	S/L Kolaczkowski
71	XR	Martlesham Heath	S/L C.G. Peterson DFC
65	YT	Debden	S/L H.T. Gilbert
111	JU	Debden	S/L G.F. Brotchie

12 Group

19	QV	Ludham	S/L Lawson DFC
412	VZ	Wellingore	S/L J.D. Morrison
616	YQ	Kirton in Lindsay	S/L C.F. Gray DFC
133	MD	Kirton in Lindsay	S/L E.H. Thomas
610	DW	Hutton Cranswick	S/L C.O.J. Pegge

13 Group

332	AH	Catterick	Maj. O. Bull
122	MT	Scorton	S/L R. Millar
81	FL	Turnhouse/Ouston	S/L R. Berry DFC

14 Group

| 603 | XT | Dyce | S/L Lord D. Douglas-Hamilton |
| 123 | XE | Castletown/Tain | S/L D.M. Jack |

82 Group

504	TM	Ballyhalbert	S/L P.T. Parsons
74	ZP	Long Kesh	S/L P.C.N. Matthews
134		Eglinton	S/L A.G. Miller

Appendix D

Spitfire V Squadrons in Fighter Command – June 1943

10 Group

Squadron	Code	Airfield	CO
132	FF	Perranporth	S/L J.R. Ritchie
412	VZ	Perranporth	S/L F.W. Kelly
610	DW	Perranporth	S/L W.A. Laurie
310	NN	Exeter	S/L E. Foit
312	DU	Church Stanton	S/L A. Vybiral DFC
313	RY	Church Stanton	S/L J. Himr
129	DV	Ibsley	S/L H.A.C. Gonay
504	TM	Ibsley	S/L J.R.C. Kilian

11 Group

Squadron	Code	Airfield	CO
485	OU	Merston	S/L R.W. Baker DFC
167	VL	Westhampnett	S/L A.C. Stewart
401	YO	Redhill	S/L E.L. Neal DFC
411	DB	Redhill	S/L B.D. Russel DFC
302	WX	Heston	S/L W. Baranski
317	JH	Heston	S/L F. Kornicki
501	SD	Martlesham Heath	S/L B. Barthold

12 Group

Squadron	Code	Airfield	CO
118	NK	Coltishall	S/L E.W. Wootten DFC
19	QV	Digby	S/L V.H. Ekins
402	AE	Digby	S/L L.V. Chadburn DFC
416	DN	Wellingore	S/L R.W. McNair DFC
315	PK	Hutton Cranswick	S/L J. Poplawski DFC
308	ZF	Church Fenton	S/L J. Zulikowski

13 Group

Squadron	Code	Airfield	CO
306	UZ	Catterick	S/L W. Karwowski
350	MN	Acklington	S/L A.L.T.J. Boussa
340	GW	Drem	Comdt J. Fournier
64	SH	Ayr	S/L M.G.L Donnet DFC CdG

14 Group

66	LZ	Skaebrae	S/L K.T. Lofts DFC
234	AZ	Skaebrae	S/L P.L. Arnott
131	NX	Castletown	S/L J.J. O'Meara DFC
165	SK	Peterhead	S/L E.G.A. Seghers DFC

RAF Northern Ireland

| 130 | PJ | Ballyhalbert | S/L W.H.A. Wright |

Appendix E

Spitfire V Squadrons in ADGB – June 1944

11 Group

Squadron	Code	Airfield	CO
64	SH	Deanland	S/L J.N. MacKenzie DFC
234	AZ	Deanland	S/L P.L. Arnott
611	FY	Deanland	S/L W.A. Douglas DFC
130	AP	Horne	S/L W.H. Ireson
303	RF	Horne	S/L T. Koc DFC
402	AE	Horne	S/L G.W. Northcott DFC
345	2Y	Shoreham	Comdt Bernard
350	MN	Friston	S/L M.G.L. Donnet DFC CdG

12 Group

Squadron	Code	Airfield	CO
504	TM	Castletown (det - Digby/Acklington)	S/L Banning-Lover

13 Group

Squadron	Code	Airfield	CO
118	NK	Skaebrae/Sumburgh	S/L P.W.E. Heppell DFC

INDEX

Names (Ranks as contemporary)

Aalpoel, P/O G.H. 64
Aitken, F/Sgt G.D. 93, 102
Alexander, F/Sgt R.L. 228
Amor, P/O 105
Anderton, Sgt C. 136, 152
Andrews, S/L D.G. 174, 176
Andrews, F/L E. 197, 202
Archer, P/O P.L.I. 25
Arnott, S/L P.L. 186, 188, 209

Bader, W/C D.R.S. 11, 17, 34, 46
Bage, F/O N. 208
Baker, F/O D. 177, 180
Bance, P/O R.A. 119
Barclay, S/L K.M. 172
Barnham, P/O D.A. 48
Bartley, F/O A.C. 8
Barwell, G/C R. 26
Bauman, Sgt V. 70
Beake, P/O P.H. 40
Beamish, G/C F.V. 73, 77
Beaumont, Sgt 73
Beer, P/O A. 136
Bell, F/Sgt P. 190
Bernard, Lt M. 191, 212
Berry, F/L T.W. 212
Binns, Sgt A.F. 40
Birchfield, S/L F.E.W. 54, 57, 60, 120
Bisdee, F/L J.D. 16, 24
Blackburn, P/O B.J. 111
Blair, Sgt I. 63

Blake, W/C M.V. 53, 116, 122
Blakeslee, P/O D.J.M. 48, 233
Bland, P/O G.R. 60
Blatchford, W/C H.P. 132, 136, 139, 141
Bocock, P/O E.P.W. 37, 74
Booth, P/O R.D. 156, 163, 166
Borne, s/Lt R. 183
Bowe, W/O 225
Bowen-Morris, Sgt H. 12, 19
Bowman, F/L H.C.F. 79
Boyd, W/C R.F. 73, 77
Boyd, Sgt R. 27
Breckon, Sgt G.F. 28
Bridgford, F/O 223
Broadhurst G/C H. 76, 199
Brown, Sgt N. 143
Brown, F/O F.T. 117, 130, 132, 136, 154, 235
Brown, F/L R.C. 90
Bruce, P/O E.A.G.C. 43
Brunier, P/O 12
Bryson, Sgt R.C. 90
Buglass, F/Sgt A. 131, 155
Burden, Sgt G.F. 155
Burley, P/O P.K. 119
Butterfield, F/L K.S. 224

Cam, Sgt 55
Cambridge, P/O F.R. 79

Cameron, P/O 55, 58, 60
Campbell, F/L 45
Campbell, S/L C.N.S. 81, 92
Campbell, W/O D.G. 93, 104
Carter, Sgt L.R. 21
Carver, S/L J.C. 52, 57, 66–7, 84
Casburn, F/Sgt R. 179
Casey, Sgt A.J. 25
Cassidy, S/L E. 169
Cassidy, Sgt G.J. 136
Chadburn, W/C L.V. 86, 143–65, 236
Chalot, Sgt J.L.A. 229
Charles, S/L E.F.J. 151, 154, 164, 173
Cermak, S/L J. 232
Chevalier, s/Lt R. 183
Childs, Sgt 59
Chilton, F/O S.N. 235
Chocholin, F/L V. 174
Choron, Lt M. 47
Christian, Sgt H.D. 90
Cleaver, S/L R.B. 203
Cleeton, F/O B.F. 222
Clifford, F/O J.T. 201
Clouston, P/O D. 78
Cochrane, Sgt 21
Cody, P/O C.T.K. 130,141
Colloredo-Mansfield, F/L E.F. 151, 154
Cooper, F/L A.G.H. 151, 171, 186, 194, 229
Coupar, P/O G.C. 191

Coward, F/O J.L. 211
Cox, Sgt H. 44
Crawford, F/Sgt 82
Crawford-Compton, S/L W.V. 78
Creedon, F/O A. 204, 206
Croxton-Davies, F/Sgt R. 147
Crist, Sgt E. 81
Croall, F/Sgt G. 131
Cross, F/Sgt A.L. 130
Cumming, Sgt W.H. 90
Currant, S/L C.F. 52, 56, 60, 70
Currie, F/Sgt R. 176

Darcey, P/O R.J. 175
Darling, F/L E.V. 93, 104–5
Davies, S/L P.R.G. 120
Davis, P/O G.J. 79
Daymond, F/L G.A. 67, 90
De Courcy, Sgt T. 69, 116, 136
Deere, S/L A.C. 92–3, 98–9, 102–3, 106
Delery, W/O F. 201
De Jana, F/O 201
De Montbron, Sgt 10
De Naeyer, P/O F. 75
De Niverville, F/L 162
De Verteuil, P/O N.J. 192, 197
De Spirlet, P/O F.X.E. 16
Denville, P/O B. 53
Dieu, F/O G.E.F. 39
Dodd, F/O W.G. 162
Dohnal, Sgt 79
Dolezal, S/L F. 119, 230
Doniger, F/L N.A. 222
Donnet, S/L M.G.L. 167
Doorly, F/O E. 228
Dougall, P/O J. 28
Douglas, S/L W.A. 185, 196, 200
Douglas, ACM W.S. 7, 107
Dowding, ACM H. 7

Drbohlav, F/O K. 230
Drossaert, P/O A.E. 70
Dubnick, Sgt H. 168, 171
Duff, P/O G.R. 221–2
Duke, P/O N.F. 17, 31, 33–4, 41–2
Duke-Woolley, S/L R.M.B. 48–9, 76
Du Monceau, P/O I.G. 27, 33, 40, 91
Duncan, F/Sgt J.D.M. 201
Dunning, F/O P.S. 147
Dunstan, Sgt B.P. 79
Duperior, *Cmdt* B. 179
Durnford, Sgt P. 80
Duval, F/L H.P. 92
Du Vivier, S/L D.A. 110

Edge, Sgt N.H. 43
Edwards, F/Sgt A.J. 175
Elcombe, F/L G. 173, 177, 179
Esmonde, Lt Cdr E. 74, 76
Evans, Sgt G.T. 21
Ewins, F/L R.H.S. 176

Fabesch, Sgt P. 183
Fairman, Sgt E.A.L. 60
Falkiner, Sgt 40, 47
Fargher, F/Sgt T.P. 199, 209–10
Farmiloe, F/Sgt S.T. 187, 195, 212–14, 217, 219
Faulkner, W/O 143
Fejfar, F/L 79
Ferguson, F/L D. 188, 193, 195, 202
Flight, P/O R.J. 134, 140, 143, 154–5
Floody, P/O C.W. 46
Foit, F/L E. 119, 230
Fokes, P/O R.H. 12
Fordham, P/O L.B. 28
Foster, S/L W. 177
Freeborn, S/L J.C. 145, 147, 156, 227
Francis, F/L G.H. 78

Gall, F/O C.N. 221
Galloway, Sgt 47
Garden, Sgt J. 74
Gardiner, P/O J.E. 93, 96
Gaskell, Sgt 12
Gentile, P/O D.S. 228
Gibbs, W/C P. 114–16, 235
Gilbert, S/L H.T. 80
Gillan, W/C J.W. 46
Gillespie, P/O E.W. 64
Gilroy, S/L G.K. 29, 40, 47–8
Glaser, F/L E.D. 54–5, 58, 61, 122–3, 226
Gleed, W/C I.R. 52, 57–8, 60, 63, 70, 84
Godlewski, P/O J.M. 25
Gordon, W/C J.A.G. 89–90
Gouby, Lt R.G. 203
Gould, F/O J.B. 168
Grant, S/L F.E. 145, 155
Grant, P/O R.J.C. 78
Graham, F/O 165
Gray, Sgt 58
Green, S/L F.E. 159
Green, Sgt M.B. 64
Green, Sgt R.E. 79
Greenhalgh, F/O D.N. 190
Grisdale, Sgt P.T. 37
Guillaume, S/L D.A. 89

Hall, F/L 40
Hamer, F/O T. 179
Handley, F/O H.G. 147
Hansell, F/O L.J. 175
Hansez, Sgt L.J.A. 91
Harbison, P/O W. 156, 226
Harley, P/O A.E. 76
Harris, F/Sgt J. 221
Harrison, Sgt C.L. 25
Harrison, P/O J. 53
Harrison, Sgt S. 31
Havercroft, Sgt R.E. 8, 18
Hawkins, F/L C.A.V. 55
Healy, F/L 136

Heighington, Sgt G.C. 90
Henderson, Sgt W.G. 21
Henderson, F/Sgt 204
Hewlett, P/O C. 81
Hicken, F/O 154
Hilken, Sgt C.G. 21
Hodgkinson, Sgt B.G. 46–7
Hogg, F/L 58
Hollingworth, Sgt J. 130, 134, 136, 150, 155
Hopkins, Sgt A. 173
Hough, Sgt F.W. 64
Howard-Williams, F/L P.I. 54
Hruby, F/Sgt 80
Hughes-Rees, Sgt J.A. 20
Hugo, S/L P.H. 79
Hunt, Sgt N.E. 93, 97
Hurst P/O D.S. 93, 105

Ingham, P/O B. 75

Jackson, F/L J. 180
Jackson, P/O J.A. 69
Jacobs, F/O W.H. 166–7
Jerabek, Sgt 66
Johnston, F/L M. 235
Johnston, Sgt W.L.H. 5, 17, 28, 34–42, 198, 208
Jones, Sgt L.H. 67
Jones, Sgt S.A. 59, 132, 148
Jones, P/O 228
Joyce, Sgt R.W. 53
Jubelin, Cdr A. 56, 84

Kasal, F/L 120
Kayll, W/C J.R. 46
Kelly, Sgt H.R. 235
Kelly, F/O 169
Kilburn, P/O M.P. 76
King, F/L K.T. 201
Kingaby, F/Sgt D.E. 8, 13, 18, 22, 25, 30–33, 44
Kingcome, F/L C.B.F. 8, 15, 75
Kohout, F/Sgt J. 232

Kopacek, Sgt V. 90
Kosinsky, F/O K. 37
Krol, P/O S.Z. 21
Kulhanek, F/L J. 76

Lack, Sgt L. 130, 134
Lamberton, Sgt W. 28
Lattimer, F/L C.H. 212
Laumans, F/O R.J.L. 91
Law, F/O 189, 201
Le Cheminant, Sgt J. 10, 31
Ledington, Sgt D. 233
Lee, Sgt A. 115
Leigh-Mallory, AVM T. 7, 109, 199
Leith, P/O C.R. 176
Levesque, Sgt J.A.O. 49, 76
Levinson, F/O H.B. 136
Lewis, Sgt R.F. 28
Liby, 2nd Lt S.K. 148, 155
Lightbourne, P/O W.R. 115
Livyns, F/Sgt G.G.A.J. 91
Lloyd, Sgt D. 25, 28
Locke, P/O 58
Lockhart, Sgt W.G. 21
Lofts, S/L K.T. 172, 177–9
Logan, F/Sgt R. 173
Long, F/Sgt R.J. 235
Love, P/O D.J. 156
Lowry, F/L E.R. 222
Loyns, Sgt R.N. 113
Lucas, W/C P.B. 151
Lund, F/O J.W. 11, 43
Lynch, P/O R.C. 57, 235
Lynn, W/C L.A. 119
Lyon, F/O E.R. 212

MacDonald, F/Sgt A.R. 111
MacDonald, F/Sgt H.D. 76
MacDonald, Sgt J.W. 233
MacDonald, P/O N. 225
Mace, W/O D. 180

Machan, Sgt S.H. 61
MacKenzie, S/L J.W. 185
MacKenzie, P/O R.W.P. 56, 84
Magwood, P/O C. 81, 98
Malan, W/C A.G. 11, 18, 29, 33–4, 37, 62
Malfroy, S/L C.E. 62
Mares, F/Sgt F. 120
Marquis, F/Sgt J. 197, 201
Mather, F/Sgt 233
Mawer, F/Sgt G.A. 114
McAuliffe, F/O L. 176
McDade, F/O P.V. 176
McGregor, F/L P.R. 201
McKay, F/L D.A.S. 85
McLeod, P/O D.N. 85
McPhie, F/Sgt 79
Merrett, Sgt J.G. 40
Metcalfe, P/O J. 211
Mileham, F/L D.E. 60
Milne, S/L R.M. 34, 37, 40, 44, 83
Miller, F/Sgt W.L. 233
Mills, Sgt W.H. 235
Mitchner, P/O J.D. 155, 159, 161–2, 166
Montet, *Capt* P. 182
Moody, Sgt V.K. 57
Moore, Sgt E.H. 235
Moore, P/O L.A. 159, 162
Morgan, Sgt 90
Morrison, Sgt D.R. 49, 76
Motycka, F/Sgt T. 121
Mrazek, S/L K. 79, 119
Mungo Park, S/L J.C. 13–15, 21
Murphy, Sgt 93–4

Nash, Sgt 136
Neil, F/L 49
Newbery, F/L R.A. 56, 66, 132–4, 143, 147–8, 150
Nioloux, *Adj* R.N. 69
Nissen, Lt V.R.E. 113
Noonan, F/O D.E. 146, 162, 166, 168

Northcott, P/O G.W. 76, 145, 150, 156, 162, 165
Novak, F/O J. 232

Offenberg, P/O J. 16, 25, 40, 47
Olver, P/O J.F. 175
Omdahl, Sgt 72
O'Neill, F/O F.H. 222
Ormston, P/O I.C. 48, 76
Ortmans, P/O V. 16, 20, 33–4, 39
Oxspring, S/L R.W. 73

Painter, F/O W. 198, 202
Palmer-Tomkinson, F/O A. 62
Park, AVM K. 7
Parker, F/O H.M. 176–7
Parr, F/O J.F. 93, 102–3
Parrack, Sgt R.E. 90
Peel, G/C J.R.A. 79
Peterson, S/L C.G. 89
Petr, W/O M. 230
Phillip, P/O R.D. 151
Pietrasiak, Sgt A. 25
Pike, P/O D.E. 85
Plagis, F/L J.A. 169, 189
Popelka, F/Sgt V. 230
Port, Sgt K.G. 43
Potelle, Sgt J.E.A. 66
Potter, P/O E.M. 90
Potter, Sgt O.C. 189
Pow, P/O L.G.D. 156
Powell, W/C P. 192
Prentice, F/O D.F. 158
Preston, P/O 69
Prihoda, P/O J. 80, 119
Pugh, W/O 197

Rabagliati, W/C A.C. 142, 151
Rae, F/L J.A. 151, 153, 156
Rae, Sgt J.D. 78
Rankin, S/L J. 9–12, 25, 30–31, 37, 39, 48
Reahill, F/O F.J. 141

Ream, Sgt 11
Redfern, Sgt J. 55
Reeder, F/O C. 178
Reid, Sgt D.T.E. 86
Richards, P/O J.R. 90
Richardson, F/L 44
Richey, F/L P.H.M. 20, 26–7
Ridings, Sgt A.L. 120
Rigler, Sgt T.C. 16
Robillard, F/Sgt 75
Robinson, S/L M.L. 10, 20, 26, 29
Rocovsky, Sgt M. 63
Roff, Sgt E.H. 36
Rosser, P/O W.J. 37
Royer, Sgt R. 120
Rumble, F/L F.D. 208
Ruprecht, Sgt V. 120
Rutherford, Sgt J. 36, 75
Ryckman, F/Sgt G.A.J. 81–3
Ryder, W/C E.N. 46

Sager, F/O A.H. 158–61, 165–6, 168, 170, 226
Sala, W/O J. 230
Sandman, P/O W.J. 15, 21
Scott-Malden, W/C F.D.S. 99, 102
Seghers, P/O E.G.A. 26
Sheen, S/L D.F.B. 22, 36–7
Shepherd, Sgt G. 64
Shepherd, F/L J.B. 115, 117, 151–2, 156
Shoebottom, P/O G.M. 203
Simmonds, F/L 135
Simon, P/O M.L. 60
Simpson, W/C P.J. 175, 177, 180
Sims, F/Sgt D. 192
Sing, S/L J.E.J. 116
Skach, Sgt A. 230
Skalski, F/O H. 36
Skinner, P/O W.M. 21
Slonski, Sgt 234

Small, P/O J.A. 46
Smolik, F/O V. 231
Somers, Sgt L.J. 83, 93, 104
Sparrow, F/O G.F. 187, 202
Sprague, F/O H.A. 48
Sprague, P/O R.S. 90
Stanbury, F/L P.J. 70, 114
Stastny, F/O J. 180
Stebbings, F/L R.D. 207
Stenger, P/O P.H. 67, 69
Stephen, S/L H.M. 52, 54
Stewart, S/L A.C. 136, 141
Stewart, Sgt 15
Stewart, F/O J.G. 115
Stockwell, F/Sgt L. 208
Stone, P/O I.S. 84
Strachan, Sgt B. 65
Strihavka, P/O J. 120
Svendson, P/O N.H. 61
Sweetman, P/O H.N. 78

Talalla, P/O C.L.F. 132, 155
Teicheira, P/O E.G. 90
Thomas, P/O 64, 84
Thomas, F/Sgt G. 173
Thompson, Lt J. 179
Thompson, Sgt S.L. 46
Thorne, Sgt J.N. 159, 162, 169
Thorpe, F/O A.T. 189
Tidy, Sgt J. 179
Tinsey, Sgt T.D. 80
Tocauer, F/Sgt S. 232
Trejtnar, F/Sgt F. 120
Trent, S/L L. 139
Truscott, S/L K.W. 77
Tummers P.N.A. Sgt 181

Van Arkel, F/O J. 141
Van Houton, Sgt C. 69
van Schaick, Sgt J.E. 39
Varey, F/O A.W. 179
Vasatko, W/C A. 119–20
Veen, P/O J. 69
Vendl, Sgt 58

Villa, S/L J.W. 70
Vinter, Sgt S.H. 28
Vrtis, Sgt K. 53, 63
Vybiral, S/L T. 232

Wade, F/O T.S. 13
Waldern, Sgt C.G. 25
Walker, F/L B. 93, 96
Walker, F/Sgt I.G. 189, 203
Walker, S/L J.H.B. 64
Walker, F/L R.H. 155, 159
Walmsley, P/O 154
Wallace, F/O C.A.B. 46
Walton, F/L W.C. 212
Ward, F/Sgt T. 203
Watkins, F/L V.E. 61
Watson, Sgt S.A. 54, 61, 110–12, 115, 137–9, 141
Webster, Sgt J.B. 60, 123
Wellman, F/O 189
Wells, S/L E.P. 77–8
Wellum, P/O G. 11, 25
Wheeler, G/C A. 229

Wheldon, P/O R. 58, 63
Whitney, Sgt G.B. 46
Wickham, S/L P.R.W. 89
Wilson, Sgt G.S. 201
Wilson, F/Sgt M.K. 201
Witney, F/O A.T. 222
Woloschuk, P/O 162
Wood, Sgt R. 83
Woods-Scawen, Sgt G.E.F. 44
Woolass, P/O R.S. 60
Wootten, S/L E.W. 68, 112, 116–17, 129–30, 134
Wozniak, P/O R. 93, 95
Wright, F/L A.R. 11
Wydrowski, F/O 60

Yorke, Sgt 15
Yule, S/L R.D. 111

Luftwaffe

Birke, *Uffz* G. 70
Brandle, *Maj* K. 167

Ebersberger, *Oblt* K. 61, 70

Ehlers, *Obfw* H. 141

Faber, *Oblt* A. 121
Fischer, *Lt* H. 171

Galland, *Obstlt* A. 46, 72
Galland, *Oblt* W-F 61, 70

Hoffman, *Obfw* H. 61

Muncheburg, *Hptm* J. 64, 70, 105

Priller, *Hptm* J. 46, 64, 90

Reiche, *Lt* H. 64
Reushling, *Uffz* W. 120

Schauder, *Lt* 44
Schmidt, *Oblt* J. 90
Schopfel, *Maj* G. 89
Seifert, *Hptm* J. 44, 90, 105
Seegatz, *Oblt* 37
Struck, *Fw* G. 12

Wickop, *Hptm* D. 139

Zimmer, *Uffz* W. 12